NINETEENTH-CENTURY AMERICAN LITERATURE AND THE LONG CIVIL WAR

American literature in the nineteenth century is often divided into two halves, neatly separated by the Civil War. In *Nineteenth-Century American Literature and the Long Civil War*, Cody Marrs argues that the war is a far more elastic boundary for literary history than has frequently been assumed. Focusing on the later writings of Walt Whitman, Frederick Douglass, Herman Melville, and Emily Dickinson, this book shows how the war took imaginative shape across, and even beyond, the nineteenth century, inflecting literary forms and expressions for decades after 1865. These writers, Marrs demonstrates, are best understood not as antebellum or postbellum figures but as transbellum authors who cipher their later experiences through their wartime impressions and prewar ideals. This book is a bold, revisionary contribution to debates about temporality, periodization, and the shape of American literary history.

CODY MARRS teaches English at the University of Georgia.

(*continued following the Index*)

NINETEENTH-CENTURY AMERICAN LITERATURE AND THE LONG CIVIL WAR

CODY MARRS

University of Georgia

CAMBRIDGE
UNIVERSITY PRESS

CAMBRIDGE
UNIVERSITY PRESS

32 Avenue of the Americas, New York NY 10013-2473, USA

Cambridge University Press is part of the University of Cambridge.

It furthers the University's mission by disseminating knowledge in the pursuit of education, learning and research at the highest international levels of excellence.

www.cambridge.org
Information on this title: www.cambridge.org/9781107109834

© Cody Marrs 2015

First published 2015

A catalogue record for this publication is available from the British Library

Library of Congress Cataloguing in Publication data
Marrs, Cody.
Nineteenth-century American literature and the long Civil War /
Cody Marrs, University of Georgia.
pages cm
Includes bibliographical references and index.
ISBN 978-1-107-10983-4 (hardback)
1. American literature – 19th century – History and criticism.   2. United States –
History – Civil War, 1861–1865 – Literature and the war.   3. War and literature –
United States – History – 19th century.   4. War in literature.   I. Title.
PS217.C58M37   2015
810.9′358–dc23   2015003105

ISBN 978-1-107-10983-4 Hardback

For Kristin, Harper, and Caleb

Contents

Illustrations

Acknowledgments

In almost countless ways, this book is the result of other people's generosity. At UC Berkeley, where this project first took root, Sam Otter guided me with such wisdom and care, I hardly know how to thank him. The following pages owe a great deal to Sam's intellect, wit, and encouragement to write – even in this day and age – about authorial careers. I'm also grateful for the many people at Berkeley who made life as a graduate student there far richer than it had any right to be: Malik Ali, Aaron Bady, Stephen Best, Munia Bhaumik, Natalia Cecire, Paul Hurh, Marisa Palacios Knox, Colleen Lye, Ted Martin, Annie McClanahan, Megan Pugh, Swati Rana, Scott Saul, Randall Smith, and Bryan Wagner.

I wrote most of this book after moving to Athens. At the University of Georgia, I've been fortunate to work with several people who are friends as well as colleagues. Doug Anderson's sagacity and friendship have been utterly crucial to me, and to this book. To Casie LeGette, Brett Szymik, Aaron Santesso, and Esra Santesso: thank you for all the late-night desserts; I don't know what I'd do without you. I'm also grateful for my exceptional colleagues who make Park Hall everything that it is: Nicholas Allen, Michelle Ballif, Cynthia Turner Camp, Nathan Camp, Roxanne Eberle, Miriam Jacobson, Tricia Lootens, John Lowe, Barbara McCaskill, Richard Menke, Ron Miller, Adam Parkes, Ed Pavlic, Chrisopher Pizzino, Jed Rasula, Channette Romero, Susan Rosenbaum, Hugh Ruppersburg, Chloe Wigston Smith, Andrew Zawacki, and Maggie Zurawski.

This book was supported by fellowships and grants from the Willson Center for the Humanities, the Office of the Vice President for Research, the Newberry Library, and, at an earlier stage, the Townsend Center for the Humanities. Those funds provided me with the time and opportunity to write the following pages. I am also indebted to the editors who allowed me to reprint two earlier essays, and to the anonymous readers who responded to those essays. Parts of Chapter 1 first appeared in *Arizona Quarterly* 67.1 (Spring 2011), pgs. 47–72, under the title "Whitman's

Latencies: Hegel and the Politics of Time in *Leaves of Grass.*" It is reprinted here by permission of the Regents of The University of Arizona. Parts of Chapter 3 first appeared in *American Literature* 82.1 (March 2010), pgs. 91–119, under the title "A Wayward Art: *Battle-Pieces* and Melville's Poetic Turn." It is reprinted here by permission of the publisher, Duke University Press.

This book also owes much to my fellow Americanists scattered around the globe, in the intellectual archipelagoes that make up our scholarly world. Philip Barnard and Dorice Williams Elliott first showed me how to read closely and widely. My collaborations with Christopher Hager, both past and present, have shaped this book and enriched my life. *Nineteenth-Century American Literature and the Long Civil War* is in many respects but a long-winded "thank you" to Chris. Coleman Hutchison, who was one of my readers, provided a brilliant response that has strengthened and sharpened my arguments; and another reader, whom I don't know, provided incisive feedback for which I'm grateful. The later parts of Chapter 3 grew out of a talk I gave at Emory University. For that, I owe a hearty thanks to Munia Bhaumik, Michael Elliott, Michael Moon, and Benjamin Reiss. Ian Finseth and Eliza Richards also responded to early, embryonic parts of this book, and their thoughts have anchored my own. I've also benefited, in one way or another, from the intelligence, kindness, and camaraderie of scholars far and wide. People like John Bryant, Kathleen Diffley, Betsy Erkkila, Jennifer Greiman, Jeffrey Insko, Michael Jonik, Robert S. Levine, Timothy Marr, Justine Murison, Michelle Neely, Basem Ra'ad, Matthew Rebhorn, Julia Stern, Ivy Wilson, and Brian Yothers make me feel lucky to be part of this profession. I also want to thank Ray Ryan and Ross Posnock for their enthusiastic support of this project, and Caitlin Gallagher, who has skillfully guided me through the production process.

Last, but certainly not least, I thank my family for all that they have given me, and for all that they continue to give. My parents, Betty and Monte, encouraged me to dream, read, and write, even when it seemed incredibly impractical. My extended family – Jay, Kim, Don, and Lynda – have been unfailingly kind and bighearted. But I owe a special thanks, one that I cannot even begin to put into words, to Kristin, Harper, and Caleb, to whom this book is dedicated. You – each of you – are my world and my cosmos. Anything worth doing must be done with love, and I have that in spectacular abundance, thanks to you.

Introduction
Transbellum American Literature

The Civil War occupies a rather strange place in the periodic imaginary
of American literary studies. On the one hand, it is frequently taken to
be the defining event of the nineteenth century – a cataclysm so vast and
transformative that it destroys one literary period and spawns another.
Much of the field is organized around the idea that because of the war's
annulling force, the century must be separated into two distinct and
largely asymmetrical eras: antebellum and postbellum; before and after.
This view of the war is reiterated at nearly every level of the discipline: in
survey courses, which frequently begin or end at 1865; in monographs,
which tend to situate themselves on either side of this grand divide; in
numerous anthologies, overviews, and companions; and in the training of
graduate students and the hiring of faculty. On the other hand, the Civil
War is also routinely marginalized in the very field that so vigorously foregrounds its influence. It often enters the curriculum only on the tail end
of courses. It receives far less attention from literary critics than the eras
that surround it.[1] And strange as it may seem, the war is deemphasized by
the periodizing practices that are specifically designed to acknowledge its
impact. Indeed, if the nineteenth century consists in a passage from the
antebellum to the postbellum, then the war is essentially an antiperiod, a
transition that matters only to the extent that it demarcates what precedes
and follows it. The conflict that Robert Penn Warren once called "our
only 'felt' history" thus functions, oftentimes, as a constitutive absence in
American literary history or, at best, as the occasion for a minor literature
that emerged between two great eras.[2]

The Civil War's paradoxical status – as both the structural pivot and
the empty center of the nineteenth century – is part of the genealogical
inheritance of our periodic terms. When "ante-bellum" and "post-bellum"
entered the American vernacular in the 1860s and 1870s, the words were
often hyphenated and italicized because they were linguistic imports
from international law. *Ante-bellum* and *post-bellum* initially functioned

as shorthand versions of longer phrases: the *status quo ante bellum* (i.e., "the state before the war") and the *status quo post bellum* (i.e., "the state after the war"), which, in treaties between warring states, were forms of resolution wherein all the newly acquired property and territory were returned or all prewar claims of ownership were renounced.[3] *Antebellum* and *postbellum* treaties thereby promoted fictions of erasure that enabled both sides to pretend either that the war had never really happened, or that history began anew with its completion. We now enlist these terms in radically different ways – as the names for discrete, overarching epochs – but "antebellum" and "postbellum" still depend on a peculiar coupling of retrospection and effacement that enables these eras to be imagined into being only by cutting out the very terminus that makes them historically distinct.

These fraught periodic categories are problematic in other ways, too. By framing literary history as an adjunct, or corollary, of national history, they contravene recent attempts to decouple literature from the state. They also bolster terms like "the antebellum novel" and "postbellum poetry," which, despite their almost axiomatic status, are remarkably poor descriptors, often functioning as placeholders for other, less epochally-bound frameworks. And as anyone who has taught a survey course knows all too well, the bellum divide also generates a weird set of curricular challenges. If a course is cut off at the war, how does one justify including a book like Frederick Douglass's *The Life and Times* (1881/1892), which, despite being composed by an "antebellum" author, was written decades after that era concluded? What does one do with intergenerational writers, like Rebecca Harding Davis and Harriet Prescott Spofford, whose careers climaxed in the midst of the war but are not typically considered to be wartime authors? And how does one even begin to properly attend to books such as *Clotel*, which was initially published in 1853 but revised on three different occasions through 1867, or *Leaves of Grass*, which was published in 1855 but significantly rewritten by Whitman, again and again, through 1891?

There are a number of ways in which literary history can be remapped without this sharp partitioning. In recent years, scholars have shifted the field's focus toward a "long nineteenth century," which jettisons traditional microperiods in favor of an expanded scale of analysis that stretches back to the eighteenth century and into the twentieth. Other critics have eschewed the Civil War almost altogether and recast the struggle not as the defining event of the era but as merely one event among many others – an option favored by many books that focus on nineteenth-century literature but have little to say about the Civil War. Both approaches have a great deal to recommend them: they draw attention to literary, cultural, and political phenomena that span several generations, and they reveal turning-points that have nothing to do with violence and war (a rare feat when it comes to periodization). Yet reading nineteenth-century literature either solely or primarily in terms of continuity risks overlooking the various ways in which that literature is indeed bound up with the Civil War – not in a linear or sequential fashion, as implied by the ante/postbellum divide, but bound up nonetheless.

This book argues for a different periodization, by looking at the Civil War as a multilinear upheaval. As an event within literary history, the war manifests not as a discrete instance of overturning but as a rupture with a stunning array of trajectories, genealogies, and afterlives. The Civil War's complex periodicity is especially evident when we read authors who not only survived the war but also wrote voluminously for decades after it. I focus on four of these writers: Walt Whitman, Frederick Douglass, Herman Melville, and Emily Dickinson. Although they are usually read as antebellum figures, these authors wrote through the Civil War and through most of the rest of the nineteenth century, often by ciphering their postwar experiences through their wartime impressions and prewar ideals. Their writings are therefore chiefly legible, I shall argue, as part of a *transbellum* literature that stretches (as the etymology implies) across and beyond the war itself.

By "transbellum," I refer to three different phenomena, which both individually and collectively index the Civil War's periodic fluidity. First, transbellum names the ways in which these writers' careers extend from the "antebellum" period, across the Civil War, and into the "postbellum" era, thereby bridging the very epochs into which American literary history tends to be segmented. It is, in this sense, a marker of this literature's multiperiodicity. Second, transbellum refers to a shared tendency to repeatedly return to the Civil War as a literary, historical, and philosophical subject long after it officially concluded. As such, it draws attention to just how continuous the war's discontinuity was as it unfolded across the century as an unresolved imaginative struggle. And, third, transbellum designates the myriad ways in which these writers recast the historicity of that conflict, often in terms that differ, quite radically, from our tendency to confine it to the period from 1861 to 1865.

Retiming the Civil War

The following pages approach the Civil War as a nonsynchronous upheaval – as a boundary, in short, that is much blurrier, and more heterogeneously constituted, than has often been assumed.[4] I begin, in Chapter 1, with Walt Whitman, who became enamored with Hegel's philosophy of history in the wake of the war. After reading Hegel (whom he declared to be the only philosopher "fit for America"), Whitman made substantial changes to *Leaves of Grass* and *Drum-Taps*, experimenting with new syntactic forms and methods of poetic organization.[5] These changes, I argue, enable Whitman to engage in rich and provocative ways with the defining struggles of the late nineteenth century, especially the conflicts between workers and capitalists in the 1870s and 1880s. Chapter 2 examines the transbellum writings of America's most famous former slave, Frederick Douglass. According to Douglass, the Abolition War (as he preferred to call it) was but a moment, or phase, in a much longer "irrepressible conflict" between freedom and unfreedom.[6] To test that idea out, he turns to theories of perpetual motion, histories of revolution, and philosophies of progress. His later speeches, essays, and autobiographies accordingly refer to a broad range of events – from sixteenth-century religious battles to nineteenth-century scientific discoveries – but they all shore up a single supposition, which he wrested from the war: that history, like everything else in this world, is immanently revisable.

Chapter 3 focuses on Herman Melville, who construes the war as part of a long cycle of internecine conflict. As Melville represents it in *Battle-Pieces* (1866), *Clarel* (1876), and *Timoleon* (1891), the Civil War repeats events that have already been repeated many times before in Europe and the Holy Land. *Battle-Pieces* elucidates this historical pattern by connecting the Civil War's defining moments – such as the draft riots of 1863 and the fights between ironclads – to ancient Roman rebellions, medieval French revolts, and other analogous instances of civil strife; while *Clarel* and *Timoleon* loosen and expand this pattern by locating similar civil wars in the earth, in the world's religions, and in the very structure of the cosmos. The war's historicity then recedes almost entirely in Chapter 4, which considers the poems that Emily Dickinson wrote from the 1860s through the 1880s. Dickinson represents the conflict as a vast undoing that is unmoored from chronology itself. Many of her poems are shot through with moments of erasure because, for her, such fading away is the Civil War's defining temporality. Unlike these other transbellum writers, Dickinson figures the conflict as a repealing of history – as an annulment that can certainly be felt, but never adequately remembered because it exceeds all of our earthly chronometrics.

As we will discover, the Civil War was an ongoing imaginative conflict across much of the nineteenth century. Or more accurately: it was a struggle that had to be continuously *re*imagined, and that is precisely what these authors did by folding the war into a raucous variety of literary timescapes. Despite the patent heterogeneity of these transbellum works – from Douglass's lectures about William of Orange to Dickinson's later poems about "Dimpled War[s]" and "finished Faces" – they each attempt to do the impossible: to secure a cogent temporality for this long, chaotic upheaval.[7] This book thereby extends the work of such scholars as Faith Barrett, Kathleen Diffley, Randall Fuller, Coleman Hutchison, Shirley Samuels, and Julia Stern, who have made a strong case for reading Civil War literature as an essential part of, rather than a violent departure from, the development of nineteenth-century United States culture.[8] In the following pages, I make that same argument from a different perspective by looking at the Civil War's transbellum influence on these purportedly antebellum writers, who try to track the war's almost untrackable history long after the fall of Richmond. And by doing so, these authors provide us with a number of rich, alternative timelines through which the war itself can be reread and replotted.

These writers' sustained efforts to figure the war underscore one of the foremost insights of recent Americanist scholarship: that literature's irregular temporalities tend to disrupt the timeframes of the clock and the nation. As several critics have demonstrated, the standardization of time in the nineteenth century – which made temporality increasingly homogeneous and measurable – was accompanied by a literature that, instead of merely archiving that transformation, actively troubled it. To account for literature's nonstandard temporalities, scholars have fashioned a robust set of interpretive models. Wai Chee Dimock has argued for a hermeneutic of deep time that is attuned to literature's "irregular duration[s] and extension[s]." Elizabeth Freeman has shown us how queer time emerged, in the nineteenth and twentieth centuries, as a kind of "arrhythmia" between "sacred, static 'women's' time and [the] secularized, progressive, nominally male national-historical time." Still other critics have examined the pluridimensionality of literature's "vehement passions"; the material and textual creation of "heterogeneous temporal cultures"; and the feeling body's ability to provide an "alternative mechanism for the collection of time."[9]

The following pages both expand on and depart from this scholarship on temporality. On the one hand, *Nineteenth-Century American Literature and the Long Civil War* extends many of the principal claims that have emerged out of this work: that time was a crucial modality of nineteenth-century political struggles; that literature played an important role in the imaginative construction of this chronopolitics; and that the temporalities enacted in literature tend to be remarkably diverse in their composition and movement. These writers' responses to the Long Civil War, we shall see, are both fueled by and structured around an abiding interest in the politics of time. They each figure that struggle in very different ways – as a revolution, or counterrevolution, or historical erasure – but they all present the war as an event that outstrips the discrete, four-year span with which it is often associated. And to understand how the war eclipses its official chronology, I turn to a different and frequently overlooked archive for thinking about time, politics, and periodicity in the nineteenth century: the less canonical works of highly canonical writers.

This author-centered focus, however, also distinguishes this book from many of its temporally-oriented companions. In studies of nineteenth-century time and literature, the analytical object is almost always a material culture, social practice, or literary genre, the defining temporalities of which point toward broader epistemic shifts in national or subnational identity. In studies of periodization (and its limits), critics often scale out, as it were, in order to reveal vast new swaths of historical time and loosened hermeneutic frameworks. These approaches have reorganized the field and yielded a stunning array of insights. Nonetheless, construing literature's temporalities primarily as evidence of discursive formations that have little to do with individual writers risks losing sight of the temporalities that hinge on the idea of authorship: the patterns that emerge across a writer's works; the timescapes that an author actively – and sometimes quite self-reflexively – assembles out of a culture's materials; and the transformations to a writer's worldview that can begin with something as simple as reading a book, or as complicated as witnessing a war. These more authorial temporalities do not require a full-scale retrieval of biography, but they do oblige us to think more rigorously about the applicability of some of this criticism's key terms – such as scaling and timing – to considerations of individual writers, and about the resources that disciplinary forms of inquiry might, in turn, bring to bear on areas of scholarship that are frequently framed as interdisciplinary, or even antidisciplinary. These chapters are designed to address these concerns by looking afresh at the later works of these four transbellum authors.

Canons and Periods

Many other writers, texts, and movements could easily be described as transbellum. Harriet Beecher Stowe, whose novel *Uncle Tom's Cabin* (1852) became such a cultural sensation before the Civil War, wrote for more than 30 years after the conflict, producing seven more novels, a book of poems, and a study of women in "sacred history." Those lions of prewar literature, the Transcendentalists, also wrote prolifically after 1865. In the wake of the war, Amos Bronson Alcott penned two books of philosophy, two volumes of poetry, and a biography; Ralph Waldo Emerson issued two more essay collections and a book of poems; and Emerson's former-associate-turned-apostate, Orestes Brownson, published so widely that when his articles were anthologized in the 1880s, it required twenty volumes to contain them.

One finds that same unyielding production among many African American writers. After the fall of the Confederacy, Martin Delany followed up his earlier antislavery writings with pamphlets for the newly freed slaves, a work of antiracist ethnography, and essays on Reconstruction. William Wells Brown not only continued to revise *Clotel*; he also wrote three books on African American history and a series of sketches about late-nineteenth-century Southern society. And slave narratives, despite their longstanding status as an antebellum genre, continued to be composed and revised into the twentieth century. In fact, more than ninety slave narratives were printed after emancipation.[10]

There is also a markedly transbellum trajectory for other types of Civil War literature. From the 1860s onward, journals and magazines throughout the United States published hundreds of fictional stories about the Civil War – more than 300 by Kathleen Diffley's count – by writers both well known (such as Louisa May Alcott and Silas Weir Mitchell) and obscure (such as Ellen Leonard and J.O. Culver). Many of the songs sung by soldiers and civilians alike continued to be sung for decades afterwards, at once shaping and preserving the conflict in Americans' cultural memory. Many Union and Confederate veterans also penned accounts of their experiences in the late nineteenth century. Memoirists included well-known generals such as Ulysses S. Grant and James Longstreet, as well as infamous captains (John Singleton Mosby), blockade runners (William Watson), bushwackers (Samuel S. Hildebrand), reefers (James Morris Morgan), spies (Allan Pinkerton), and confused privates (Mark Twain).[11] That collective attempt to create a usable and readable past for the struggle also generated a stunning array of other texts, including – though hardly limited to – pictorial records, newspapers compendiums, day-by-day chronicles, popular histories, regional histories, state histories, regimental histories, encyclopedias, anthologies, almanacs, and biographies.[12]

Rather than examining this broad range of transbellum literature, I focus on the long careers of just four writers. I do so for a few related reasons. First of all, Whitman, Douglass, Melville, and Dickinson are among the most canonical of "antebellum" authors, and I think that this matters. Not because their writings are inherently better (although some of them are indeed unusually rich and intricate), but because their canonical status both shapes and is shaped by the narratives that critics use to frame the periods to which they belong. The very conceptual salience of such terms as antebellum and postbellum hinges in no small part on their identification with a particular set of authors; hence the difficulty of thinking about the British Renaissance without Shakespeare, or the Victorian period without Dickens. Such terms are also, as Marshall Brown notes, "relational" categories: instead of naming a particular zeitgeist like the nomenclature of movements (for example, "Imagism," or "Naturalism"), they denominate a transition, a before-and-after that grants each category its semantic and historical content.[13] In studies of nineteenth-century American literature and culture, these two tendencies – the condensing of an entire period into certain authors and the narrativized reading of a period – are often fused. The passage from antebellum to postbellum has long been framed as a story of generational succession: Hawthorne gives way to James; Melville to Twain; and so forth. This story has many different versions – for example, as a narrative about generic displacement, or the collapse of idealism, or the modernization of copyright law – but there is an abiding authorial dimension in many of these accounts.

Jonathan Arac offers a particularly compelling version of this succession story in his book, *The Emergence of American Literary Narrative* (2005). Arac rigorously traces the evolution of prose forms in the United States prior to the Civil War, arguing that almost all of the era's narratives, both major and minor, can be grouped into four generic categories: personal, local, national, and literary. The first three categories emerged as competing efforts to find a narrative structure capable of articulating the fragile, heterogeneous structures of belonging in the prewar United States. National narratives, such as James Fenimore Cooper's "Leatherstocking Tales" (1827–41) and George Bancroft's *History of the Colonization of the United States* (1841) "told the story of the nation's colonial beginnings and looked forward to its future as a model for the world," while local narratives, such as the tales of

Washington Irving and Edgar Allan Poe, and personal narratives (for example, Richard Henry Dana's *Two Years Before the Mast*, Herman Melville's *Typee*, and Frederick Douglass's 1845 *Narrative*) provided alternative accounts of experience that often elided the nation and forged other visions of connection. When the more explicitly literary works – *Moby-Dick* (1851) and *The Scarlet Letter* (1850) are Arac's chief examples – appeared in the early 1850s, they effectively remixed these earlier forms into a new narrative genre, one that created a "world elsewhere" yet remained engaged with the world itself, and thus seemed to "not only differ from but [...] also to transcend and, implicitly, to criticize [...] common life."[14]

Arac's account admirably marshals disparate strains of literary history into a cogent narrative about narrative. What I want to bring attention to, however, is the end, which is foreshadowed in the book's chronological frame: 1820–60. This pattern of prose development was evidently completely undone by the Civil War. The latter "sanctified" the state by transferring "the prestige that had previously been reserved for 'Union' and the 'People'" to the state. This transformation, Arac argues, "debilitated" literary writers such as Hawthorne and Melville and "inhibited literary narrative" itself, thereby giving rise to a new narrative dispensation epitomized by Twain and Parkman:

> Faced with the "convulsive action" of the Civil War, [...] Hawthorne could no longer effectively commit himself to this faith in romance as progress without agency, which had made possible the independent worlds of his literary narratives [...] but it did not prevent all new narratives. The greatest talent to emerge during the war was Mark Twain. His first books clearly link him to the traditions of local and personal narratives: *The Celebrated Jumping Frog of Calaveras County and Other Sketches* (1867), *Innocents Abroad* (1869), and *Roughing It* (1872), which the preface characterizes as "merely a personal narrative." During the war, Francis Parkman recovered from his nearly two decades of debility and renewed his national narrative [...] Over the last decades of the century, until his death in 1893, he completed his series on "France and England in North America," to which *The Conspiracy of Pontiac* had formed a proleptic coda.[15]

What interests me about this claim is the connection – quite explicit here – between the Civil War's impact and the succession of authorship that accompanies it. The transition from literary narrative in the 1850s to new local and national narratives after 1865 is not just generic but authorial: Hawthorne and Melville recede just as Twain emerges and Parkman resuscitates his historical project.

This claim is actually a very old one. Versions of it appear in a number of combinations across twentieth- and twenty-first-century criticism (although, curiously, Twain is often taken up by critics as the postbellum writer *par excellence*). Here is Norman Foerster, writing in 1928:

> [The Civil War] destroyed New England as completely as it did the South. Two aristocracies simultaneously fell into ruins. Following it there flooded into the East a second wave of Western vulgarity, a new humor, a new literary form – the native type of short story – a new realism that scorned Europe and the East [...] The era of Mark Twain had dawned. Literature began to spring from life, from the people, from the spirit of the epoch.

Edmund Wilson, in 1962:

> [After 1865,] the whole style of prose-writing changes. In the field of prose fiction before the war, the American writers, both North and South, had a verbose untidy [style ...] Hawthorne and Melville and Poe [...] always embroidered, or, perhaps better, coagulated, their fancies in a peculiar clogged and viscous prose [...] But a change in American style takes place in the middle of the century. The plethora of words is reduced; the pace becomes firmer and quicker; the language becomes more what was later called "efficient," more what was still later called "functional."

Martha Banta, in 1988:

> Considered in terms of its most noted writers, the change in American literature between the earlier and later halves of the nineteenth century is strongly marked. With the deaths or retirements from authorship of the generation of Hawthorne, Melville, Emerson, and Poe in the 1850s and 1860s, then the emergence, just after the Civil War, of such new figures as Henry James, William Dean Howells, and Mark Twain, American literature undergoes one of the most thoroughgoing changes of the guard in its entire history.

Louis Menand, in 2001:

> The Civil War swept away the slave civilization of the South, but it swept away almost the whole intellectual culture of the North along with it. It took nearly half a century for the United States to develop a culture to replace it, to find a set of ideas, and a way of thinking, that would help people cope with the conditions of modern life. That struggle [...] runs through the lives of [...] Oliver Wendell Holmes, William James, Charles S. Peirce, and John Dewey. These people [...] were more responsible than any other group for moving American thought into the modern world.

And Randall Fuller, in 2011:

> In many ways, the task of assimilating the war imaginatively – of construct-
> ing a coherent narrative about the conflict that would make sense of its
> bitter costs and enable Americans to adapt to a changed national land-
> scape – would fall less upon Emerson and his contemporaries than upon
> the next generation of authors. Mark Twain, Stephen Crane, and Ambrose
> Bierce were just a few of the many writers who participated in an epic rei-
> magining of the war in the last third of the nineteenth century. For them,
> the war was a tragic farce, a sick joke that belied the lofty rhetoric of writers
> and politicians from the previous generation.[16]

These arguments are hardly interchangeable, but they do share a common periodizing framework (even if it is not named as such) that presents
the war as the limit-point of literary careers. The rub, of course, is that
many prewar writers did not suddenly disappear. Although Thoreau and
Hawthorne did not survive the struggle, and Poe and Fuller met their
untimely deaths before it even commenced, many other authors continued writing and revising for generations afterwards, and what they produced in the wake of the war is just as intricate, layered, and engaged as
anything they produced before it. The long integration (and disintegration) of *Drum-Taps* into *Leaves of Grass*, the later orations of Frederick
Douglass, the coiled histories of *Battle-Pieces*, *Clarel*, and *Timoleon*, and
the remarkable poems of Dickinson's final years all make it abundantly
clear that, in certain crucial respects, there was no passing of the guard.
These writers, and their powerful imaginations, did not suddenly fade and
curl "in[to] Capricorn" (F 233). Rather, they continued to write alongside
the authors who purportedly replaced them, crafting verbal timescapes
that traverse the war and our standard chronologies of the nineteenth
century.

The Renaissance after the Renaissance

I am also interested in these four writers because of the particular histories
of their canonization. Two of them (Whitman and Melville) are original
members of F.O. Matthiessen's American Renaissance, and the other two
(Douglass and Dickinson) were added decades later, when critics challenged the numerous exclusions – racial, regional, gendered, and generic –
that demarcated the Renaissance and the national literature it purportedly
inaugurated.[17] Even though the idea of the American Renaissance has by
and large been replaced by more capacious models that emphasize this literature's connections to various subnational and transnational formations,

the periodization upon which that seminal category was based remains very much intact. These four authors continue to be identified with the 1850s because of a chronological segmentation of the field that has been around for quite some time, a segmentation that does not simply slice the century into two halves but presents that earlier half as climaxing in the decade or so immediately preceding the Civil War.

This microperiodization of the antebellum period received its fullest and most popular elucidation in F. O. Matthiessen's *The American Renaissance: Art and Expression in the Age of Whitman and Emerson* (1941). Our periodizing practices are undoubtedly determined by a number of different phenomena, from professional and curricular obligations to the evolution of ideas in American literary studies, but Matthiessen's famous study has played a pivotal role, even for his most vocal critics, in dividing and organizing nineteenth-century literary history. When it was published in 1941, *The American Renaissance* crowned the institutionalization of American literary studies in the academy, a process completed, in part, by importing the periodic categories that critics typically associate with British literature.[18] (Hence, an American Renaissance that competes with its British equivalent.) Matthiessen's book celebrated the "literature for democracy" launched in the "age of Emerson and Whitman," a literature that provided a robust, if belated, cultural complement to the Revolution of 1776.[19] But what defined the period for Matthiessen was not simply the democratic form and content of such books as *Moby-Dick*, *Leaves of Grass*, and *The Scarlet Letter*, but the extraordinarily brief window of time in which they were created: between 1850 and 1855. The Renaissance was the Renaissance precisely because of its strange pairing of beauty and brevity – its sudden, almost miraculous emergence, and its equally sudden collapse.

Matthiessen's contribution to intellectual history, however, lies less in chronology than in nomenclature. In almost every respect, from its authorial selections to the concentrated span of its chronology, Matthiessen's American Renaissance was simply a rechristened version of the New England Renaissance that critics had already been anthologizing and celebrating for more than 40 years. In his *Literary History of America*, published in 1900, Barrett Wendell argued that the most far-ranging movement in nineteenth-century literature was the "Renaissance of New England," a fluorescence of poetry, oratory, and fiction that was spawned by Emerson, Thoreau, Whittier, Longfellow, Holmes, and Hawthorne in the 1840s and 1850s but then decimated by the war. "The intellectual hegemony of Boston," Wendell posited, "may roughly be said to have lasted until the Civil War. That great national convulsion affected the Northern States somewhat as an electric current affects temporarily isolated chemicals; it flashed the Union into new cohesion." In his 1915 study, *A History of American Literature Since 1870*, Fred Lewis Pattee likewise identified a "New England Period" that emerged between the "Knickerbocker Period" of the early republic and the "National Period" of American literature after 1865. The Civil War, as Pattee put it, "marks a dividing line in American history as sharp and definitive as that burned across French history by the Revolution [...] A totally new America grew from the ashes of that great conflict." And this same periodization proved instrumental to other early overviews of American literary history, from Norman Foerster's *The Reinterpretation of American Literature* (1928), which describes the war's destruction of "The New England Renaissance," to Granville Hicks' *The Great Tradition* (1933), which traces the emergence of a "new [literary] spirit" in the 1850s and its wartime decline. As Hicks puts it, books like *Moby-Dick* and *Leaves of Grass* "were the consummation of an epoch that, by 1865, was ended."[20]

Matthiessen's greatest debt, however, was to Van Wyck Brooks. The latter's study, *The Flowering of New England, 1815–1865* (1936), had already gone through dozens of printings and won the Pulitzer Prize by the time that Matthiessen's own account was published, and it pivoted on the same microperiodization of the antebellum era. According to Brooks, the war "brought to a head, however inconclusively, a phase of American literature that later times described as the New England 'renaissance.'" Although some of these authors continued to write, they had all "given their measure before the war, and several had disappeared before it." Writers such as Melville, Whitman, Emerson, and Hawthorne, he explains, had unquestionably "stood for some collective impulse, exceptional in the history of the national mind [...] Whether this impulse was a 'renaissance' or only an 'Indian summer,' as Mr. Santayana has called it, a 'golden age' or a 'golden day,' the impulse existed and the movement was real." Nonetheless, this movement proved to be wholly incompatible with the postwar world. Brooks accordingly begins his subsequent study, *New England: Indian Summer, 1865–1915* (1940), with the following anecdotal description: "In the early spring of 1866, a young man named William Dean Howells quietly slipped into Boston. He was twenty-nine years old, slight, with a black moustache, mild in his manner and modest in appearance. One saw that he had delicate perceptions and a shrewd gift of observation, and he gave one a marked impression of will and purpose. The brooding look in his eyes betokened a future."[21]

Matthiessen's reading of the American Renaissance thus nationalized a regional literature while preserving the phased chronology and accompanying narrative of generational change through which earlier critics had defined that literature. Those two levels of Matthiessen's analysis are codependent. Transforming the New England Renaissance into an American variant required a story of national emergence, and that is precisely what the temporal narrowing of the period provides: it converts this literature into a brief but paradigmatic expression of the state itself. The chronology for the nineteenth century that is so memorably crystallized in *The American Renaissance*, and that continues to bound criticism and teaching in the field, therefore substantiates Kathleen Davis's claim that periodization is never really just a struggle over historical limits but a struggle "over the [very] definition and location of sovereignty."[22] Because they segment historical time by stipulating beginnings and endings, and moments of emergence and decline, periods inevitably narrate – or at least gesture toward – the story of a sovereignty coming into being. This is a vital consideration when thinking about the Civil War's periodic status. The very act of splitting the century into two sequential halves redeploys the myriad narratives of national development upon which the state's sovereignty fictively rests. This is in fact what's at stake in the antebellum/postbellum partitioning upon which so much scholarship is predicated: to the degree that it slices the century into a neatly delineated before and after, it provides fictions of American sovereignty with a nineteenth-century origin story, a narrative of tragic but necessary development that is indelibly inscribed in the nation's literature.[23]

We can better understand the politics of this narrative if we return briefly to Brooks. For the latter, the Renaissance, in all its short-lived glory, was indicative of a much grander pattern of historical development:

> One finds in it the same succession of phases that one finds in the great culture-cycles [...] Here we have a homogeneous people, living close to the soil, intensely religious, unconscious, unexpressed in art and letters [...] One of its towns [then] becomes a "culture-city," for Boston, with Cambridge and Concord as its suburbs, answers to this name [...] There is a springtime feeling in the air, a joyous sense of awakening, a free creativeness, [... and] the mind begins to shape into myths and stories the dreams of the pre-urban countryside. There is a moment of equipoise [...] Then gradually the mind, detached from the soil, grows more and more self-conscious. Contradictions arise within it, and worldlier arts supplant the large, free, ingenuous forms through which the poetic mind has taken shape. What formerly grew from the soil begins to be planned. The Hawthornes yield to the Henry Jameses. Over-intelligent, fragile, cautious and doubtful, the soul of the culture-city loses the self-confidence and joy that have

marked its early development, – it is filled with a presentiment of the end; and [eventually ...] Boston surrenders to New York.[24]

This passage probably strikes most twenty-first century readers as both strange and familiar. Brooks recounts a story of modernization that we have all heard (the countryside gives way to the city, and pre-urban harmony to modern antagonism), capped by a narrative of authorial substitution ("The Hawthornes yield to the Henry Jameses"). But what should we make of those odd hyphenated phrases, the "culture-city" and "culture-cycle"? Or his ideas about collective "myth[s]" and "dreams"? Brooks offers us a clue when, immediately before launching into this description, he claims that this New England Renaissance "obvious[ly]" followed "the typical pattern of the 'culture-cycle,' as Spengler has convincingly described it."

The Spengler to whom Brooks refers is Oswald Spengler, the German doomsayer and philosopher of history whose book *The Decline of the West* (1918–1922) gained a wide readership in the interregnum between World War I and World War II. Despite the book's title, Spengler's subject in *Decline* is not just declension – although that looms throughout, since he frames the twentieth century as the final act of "West-European-American civilization" – but emergence. According to Spengler, human development proceeds through "a series of stages which must be traversed, and traversed moreover in an ordered and obligatory sequence," and literature and art are the most symptomatic expression of this uniform progression. "Each Culture," he reasons, "has its own new possibilities of self-expression which arise, ripen, decay, and never return [...] These cultures, sublimated life-essences, grow with the same superb aimlessness as the flowers of the field." This evolutionary philosophy appears to be organic, even vitalist – hence Brooks's vegetative title, *The Flowering of New England* – but Spengler insists that this aimlessness cannot last because cultures evolve through distinct "wave-cycles," which

> appear suddenly, swell in splendid lines, flatten again and vanish, and the face of the waters is once more a sleeping waste. A Culture is born in the moment when a great soul awakens out of the proto-spirituality of ever-childish humanity, and detaches itself, a form from the formless, a bounded and mortal thing from the boundless and enduring. It blooms on the soil of an exactly-definable landscape, to which plant-wise it remains bound. It dies when this soul has actualized the full sum of its possibilities in the shape of peoples, languages, dogmas, arts, states, sciences, and reverts into the proto-soul [...] The aim once attained – the idea, the entire content of inner possibilities, fulfilled and made externally actual – the Culture suddenly hardens, it mortifies, its blood congeals, its force breaks down, and it becomes *Civilization*.[25]

Culture and Civilization, according to Spengler, are connected through a distinct sequence of development: when a Culture emerges (often through the visionary work of a single "great soul"), it yields a splendid array of art and literature, but it inevitably "mortifies" and becomes the very thing that eventually negates it: a Civilization. (It is a rather Faustian model, wherein one's gifts are but precursors to one's demise.) When Brooks – and after him, Matthiessen and others – describes the sudden rise and fall of the American Renaissance, it is thus a rearticulated version of this wave-cycle, with the antebellum literature of Emerson and Hawthorne comprising the cultural bloom and postbellum realism comprising the civilizational literature that supplants it after the mortification of war.

This importation of Spengler occurred nearly 80 years ago, but it still continues to frame our conceptions of nineteenth-century American literature. Brooks's reading of Renaissance, and its popularization by Matthiessen, has been vigorously critiqued in recent decades, as critics have "reconsidered" the category's myriad exclusions and looked "beneath" its history and politics, but its basic periodization – which traces a literary rise and fall neatly separated by the Civil War – abides. Perhaps this is due to the tendency for periods to "become their own agents," as Timothy J. Reiss writes, and "get naturalized as homogeneous structures whose motor is as lawfully ruled as the mechanical structure [that] Newtonian science took to regulate the physical world."[26] Yet regardless of how or why this periodization became so naturalized, the fact is that the Civil War is a very different kind of literary event than Brooks, Matthiessen, and many other critics have presumed. It is undoubtedly a turning-point for literary history, but it is impossible to locate on a single, chronological timeline. It is certainly a boundary for American culture, but it is also remarkably elastic and unsettled. And that unsettledness is precisely what makes the Civil War exceed, and even trouble, the nationalist narratives into which it is so often merged, which frame the conflict as the discrete, self-contained crucible out of which modern America was born.

Periodization and the Career

Given the war's porousness as a literary and historical marker, one could certainly argue – as several critics recently have – that perhaps periodization itself should be jettisoned. Literary periods, Caroline Levine points out, are inherently "leaky containers," and the reason for this leakage is form: by seeking "to reveal rooted and local historical specificity, pre-cisely in opposition to abstract and timeless organizing principles," peri-odization is the "strange form that antiformalism often takes." For Eric Hayot, periodization is an immanently ideological exercise, the very persistence of which "amounts to a collective failure of imagination and will on the part of the literary profession." Still other scholars have cas-tigated periodization for its "presentism"; its "antiquarianism"; and for its tendency to foreclose readings that emphasize the "sense of lasting trauma, rupture, and profound vulnerability that often accompanies historical events."[27]

Despite its many problems and limitations, periodization will not go away anytime soon – nor should it. There is no way to organize literary history without positing, however tenuously, some kind of story about that history. Even the most microhistorical study or generically centered survey course enlists some mode-of-emplotment to establish connections and disconnections between literary phenomena. Literary history is sim-ply not thinkable without beginnings, endings, gaps, and divergences. Thus, instead of renouncing periodization, the following chapters move in the opposite direction and consider the remarkable *variety* of periodic ideas and figures that emerge out of transbellum writing. Periodization is not an intellectual project invented by latter-day literary professionals; for each of these authors, it is an important imaginative act that enables them to process the Civil War. When Whitman, for instance, enlists Hegel to reframe the war as part of a long dialectical struggle, or when Melville ties the conflict to the violent history of the Holy Land, they are construct-ing accounts of the struggle that hinge, in no small part, on the idea of periodicity.

These writers' transbellum efforts to time and retime the war are part of a broad range of nineteenth-century periodizing practices. Periodization, as we now think of it, derives from Enlightenment-era models of his-toriography that divided up the past so as to better understand the dif-ference of the Enlightenment moment. The Enlightenment was defined partly by its temporalization of historical time, which condensed the plu-ral and cyclical histories that hitherto prevailed into a "collective singu-lar," a History that was unilinear and sequential.[28] The subsequent shift from the Enlightenment to Romanticism produced something like a shift in periodization itself – a grafting, or transfer, of history's phased struc-ture onto an understanding of art and literature. It is hardly coincidental that Romanticism's most celebrated essays and manifestos – like Shelley's "Defence of Poetry" (1840), Emerson's "The Poet" (1844) and Whitman's

1855 preface – are keenly interested in the patterned connections between history and literature: they are designed to take the pulse of the present and measure its distance from the past. Indeed, as James Chandler has argued, Romanticism's historical imaginary – and in particular, the epochal concepts that emerged out of Romanticism's "urgent sense of contemporaneity" – was what made modern-day periodization both thinkable and practicable.[29]

Many of the transbellum works we will consider in the following pages grow out of these periodization practices. But these writers also reveal just how malleable and imaginative such practices could sometimes be prior to their institutionalization. Throughout much of the nineteenth century, periodization was not simply a scholastic affair but a historicizing impulse that acquired a wide array of literary, artistic, and philosophical forms. Melville's "Battle of Stone River, Tennessee" (1866), for instance, marshals many of the things we now tend to associate with periodization – an interest in history's developmental patterns, a focus on epochal differences and similarities, and so forth – into a poem about the Civil War's historical precedents:

> With Tewksbury and Barnet heath
>   In days to come the field shall blend,
> The story dim and date obscure;
>   In legend all shall end.
> Even now, involved in forest shade
>   A Druid-dream the strife appears,
> The fray of yesterday assumes
>   The haziness of years.
>   In North and South still beats the vein
>   Of Yorkist and Lancastrian.
>   [...]
> But where the sword has plunged so deep,
>   And then been turned within the wound
> By deadly Hate; where Climes contend
>   On vasty ground –
> No warning Alps or seas between,
>   And small the curb of creed or law,
> And blood is quick, and quick the brain;
> Shall North and South their rage deplore,
>   And reunited thrive amain
>   Like Yorkist and Lancastrian?[30]

This poem – or "View from Oxford Cloisters," as the subtitle puts it – offers up a cross-epochal perspective wherein the nineteenth-century conflict between the Union and the Confederacy seems to either revive or restage the fifteenth-century conflict between the Houses of York and Lancaster. In certain respects, the American Civil War is but another War of the Roses: now, as then, rival sides are carried away by tribalistic passion; kill each other in the most pastoral of settings; and consider that bloodletting to be both morally justified ("[they] warred for Sway – / For sway, but named the name of Right") and divinely sanctioned ("Monks blessed the fratricidal lance"). Yet Melville is less interested in simply evoking an interesting historical parallel than in meditating on the complex periodicity of fratricidal violence. The opening and concluding stanzas (quoted above) differentiate as much as they connect, suggesting that these battles will "blend" only in the hazy "legend" that eventually enshrouds all wars, and that America's War of the Roses might not end as harmoniously as its English antecedent, since the "sword has plunged so deep" here and neither "creed" nor "law" can assuage "deadly Hate." The poem thereby unfolds, in certain respects, as an exercise in periodization that simultaneously merges the Civil War into a protracted historical sequence *and* gauges its distance from that sequence. Melville vivifies that history in a manner that is all his own, but we will find that all of these transbellum writers draw upon an array of periodic claims and historical ideas in order to represent the Civil War and account for its non-synchronicity.[31]

By examining the transbellum timescapes imagined into being by these ostensibly "antebellum" authors, I hope to amend some of the recent, incisive scholarship on the links between prewar and postwar literature. In certain respects, my argument parallels the counternarrative for the period that Michael T. Gilmore carves out in *The War on Words: Slavery, Race, and Free Speech in American Literature* (2010). In a series of elegant readings that range from Emerson's *Nature* (1836) to Dixon's *The Leopard's Spots* (1902), Gilmore contends that the antebellum and postbellum periods are in fact connected through a common predicament: the censorship of language effected by debates about slavery (before the war) and race (after the war). This linguistic policing, Gilmore argues, "began in earnest by targeting abolitionism in the 1830s, was briefly overthrown during and after the Civil War, and, redirecting its animus toward racial equality, acquired fresh life and lasted into the next century." In the 1840s and 1850s, when the planter class controlled much of the government and "used legislation and bullying to stifle agitation against the South's labor regime," this censorship acquired real material force, and it is apparent in the silences and gaps that proliferate in prewar writing, from Melville's "Benito Cereno" (1855) to Poe's "Murders in the Rue Morgue" (1841). The war, rather than ending this deterrence, simply shifted its legal and perceptual contours. Postwar literature in general, and realism in particular, Gilmore argues, internalizes this "contraction of discursive possibility" – a narrowing legible in the "encoded communication" of George Washington Cable's *The Grandissimes* (1880), in Henry James's fascinating silences, and in the ethical dilemmas of language that are grimly staged in *Billy Budd* (1888–91).[32] While I am less convinced than Gilmore is about the later political apostasy of these prewar writers, my account of the nineteenth century traces a similar trajectory for the period, according to which the war is less a terminus than a transition.

If for Gilmore the continuity between antebellum and postbellum literature resides in the lasting restrictions on free speech, for Maurice Lee it inheres in American writers' abiding interest in and anxieties about chance. As he argues in *Uncertain Chances: Science, Skepticism, and Belief in Nineteenth-Century American Literature* (2011), although the discourse of probability is often associated with late-nineteenth-century philosophy and the ascent of scientific positivism, it originated in earlier American culture. The "rise of chance and the spread of the probabilistic revolution" is first evident not in the pragmatism of William James and Oliver Wendell Holmes, Jr., but in prewar writing, from Poe's detective stories (which continuously – indeed, *obsessively* – enlist the discourse of probability) to Douglass's essays and speeches (which sometimes overflow with statistics) and Melville's fiction (which, from *Moby-Dick* to "Bartleby," explores the limits and possibilities of ethical action in a world governed by chance). This connection between probability and literature, Lee argues, lasts through and even after the war. The "complexity, chaos, and violence of the conflict put increasing pressure on providential accounts of the war, but [...] in the lead-up to the conflict and during its course, many commentators figured the possibilities of war in terms of fortune, risk, luck, gambling, unpredictable weather, and unknowable causation." Lee's account thereby enables us to view the war not as a sudden, epistemic rupture but as a conflict that amplified the ideas and concerns regarding probability that were already deeply embedded in prewar American culture.[33]

Critics have also challenged – or at least elided – the antebellum/postbellum divide by examining the fluid development of literary genres; the self-periodizing capacity of the affects; and the long history of poetry's political and print cultures.[34] As this scholarship has demonstrated, the split chronology encapsulated by the terms antebellum and postbellum cannot trace the diachronic patterns of American literary history and must be supplanted by models of literary correspondence that are better equipped to account for those patterns' dynamism and irregularity. This book contributes to this project by reconstructing the transbellum shape of these writers' careers, and it is indeed the career as a hermeneutic category in which I am most invested. By their very nature, careers bridge the historical and the transhistorical, unfolding in ways that disclose the influence of particular events on given works and, at the same time, the broader imaginative connections with which those works are bound up. Careers thereby enable us to read multilinearly across eras and genres that are often kept quite separate from one another, and this perspective is utterly crucial when it comes to the Civil War. Throughout their careers, the ways in which these writers figure time – as a lived experience, political modality, and matter of literary form – shift and evolve, and these changing practices of chronopolitical imagining offer us a different point of access not only to the defining transitions in these authors' lives but also to the shape and impact of the war itself.

One such measure of the career's value as a hermeneutic standpoint is the emphasis it places on what a writer actually read. Whitman, Douglass, Melville, and Dickinson were not simply prolific authors; they were voracious readers and autodidacts whose writerly output was directly tied to their readerly entanglements. In these chapters, I thus linger with some of the texts that fascinated these writers: Frederic Hedge's *The Prose Writers of Germany* (1848), which Whitman treasured; John Lothrop Motley's *The Rise of the Dutch Republic* (1856), which Douglass mined for transbellum history; Arthur Schopenhauer's *The World as Will and Idea* (1818), which provoked and inspired Melville late in life; and the poems and periodicals that were important to Dickinson throughout the Long Civil War. Such intertextual engagements are often approached as evidence of broad print networks or discursive formations – and so they are. But they are also evidence of reading, which, as every bibliophile knows, can yield new ideas, subvert old ones, and produce an almost infinite variety of pleasures, doubts, and surprises.[35] That raw volatility which derives from reading and responding to that reading only becomes legible if we take the idea of the authorial career seriously.

Careers also oblige us to move between – and in so doing, put pressure on – the moments and movements that ostensibly encapsulate writers. The protracted careers of Whitman, Douglass, Melville, and Dickinson conjure up a wide array of categories that their writing actively remixes and reassembles. In the cyclical timespace of *Battle-Pieces*, the cryptic lines of Dickinson's late poems, the raucous history of Douglass's lectures, and the anticipatory deferrals of the later *Leaves*, categories such as "antebellum," "postbellum," and "wartime" both crystallize and dissolve, yielding a literature that crosses through the conflict and far beyond it – a literature, in sum, that can only be called transbellum.

CHAPTER I

Walt Whitman's Dialectics

When Whitman was preparing the final, deathbed edition of *Leaves of Grass* for publication in 1891, he wrote an essay about the literary labor that had consumed the past 40 years of his life. As he recounts the long evolution of *Leaves*, he quickly discovers that this most protean book of songs (and bodies, and glances, and selves, and vegetation) is exceedingly difficult to sum up. So he tests out a variety of definitions. *Leaves of Grass*, he suggests, is perhaps best viewed as "my definitive *carte [de] visite* to the coming generations of the New World," a verbal record of "one man's – the author's – identity, ardors, observations, faiths, and thoughts." Or, maybe, as a poetic experiment that redoubles the political experiment of the American Revolution. Or, perhaps, as a "sortie" for unrhymed verse. Or "modern science." Or the New World "ego." Or "Sex and Amativeness." Or "the working-man and the working-woman."[1]

Although it is nearly impossible for Whitman to categorize this "multitudinous" book, he does make one thing quite clear: that whatever one calls *Leaves*, and however one classifies it, it is inarguably a document of the Civil War:

> [It was] only from the occurrence of the Secession War, and [...] from the strong flare and provocation of that war's sights and scenes [that my ...] autochthonic and passionate song definitely came forth. I went down to the war fields in Virginia (end of 1862), lived thenceforward in camp, [...] partook of all the fluctuations, gloom, despair, hopes again arous'd, courage evoked – death readily risk'd – *the cause*, too – along and filling those agonistic and lurid following years, 1863-'64-'65 – the real parturition years (more than 1776-'83) of this henceforth homogeneous Union. Without those three or four years and the experiences they gave, "Leaves of Grass" would not now be existing. (*PW*, 2: 724)

The "real parturition years" not only spawned the modern American nation; they also occasioned Whitman's own "passionate song" and inspired him to compose *Leaves of Grass*. His celebratory chant thus originated not in a moment of peaceful repose but in the midst of this internecine conflict, with all of its "fluctuations, gloom, [and] despair."

This description of Whitman's massive debt to the Civil War is stirring and beautiful. It is also patently untrue. Prior to the outbreak of violence in 1861, Whitman had already issued three separate editions of *Leaves of Grass*, and those prewar books were the byproduct of more than a decade of reading and writing about history, politics, slavery, language, music, and aesthetics. When he claims that "my 'Leaves' could not possibly have emerged or been fashion'd" without "the absolute triumph of the National Union arms" (*PW*, 2:718), he expunges dozens of years and hundreds of pages from *Leaves*' actual compositional history. And yet, despite the chronological erroneousness of Whitman's retrospection, it does underscore a crucial fact about *Leaves*: that it is indeed a very different book after "the strong flare and provocation of that war's sights and scenes." In the later editions (that is, 1867, 1871, 1881, and 1891), there are fewer artisans, and more soldiers; fewer catalogs, and more apostrophes; and the poems, as well as the volumes themselves, tend to be more tightly sequenced and organized.

Whitman made these changes to *Leaves of Grass* over the course of the 26 years following the Confederacy's defeat. During that time, he also published two probing memoirs about the conflict, *Memoranda during the War* (1876) and *Specimen Days* (1882), as well as numerous essays that he later collected in *Notes Left Over* (1881) and *November Boughs* (1888). Whitman's career thus bridges the very epochal boundaries and periodic subsets that have long structured American literary studies; it is not so much antebellum or postbellum as it is interperiodic – or more accurately, what I am calling transbellum. Like these other authors, Whitman writes prodigiously across the nineteenth century by continually retiming the war in his poems and prose. And that retiming is what enables him to account for this event which, as Peter Coviello, Robert Leigh Davis, Betsy Erkkila, Michael Moon, and M. Wynn Thomas (among others) have shown us, profoundly impacted his sense of national, authorial, and sexual identity. As Whitman himself once put it, the war was "the centre, circumference, umbilicus, of my whole career."[2]

The word "umbilicus" – a Latinate version of "navel" that also means "core" or "heart" – is an appropriate one for Whitman, who repeatedly returns to the conflict as a kind of natal scene.[3] Although he frequently claims in his later works that "the war, the war is over" (*LG*, 1:210), that struggle comes back again and again in these writings, and often when you least expect it: in essays about Shakespeare; poems about workers; and discussions of his "gray-blurr'd old shell" of a body (which he attributed not to the strokes that progressively immobilized him but to his "too over-zealous [...] bodily emotional excitement and action through the times of 1862, '3, '4, and '5" [*PW*, 2:737–8]).[4] The war's abiding presence in these works is frequently called "nostalgic," but in Whitman's later writings retrospection almost always yields to projection. In fact, the predominant temporal framework of his transbellum writing is a peculiar kind of anticipation in which the recent past gives way to an imminent future that is only beginning to unfold.[5] This sense of time bears less resemblance to nostalgia, which empties out the present in order to make way for the past's return, than to Hegel's philosophy of history, which construes the past and the present as – in Whitman's words – "different steps or links" in "the endless process of Creative thought, which, amid number-less apparent failures and contradictions, is held together by central and never-broken unity" (*PW*, 1:259).

That resemblance is hardly coincidental. During and after the Civil War, Whitman became increasingly interested in Hegel and often used dialectics to write new poems, rewrite old ones, and revise his thoughts about that bloody struggle. This chapter is about how and why this shift in Whitman's career occurs. I begin with *Drum-Taps*, which enlists an array of temporal scales to represent the war, and then move through the editions of *Leaves* into which that book was subsequently integrated. The Civil War, we will find, takes shape across these transbellum works not as a discrete upheaval but as a complex rupture that is just as protracted, and just as multitudinous, as Whitman's own *carte de visite*. And that is what makes the later *Leaves* so remarkable: they reframe that conflict as part of a dialectical history that outstrips the periodizing categories through which Whitman and these other transbellum writers are so often grouped.

Drum-Taps and the Chaos of War

For Whitman, the Civil War's greatest surprise came in the winter of 1862, when he received word that his brother George, an infantryman with New York's 51st, was among the nearly 10,000 Union soldiers wounded in the recent battle at Fredericksburg. Walt immediately took the train to Washington and spent two straight days "hunting through the hospitals, walking all day and night, [...] trying to get information" but without acquiring "the least clue to anything."[6] When he finally reached George, he discovered that his brother was relatively unscathed. An exploding shell had cut open his cheek, but he was convalescing quickly and could soon return to his regiment.

Whitman, however, decided to stay behind. In the hospitals, he discovered that there were countless other soldiers – brothers all, in his *Calamus*-like estimation – who needed his care. So for the next 3 years, he volunteered his services as a nurse, swapping out bandages, comforting the wounded, and writing letters home for those who could no longer write for themselves. "[N]ever before," he attested, "had my feelings [been] so thoroughly and [...] permanently absorbed, to the very roots, as by these huge swarms of dear, wounded, sick, dying boys – I get very much attached to some of them, and many of them have come to depend on seeing me, and having me sit by them a few minutes, as if for their lives." Throughout the day, Whitman often recorded what he witnessed in stray lines and memoranda, writing – as he later recalled – "by fits and starts, on the field, in the hospitals, as I worked with the soldier boys. Some days I was more emotional than others, then I would suffer all the extra horrors of my experience – I would try to write, blind, blind, with my own tears."[7]

Over the course of the ensuing decade, Whitman expanded these loose notes into a series of searching meditations that span from *Drum-Taps* (1865) to *Specimen Days* (1882) and *Memoranda during the War* (1876). I want to focus primarily on *Drum-Taps* (and its subsequent merger into *Leaves*) because of its transbellum scope. It originated during the war and then acquired a variety of different forms: a book (1865), a sequel (1865–6), an addendum (1867), and a series of clusters (1871, 1881 and 1891). Across these textual instantiations, *Drum-Taps* continually evolves as Whitman tries, again and again, to represent this long and bloody war.

When it first appeared, *Drum-Taps* met a rather mixed reception. Reviewers liked some of the poems, especially "When Lilacs Last in Dooryard Bloom'd," but considered the book overall to be rather poorly designed and hastily executed. "The trouble about it," William Dean Howells opined, is that it is "music[al]" but "inarticulate"; it does not endow thought or experience with "a portable shape" and fails to provide a cogent vision of the war. The most biting criticism came from a young Henry James, who deemed *Drum-Taps* a melancholic and unpoetic hodge-podge. According to James, every poem – nay, every line of every poem – "stands off by itself, in resolute independence of its companions, without a visible goal," furnishing but a wild "medley" of impressions that never converge into "a single idea."[8] Such reviews, of course, probably tell us less about Whitman's poetry than they do about the importance of a unified artistic consciousness to budding realists like James and Howells. But they are right, in a certain sense, about *Drum-Taps'* structural heterogeneity. Whitman's book is an astonishingly fragmented affair. Unlike Melville's *Battle-Pieces* (1866), which proceeds – as we shall see in Chapter 3 – through historical time, *Drum-Taps* unfolds through perspectival shifts. The poems also enlist a broad range of affective, aesthetic, and experiential registers, from the imagistic ("Cavalry Crossing a Ford," "Mother and Babe," "A Farm Picture") to the prophetic ("Over the Carnage"), all of which are articulated through assorted metaphors of movement (marching, stopping, waiting, walking) and sound (the martial tap, the funereal dirge, the bugle's wail).

This disorder is partly the result of Whitman's process of composition. *Drum-Taps* is not a retrospective meditation on a conflict that has just concluded but a book penned amidst the war that it so beautifully and variously records. Whitman published a version of "A Broadway Pageant" in the *New York Times* in 1860. And the poems "Beat! Beat! Drums!," "I Heard You Solemn-Sweet Pipes of the Organ," and "Old Ireland" all appeared in periodicals shortly afterwards, in 1861. Critics who have studied *Drum-Taps'* publication history have also argued that the book's chaotic arrangement was something of a forced choice: Whitman's contract allotted him only seventy-two pages, and the economics of wartime publishing compelled him to cram as many poems as he could into these limited "leaves."[9] Nonetheless, if there is one thing we know about Whitman, it is that he conceived of his books as extensions of himself and of the world more broadly. No writer who refers to his poems as "autochthonous song[s]," or who conceives of the United States as "essentially the greatest poem," would issue a book of verse that was not carefully and lovingly designed (*PW*, 2:731, 434). Upon the eve of *Drum-Taps'* publication, he also told a friend that the book's disorderliness was what made it "*superior* to *Leaves of Grass* – certainly more perfect as a work of art." "I feel at last," he declared, "& for the first time without any demur, that I am [...] content to have it go to the world verbatim." Although "the ordinary reader," he added, will think it was "let loose with wildest abandon," *Drum-Taps* but expresses the raw heterogeneity of "this *Time & Land we swim in*, with all their large conflicting fluctuations of despair & hope, the shiftings, masses, & the whirl & deafening din, [...] the unprecedented anguish of wounded & suffering, the beautiful young men, in wholesale death & agony, everything sometimes as if in blood color, & dripping blood."[10]

Drum-Taps tends to figure these "shiftings" and "fluctuations" temporally. Eschewing the idea that a single vision can be wrested from the war,

Whitman uses a variety of proliferating timeframes, from the calendrical ("1861," "Year that Trembled and Reel'd Beneath Me") to the musical ("Beat! Beat! Drums!") and the astronomical ("Year of Meteors"). Although he occasionally flirts with ideas of fated emergence, *Drum-Taps* tends to immerse the reader in a stunning array of disparate temporalities. The war thereby emerges in Whitman's poems as a polyvalent and multilinear event that is most amply recorded not in combat but in the volatile temporalities of grief and pain, in the cadences of the march, and in the pauses required for wonderment.

Drum-Taps' discordant temporalities made the book, as Michael Warner has argued, a rather "unusual piece of war discourse." Whereas most Civil War poetry reflected on the war's defining battles and ideas, *Drum-Taps* shuttles "between different layers of composition and different rhetorics of time." Some of the poems, Warner points out, are addressed to specific "years, recreating and commenting upon historical frames of expectation and uncertainty," but the underlying suggestion of the volume is that "the calendar itself has been rendered directionless and nonnumerically suggestive." *Drum-Taps*, he writes, "does not exactly record history; events have been pushed to the margin along with the historical god who is usually thought to direct them. Its oddly looped narrative time is registered through a kind of trembling before history."[11] This description of temporality in *Drum-Taps* as "oddly looped," and of history in the volume as "trembled before" rather than recorded, helps us understand just how transformative the war must have been for Whitman. The "red business" of the "Secession War" extinguished his vision of America's temporal and political harmony, and he responds in *Drum-Taps* by fashioning a series of unbound, nonlinear timeframes (*LG*, 2:455).[12]

Warner's account also helps us make sense of one of the more peculiar dynamics in *Drum-Taps*: the relative absence of violence in this volume that was written, in Whitman's words, with "the bayonet's flashing point" for a pen and "streams of blood" for ink (*LG*, 2:458). If Whitman is more interested in fragments than in totality, it makes sense that violence manifests only as something that is expected, remembered, or mourned over. Bullets and "slugs whizz" (*LG*, 2:458) not in battle itself, but in the anticipatory timespace of the recruitment poems ("Drum-Taps," "First O Songs for a Prelude") and in the vivid memories of aged nurses ("The Wound-Dresser") and veterans ("The Veteran's Vision"). The only bodies that are opened up, showing us precisely what war does to the divine human corpus, are either undergoing surgery or are already buried, having been transformed through violence into "white skeletons" and "debris"

(*LG*, 2:538). These elliptical representations of the dead, Warner helps make clear, mimic the broader structural architecture of *Drum-Taps*, which tends to break the war into pieces because for Whitman no vision of its historical totality is poetically thinkable or philosophically tenable.

Nonetheless, I am far less convinced than Warner is that *Drum-Taps'* assorted frameworks have an "implicitly and sometimes explicitly religious cast."[13] The volume's chaotic temporalities certainly touch on matters of religiosity, particularly in "A Child's Amaze" and the "Hymn of Dead Soldiers," but most of the poems consider very different types of experience, like the processes of reading and learning ("Shut Not Your Doors," "Beginning My Studies"), the meanings of flags and other signs ("As Toilsome I Wander'd Virginia's Woods," "Thick-Sprinkled Bunting," "World, Take Good Notice"), and the power of memory ("The Wound-Dresser"). Even when Whitman claims to have learned a lesson from the war, as he does in "Solid, Ironical, Rolling Orb," it is framed as a secular insight:

> Solid, ironical, rolling orb!
> Master of all, and matter of fact! – at last I accept your terms;
> Bringing to practical, vulgar tests, of all my ideal dreams,
> And of me, as lover and hero.
>
> (*LG*, 2:522)

What Whitman accepts here is not some Providential faith but the raw destructive power of the earth's perpetual revolutions: this is the cosmological "fact" that "tests" his democratic "dreams."

If one construes time in *Drum-Taps* as theologically inflected, it is also difficult to understand why so many of the poems are more interested in things like ships, faces, and moonlight than they are in gods or creeds. Several poems, for instance, are primarily concerned with water during wartime. In "The Torch," Whitman envisions a lake near the Pacific:

> On my Northwest coast in the midst of the night a
> fisherman's group stands watching;
> Out on the lake, expanding before them, others are
> spearing salmon;
> The canoe, a dim shadowy thing, moves across the
> black water,
> Bearing a Torch a-blaze at the prow.
>
> (*LG*, 2:503)

Here we are almost entirely removed from the world of Gettysburg and Shiloh. The war itself seems like a "dim shadowy thing" in these four lines, which replace the temporalities of battle with the more melodious experiences of "watching" and "spearing" (which, not coincidentally, are poetic as well as water-borne acts). A similar sense of momentary peace is cultivated in the concluding stanza of "The Ship":

> Lo! the unbounded sea!
> On its breast a Ship, spreading all her sails – an ample
>   Ship, carrying even her moonsails;
> The pennant is flying aloft, as she speeds, she
>   speeds so stately – below, emulous waves press
>   forward,
> They surround the Ship, with shining curving motions,
>   and foam.
>
> (*LG*, 2:512)

Whitman, of course, was always drawn to the water: "Song of Myself" features a crucial nautical section, and both "Crossing Brooklyn Ferry" and "Out of the Cradle Endlessly Rocking" depict *Leaves* as an oceanic poem and performance. During the war, the "unbounded sea" seems to have provided Whitman with a natural analogue for the Union's war effort. And it is precisely by forging this sense of liquid cadence that Whitman's maritime poems feed back into the volume's broader temporal looping, which ties these moments of undulation to a broad array of other perspectives and frameworks.

Across *Drum-Taps*, Whitman is particularly interested in the temporalities of wartime movements, and none more so than the march. The book draws its very title from the rhythmic drumming that led the armies, in unison and *en masse*, from the camp to the battlefield and back. Throughout the poems, as Whitman sings about the soldiers' "unknown road[s]," "the world of labor and / the march," and the sight of men "countermarching by swift millions," it becomes clear that marching is not simply a form of martial kinesis but an emblematic mode of collective action (*LG*, 2:494, 475, 504). To march, the same actions must be repeatedly and serially enacted; it is a ritualized absorption into a group whose membership is felt and gauged in the measured motions of the body. In *Drum-Taps*, marching is a secularized congregation of movement, a joint practice of devotion that solidifies an embodied covenant with the Union and its representative army.

Marching also manifests as a literary rhythm that encapsulates Whitman's own *ars poetica*. This connection between marching, poetics, and violence is most explicit in "Spirit Whose Work is Done":

Spirit of gloomiest fears and doubts, (yet onward ever
    unfaltering pressing;)
[...]
While I look on the bayonets bristling over their shoulders;
While those slanted bayonets, whole forests of them,
    appearing in the distance, approach and pass on,
    returning homeward,
Moving with steady motion, swaying to and fro, to the right
    and left,
Evenly, lightly rising and falling, as the steps keep time:
– Spirit of hours I knew, all hectic red one day, but pale as
    death next day;
Touch my mouth, ere you depart – press my lips close!
Leave me your pulses of rage! bequeath them to be! fill
    me with currents convulsive!

                            (*LG*, 2:542–43)

Although this poem directs itself apostrophically to the war, its true subject (as is so often the case with Whitman) is Whitman. The lines focus not
on the generals, or the soldiers, or the bloodshed, but on what Whitman
sees: the patterns of relation forged by the march, as "whole forests" of
bayonets sway back and forth, blending in perfect unison, as though pul-
sating to the beat of a single heart. The poem then turns toward a fictive,
wished-for encounter between Whitman and the war's "Spirit," capped by
a single impossible kiss that will miraculously convey to him the struggle's
"currents convulsive." The poem thus represents Whitman as the war's
most adequate conduit, and what comes from this imagined transfer is an
identification of the war almost exclusively with the march and the particular manner in which it "keep[s] time."

    For Whitman, as for many Civil War soldiers, marching provides a way
to momentarily take leave of all the war's terrifying temporalities – the
anticipations of violence, the fraught timeframes of grief and mourning, the surprises of combat and destruction – and be swept up, in their
absence, by a hypnotic rhythm. If, as Cheryl Wells has posited, the Civil
War scrambled the temporalities that had hitherto prevailed in the United
States by introducing "battle time," which "impinged on, overrode, and
rearranged" other chronometrics, it is possible to view Whitman's turn
to the march as an attempt to keep time, in the midst of such upheaval,
by focusing on the thing that he treasured the most: the human body. In
other parts of *Drum-Taps,* the divine body is profoundly at risk. In "The
Wound-Dresser," we encounter lacerated necks, shattered knees, amputated hands, and crushed heads. (As Whitman later attested, when he

first went to the hospitals he was greeted by a giant "heap of amputated feet, legs, arms, hands, &c., a full load for a one-horse cart."[14]) But in the marching poems the body is returned to its original, beautiful totality. Arms, feet, and faces advance in unison, generating a shared rhythm – a processional, embodied timescape – which makes momentary order out of chaos.

Whitman also inscribes that beat of the march into the very structure of his poems. Both "Pioneers! O Pioneers!" and "Dirge for Two Veterans" enlist quatrains that encase the most unwieldy of experiences – generational passage and mourning, respectively – in a pattern of doubled return. Whitman's famous, rhymed dirge for Lincoln, "O Captain! my Captain!," measures time with the same pulse as soldiers' marching feet:

> O Captain! my Captain! our fearful trip is done;
> The ship has weather'd every rack, the prize we sought is won;
> The port is near, the bells I hear, the people all exulting,
> While follow eyes the steady keel, the vessel grim and daring:
> But O heart! heart! heart!
> Leave you not the little spot,
> Where on the deck my captain lies,
> Fallen cold and dead.
> (*LG*, 2:540–1)

This poem has enjoyed such a long afterlife because it is the most orderly of elegies. The iambs strike almost like taps on a drum and the rhymes advance in a steady, paired procession (*aabb*). The poem's quartets also establish two intertwined movements – one that is longer and more narrativized, and one that is shorter and more exclamatory – which alternate, lockstep, until the final grim statement (which is also a refrain): "But I with silent tread, / Walk the spot my captain lies, / Fallen cold and dead." These formal choices have been described as integral to "a communal rhetorical strategy, appealing in [their] memorizable simplicity to a broad base of readers," and that strategy is successful precisely because the poem draws on the beat of the march in order to contain the uncontainable.[15]

Marching, however, is only one of many different timeframes in *Drum-Taps*. Several of the poems, such as "Camps of Green," "Mother and Babe," and "When I Heard the Learn'd Astronomer," are about what happens when there is nothing to march to or from. "A Farm Picture," for instance, pivots not on action, whether individual or collective, but on pausing and looking:

Through the ample open door of the peaceful country barn,
A sunlit pasture field with cattle and horses feeding,
And haze and vista, and the far horizon fading away.

(LG, 2:497)

Here we witness light's gorgeous diurnal rebirth. As the sunlight fills the pasture and then dissipates into "haze and vista," the war – like the darkness that precedes the morning – seems to fade away at the horizon. This "picture" finds a fitting companion in "Bivouac on a Mountain Side":

I see before me now, a traveling army halting;
Below, a fertile valley spread, with barns and the orch-
　　ards of summer,
Behind, the terraced sides of a mountain, abrupt in
　　places, rising high;
Broken, with rocks, with clinging cedars, with tall
　　shapes, dingily seen;
The numerous camp-fires scatter'd near and far, some
　　away up on the mountain;
The shadow forms of men and horses, looming, large-
　　sized, flickering;
And over all, the sky – the sky! far, far out of reach,
　　studded with the eternal stars.

(LG, 2:526)

The "halting" at the poem's outset seems to promise some insight – a clue, perhaps, to where this why this "army" is "traveling." The only thing yielded by this cessation, however, is a scene of pastoral (and then astral) beauty. As the lines slide from the traveling corps to the valleys, orchards, terraces, and cedars, they erase the lines of battle (it is even ambiguous whether this is a Northern or a Southern army), and the war vanishes into the stars. Both of these poems temporarily suspend the very conflict whose devastation not only fills the volume but also limns these brief stunning scenes. In the initial versions of *Drum-Taps* (i.e., the editions published between 1865 and 1867), "A Farm Picture" immediately follows Whitman's discovery of three anonymous corpses – an old man "all sunken about the eyes," a young boy "with cheeks yet blooming," and a middle-aged man with a "calm" visage – by a hospital tent (*LG*, 2:496); and "Bivouac" is placed just before a poem about the mass deaths of the battlefield ("Pensive on Her Dead Gazing, I Heard the Mother of All"). What makes these scenes so beautiful and so moving has less to do with their particular contents and than with their timing: these are pauses before and after loss, moments that either precede or follow death.

These poems, like countless others in *Drum-Taps*, imaginatively retrace Whitman's lines of vision. In "A Farm Picture," his gaze is photographic and horizontal: the observer sees the light catch the earth through the barn's "open door"; his sight is bounded by a square frame, just as in the daguerreotypes that Whitman loved and cherished. Similarly, in "Mother and Babe" –

> I see the sleeping babe, nestling the breast of its
>   mother;
> The sleeping mother and babe – hush'd, I study them
>   long and long.
>
> (*LG*, 2:491)

– he looks directly at the war-torn world around him and records it as if it were a photograph, "catching life on the run, in a flash."[16] In other poems, Whitman directs his gaze downwards, either at the ground ("Quicksand Years," "Rise O Days from Your Fathomless Depths") or at the corpses and near-corpses that will soon fill it ("Vigil Strange I Kept On the Field One Night," "A March in the Ranks"). A vast majority of the poems in the volume, however, tend to tilt their vision upwards. The great western "orb" in "Lilacs"; the stars in "Bivouac"; the mountains in "Lo! Victress On the Peaks!"; and the astronomical bodies of "Look Down Fair Moon," "Year of Meteors" and "Give Me the Splendid Silent Sun" all direct Whitman's sight, and our own, away from the earth and toward the heavens. This stargazing is most finely captured in "When I Heard the Learn'd Astronomer":

> When I heard the learn'd astronomer;
> When the proofs, the figures, were ranged in columns
>   before me;
> When I was shown the charts and diagrams, to add,
>   divide, and measure them;
> When I, sitting, heard the astronomer, where he
>   lectured with much applause in the lecture-room,
> How soon, unaccountable, I became tired and sick;
> Till rising and gliding out, I wander'd off by myself,
> In the mystical moist night-air, and from time to time,
> Look'd up in perfect silence at the stars.
>
> (*LG*, 2:483)

This is surely one of the weirdest of all war poems. Meditating on the stars rather than the struggle at hand, "When I Heard the Learn'd Astronomer" seems to be almost entirely disconnected from not only from the Civil

War but also from the volume of poems in which it appears. The poem's ideational movement is nonetheless exceedingly familiar. As Whitman moves from the lecture room to the open air, measurement gives way to wonder, and that ensuing sense of astonishment – of being stunned into silence by the immeasurable – is in many respects the prevailing affect in *Drum-Taps*.[17] It is repeated almost every time he sees a corpse, or aids in a surgery, or gazes up through "the mystical moist night-air."

In certain respects, this silent amazement is a kind of eloquent refusal. By the time *Drum-Taps* first appeared in print, various forms of demographic and statistical accounting had emerged to record, quantify, and assess the war's costs. The Union and Confederate governments scrupulously tracked the numerical categories that indexed victory and defeat: revenues and expenditures, soldiers killed and conscripted, munitions depleted, armaments produced. Regional newspapers regularly printed lists of the local dead and presumed dead, and national periodicals routinely used statistics to explain assorted routs, setbacks, and impasses. Although these accounting practices originated long before the Civil War, that conflict's unprecedented scales of loss and destruction made such numerical measurements indispensable for imagining and reckoning the war. This collective impulse to cognitively map the struggle by way of numbers was markedly unstable, however. As Max Cavitch points out, "the scientific tallying of the dead" often had the paradoxical effect of underscoring its own inadequacy, since it promised to "redeem unidentifiable and unlocatable bodies for a symbolic totality of otherwise immeasurable sacrifice, while at the same time highlighting the pace at which the war was outstripping both the psychic and material resources of individuated mourning."[18]

Much of the literature that surrounds the war views these accounting practices with skepticism. Melville and Douglass locate the war's meaning in the deep patterns of history rather than the calculated present, and Dickinson's poems repeatedly challenge the idea that the war can be historically or cognitively mapped at all. In *Drum-Taps*, Whitman constructs a kind of antistatistical vision of the war, a poetry of incalculability that recalls his well-known description, in *Memoranda*, of the war's countless "strayed dead" who lay, unburied and unremembered, in the nation's "fields and woods and valleys":

[T]he estimate of the War department is 25,000 National soldiers kill'd in battle and never buried at all, 5,000 drown'd – 15,000 inhumed by strangers or on the march in haste, in hitherto unfound localities – 2,000 graves cover'd by sand and mud, by Mississippi freshets, 3,000 carried away by caving-in of banks, &c., [...] the dead, the dead, the dead – *our* dead [...] Some where they crawl'd to die, alone, in bushes, low gulleys, or on the sides of hills – (there, in secluded spots, their skeletons, bleach'd bones, tufts of hair, buttons, fragments of clothing, are occasionally found, yet) [...] the general Million, and the special Cemeteries in almost all the States – the Infinite Dead – (the land entire is saturated, perfumed with their impalpable ashes' exhalation in Nature's chemistry distill'd, and shall be so forever, and every grain of wheat and ear of corn, and every flower that grows, and every breath we draw,) – not only Northern dead leavening Southern soil – thousands, aye many tens of thousands, of Southerners, crumble to-day in Northern earth.[19]

This chemistry cannot be grasped through science. (Hence the progression, in Whitman's language, from the wholeness of numbers to the fragmentation of bodies.) The only proper way to register these deaths is to experience the same kind of astonishment that Whitman feels upon leaving the astronomer's lecture. That decision to glide out and wander by himself is a decision to gaze rather than add or divide. When Whitman looks up in *Drum-Taps*, as he so frequently does, it is to acknowledge the war's patternlessness, which can be partially beheld but never fully assessed.

Whitman's war poems thereby contravene epochal categories such as "antebellum" and "postbellum," which hinge on a neat and progressive segmenting of historical time. First published in 1865, *Drum-Taps* entered the world around the same moment that, according to our prevailing model of periodization, the postbellum era began to come into being. This is supposed to be the moment of realism's embryonic birth and Romanticism's eclipse. This is the moment when the war ostensibly "swept away" the "whole intellectual culture of the North" and created the conditions for modern life and American pragmatism. This is the moment when, according to most American literature anthologies and surveys, there is a macrohistorical passage from prewar to postwar, a progression from everything that was antebellum to everything that came after it.[20] And yet that moment never materializes in *Drum-Taps*. Instead of witnessing a tectonic shift in the structure of historical time, we gaze at the stars. Or we wait, or march. Or we see Whitman nursing, or taking pictures.

This prodigious mixture of timescales in *Drum-Taps* mirrors the various modes of cross-identification that fill out Whitman's other Civil War writings. In *Specimen Days* and *Memoranda*, Whitman tends to represent himself, as Roy Morris, Jr. and Robert Leigh Davis remark, as both "doctor and nurse, mother and father, friend and lover, angel and Death," folding different identities into one another so that "'enemies' are at the same time 'brothers,' 'sisters,' 'fathers,' 'friends,' and 'lovers.'" A similar dynamic unfolds across *Drum-Taps*, but Whitman's cross-perspective here pivots less on identity than on time, as his "splintered, centerless point of view" weaves together a heterogeneous array of temporal frameworks, feelings, and perceptions.[21] The Civil War thereby becomes spectacularly diffuse, manifesting in these poems not as a single upheaval that can be confidently timed and measured but as a variety of sounds, processions, pauses, and surprises, which Whitman weaves into a chaotic series of exquisite songs.

Leaves of Grass, before and after *Drum-Taps*

Whitman, of course, had always been fascinated by time's plurality. In the notebooks that he composed prior to *Leaves of Grass*, he reflects at length on the soul's unceasing growth ("I think the soul will never stop, or [... reach a point] beyond which it shall not go"); the immediate insights yielded by bodily contact ("touch" provides "me a library of knowledge in an instant"); and the ideal poet's peculiar conflation of timeliness and untimeliness ("I do not lag – I do not hasten [...] I exist in the void that takes uncounted time and coheres to a nebula").[22] Across its first three editions, *Leaves of Grass* is similarly replete with timeframes that are just as diverse as Whitman's protean poetic self. When reading these poems, one continually encounters a broad and sometimes overwhelming array of temporalities: fantasies of whispered intimacy and instantaneous connection (*Calamus* and *Messenger Leaves*); long regenerative cycles ("Song of Myself" and "Crossing Brooklyn Ferry"); photographic snapshots ("Leaf of Faces" and "A Hand-Mirror"); temporal fragments ("Debris"); revolutionary moments and memories ("Europe, the 72nd and 73rd Years of These States" and "To a Foiled Revolter or Revoltress"); and probing meditations on both commencement ("Beginners" and "Salut au Monde!") and conclusion ("Burial Poem," "To One Shortly To Die," "So Long!").

In his pre-*Drum-Taps* poetry, however, these temporalities all tend to synchronize. For Whitman, fashioning order out of disorder was a crucial part of the poet's task. As he claimed in the 1855 preface, poets must show how the "past and present and future are not disjoined but joined" by forming "the consistence of what is to be, from what has been and is" (*PW*, 2:443). To disclose time's underlying equilibrium, which makes the "universe" a great "procession with measured and beautiful motion,"

Whitman enlists a variety of poetic techniques (*LG*, 1:128). His famous catalogs fold the most disparate of events into a single, elastic moment; his syntax, which is based almost entirely on present-tense verbs and prepositions, continually places the reader in that moment; and he moves repeatedly between modes of address, sliding from "I" to "others" and "you" so as to make time's consistence both felt and imaginable.[23]

All of these temporal techniques and ideas converge in "Crossing Brooklyn Ferry" (or, as he initially titled it, "Sun-Down Poem"), Whitman's 1856 poem about the generational cycles of the United States. Standing on the shore of the East River, he presents the water as an ideal metaphor for temporal change:

> Flood-tide of the river, flow on! I watch
>   you, face to face,
> [...]
> The impalpable sustenance of me from all things
>   at all hours of the day,
> The simple, compact, well-joined scheme – my-
>   self disintegrated, every one disintegrated,
>   yet part of the scheme,
> The similitudes of the past and those of the
>   future,
> The glories strung like beads on my smallest
>   sights and hearings – on the walk in the
>   street and the passage over the river,
> [...]
> What is it then between us? What is the
>   count of the scores or hundreds of years
>   between us?
>
> Whatever it is, it avails not
>   (*LG*, 1:217–18, 220)

But "change" here is almost a misnomer. Differences certainly arise as people and things "disintegrate," but time's "scheme" ensures a continuous reintegration of experience. In fact, the poem depicts the "past and present and future" as not simply "joined" but utterly transposable, since each moment stretches forward and backward through history, like the tides of the water. The very thing that makes the poem so undeniably strange – Whitman's abiding and indelible presence, which he cultivates across the "scores or hundreds of years / between us" – thus restages the poem's philosophy of time, according to which every instant is part of a vast present that cycles on and on without end.

"Crossing Brooklyn Ferry" tends to be classified as an antebellum work, as though it predates the Civil War in its entirety. However, Whitman crafted this harmonious vision as a poetic response to the same interregional political divides that eventually led to the war. The United States in the 1850s was in many respects an interwar rather than a prewar culture. The Compromise of 1850, rather than resolving the political fallout from the Mexican War, forged what historians have termed a short-lived "armistice" between the North and the South, and even that was not much of an armistice: violent conflicts erupted in Kansas and Missouri; on the Senate floor (when Preston Brooks, a South Carolinian, beat Charles Sumner with his cane); and in Virginia (when John Brown led his "antebellum" raid on Harper's Ferry).[24] Written and rewritten amidst this turmoil, *Leaves of Grass* seeks to create a sense of imaginative transcendence, and that is why the poems overflow with temporalities that drift away and then merge together: that movement reframes antagonism as something that leads not only to unity but to growth and rebirth.

What makes *Drum-Taps* so astounding, and so vital to any discussion of Whitman's career, is the way that it does *not* stage such synchronized mergers. Instead of joining, time in *Drum-Taps* simply proliferates. Instead of immersing the reader in a cosmic and resplendent now, the poems tend to split the present apart. The social harmony of the early *Leaves* still enters *Drum-Taps*, but only in bits and pieces – in the soldiers' marches, for instance, and in the lovely image of "Mother and Babe." Even that most peaceful of Whitman's war poems, "When I Heard the Learn'd Astronomer," finds harmony in the stars rather than on earth, where "charts," "diagrams," and "columns" are used to plan and execute an almost unimaginable war. If *Drum-Taps* shuttles between an eclectic array of unmerged timescapes, that is because now, when the "land entire is saturated" with blood and the war's "Infinite Dead" are subjected to "Nature's chemistry," it is no longer possible to view time itself as a perfect and beautiful "procession" (*LG*, 1:128).

Whitman was quite aware of this tension between *Drum-Taps* and *Leaves of Grass*. Initially, he even considered them to be completely separate productions. As he confided in early 1865, he deemed *Drum-Taps* to be more fully realized, and more self-contained, than *Leaves*. The latter, he added, is still "dear to me, always dearest to me, as my first born," but if it is to continue to mature and grow, many of the lines will need to be "carefully eliminate[d] in the next issue" or "considerably change[d]."[25] And that recomposition, carried out in the transbellum world made by the war, is exactly what Whitman devoted himself to in the ensuing years. Until his death in 1892, he repeatedly tried to merge *Drum-Taps* into *Leaves* and thereby assimilate the war into his life's song, which he began "in ripen'd youth and steadily pursued" across the nineteenth century (*LG*, 3:748).

Why, then, did Whitman fold *Drum-Taps* into *Leaves*, rather than vice versa? That decision is a bit less baffling when we consider *Leaves'* insatiable appetite for assimilation. Whitman altered, expanded, and reorganized this book for nearly 40 years, issuing seven major editions (in 1855, 1856, 1860, 1867, 1871–2, 1881–2, and 1891–2), as well as other, supplemental additions (*Passage to India* [1871], *As a Strong Bird on Pinions Free* [1872], *Two Rivulets* [1876]), and collections of prose (*Democratic Vistas* [1871], *Notes Left Over* [1881], *Specimen Days and Collect* [1882], *November Boughs* [1888]), which he eventually incorporated into the singularly capacious pages of this volume. This protracted labor of adding, deleting, and editing lines, of composing new poems and rearranging clusters, led his friend and biographer John Burroughs to declare that *Leaves*, properly understood, is not a book at all but a "series of growths, or strata, rising or starting out from a settled foundation or centre and expanding in successive accumulations."[26] And Whitman's incorporation of the Civil War into *Leaves* is the signal event in its recomposition – the foundation, as it were, of the book's later strata.

When *Drum-Taps* first appears in the fourth edition (1867), it is a kind of poetic addendum to *Leaves*. It is simply attached, with only minor changes, to the back of the book. As Ed Folsom remarks, "Whitman performed his own textual version of healing surgery, suturing the leftover and still-unbound pages of *Drum-Taps* and *Sequel to Drum-Taps* into the back of his new volume, thus binding the poetry of the war into *Leaves of Grass*."[27] But in the following years, as Whitman expands *Leaves* and revises his wartime memoranda, these war poems split up and disperse. In the fifth edition (1871), Whitman – taking seriously his claim that "my book and the war are one" (*LG*, 3:628) – moves *Drum-Taps* into *Leaves* proper and scatters many of the original poems. He relocates most of the marching pieces to *Marches Now the War is Over*; the flag poems to *Bathed in War's Perfume*; "Years of the Unperform'd" and "When I Heard the Learn'd Astronomer" to *Songs of Parting*; and several others to *Leaves'* own subsections. Some of the poems, such as "Mother and Babe" and "A Farm Picture," become unaffiliated with the war altogether, appearing within the sequences between Whitman's clusters. This dispersion is then amplified in the sixth edition (1881), in which Whitman adds new poems to the *Drum-Taps* cluster (including the one poem that explicitly addresses slavery, "Ethiopia Saluting the Colors") and rearranges the others, folding many of his war poems into *Inscriptions, Birds of Passage, Autumn Rivulets,* and *Songs of Parting.* "Weave In, Weave In, My Hardy Life" and "Thick-Sprinkled Bunting" now appear in *From Noon to Starry Night*; "Quicksand Years" and "A Paumanok Picture" in *Whispers of Heavenly Death*; and several others appear in *By the Roadside,* thus leaving "A Broadway Pageant" as the only unresituated and unclustered remainder.

These organizational changes are accompanied by marked shifts in Whitman's temporal representations of the war. As he transforms *Leaves* into "a veteran's testimony" (in the words of M. Wynn Thomas), Whitman alters the very chronopolitical vision that gave rise to *Drum-Taps* in the first place, reframing the war as a transition-point in democracy's long teleological progression.[28] As he explains in the 1876 preface, the "death of President Lincoln" coincided with the death of "feudalism" itself, "drop[ping] on [it], suddenly, a vast, gloomy [...] separating curtain" (*PW*, 2:470). The later *Leaves* accordingly deemphasize the experiential chaos of the war and inject the edited and relocated poems with a far more anticipatory temporality. "Years of the Unperform'd," for instance, becomes "Years of the Modern," and that same sense of imminent change and growth is revoiced in "Turn O Libertad" (1865), which portrays the war as an epochal transition:

> Turn from lands retrospective, recording proofs of the past,
> From the singers that sing the trailing glories of the past;
> From the chants of the feudal world, the triumphs of
>   kings, slavery, caste,
> Turn to the world, the triumphs reserv'd and to come –
> [...] and do not be alarm'd, O Libertad – turn
>   your undying face,
> To where the future, greater than all the past,
> Is swiftly, surely preparing for you.
>
>   (*LG*, 2:525)

In the late-1860s, Whitman amends this verse by adding a line that amplifies the assertion that "the war is over": "From it and all henceforth expanding, doubting no more, resolute, sweeping the world." Dealing a deathblow to all the "proofs of the past," the war now is not simply an instance of freedom's unfolding – it is the latter's pivotal event.

Leaves of Grass is reborn through slaughter and restructured through a new emphasis on futurity. In *Drum-Taps,* the future is almost entirely absent, and in the early *Leaves* it is often a repetition of the present, but in the later *Leaves* Whitman tends to depict the still-to-come as coextensive with freedom. In the 1872 poem "As A Strong Bird On Pinions Free," he sings in the conditional, addressing his chant to a people not yet born and a nation still unrealized. "For thee, the future," Whitman writes, "the peerless grandeur of the modern" will bear its face:

> Equable, natural, mystical Union thou, (the mortal
>   with immortal blent,)
> Shalt soar toward the fulfillment of the future – the
>   spirit of the body and the mind,
> The Soul – its destinies.
>
> The Soul, its destinies – the real real,
> (Purport of all these apparitions of the real);
> In thee America, the Soul, its destinies;
> Thou globe of globes! thou wonder nebulous!
> By many a throe of heat and cold convulsed (by
>   these thyself solidifying);
> Thou mental, moral orb! thou New, indeed new,
>   Spiritual world!
> The Present holds thee not – for such vast growth as
>   thine – for such unparallel'd flight as thine,
> The Future only holds thee, and can hold thee.
>   (*LG*, 3:634, 641)

Whereas in "Crossing Brooklyn Ferry" the future is practically indistinguishable from the present that precedes it, here it is the result of a profound historical transition. All of "history's cycles," Whitman writes, are now "acceding from [...] gestation" so as to produce "a freer, vast, electric world" (*LG*, 3:638). Since this coming global union, which will endow each soul with its destiny and reality with its kernel ("the real real"), is still on the horizon, the present is structured through a not-yet and history itself appears to be a unidirectional process.

These changes represent a dramatic shift in Whitman's view of the Civil War. Instead of unfolding nonlinearly through an eclectic array of timeframes, that conflict emerges, in *Leaves'* transbellum reframing, as the prime moment in democracy's historical advance. This transition in Whitman's poetic and historical representation of the struggle is surely attributable to a variety of influences: the trauma of those hospitals; the ideological and discursive pressures of debates about Civil War memory; and Whitman's abiding prophetic impulse. But what gives these revisions their particular shape and flavor is, more than anything else, Whitman's transformative encounter with Hegelian philosophy right after the Civil War. That encounter, in the mid- to late-1860s, prompted him to reconceptualize history as a unitary process and the war as a sublative event – or, as he once put it, as a struggle not "of two distinct and separate peoples, but a conflict [...] between the passions and paradoxes of one and the same identity – perhaps the only terms on which that identity could really become fused, homogeneous and lasting" (*PW*, 2:426–7).

Whitman's knowledge of Hegel likely came from three sources: Frederic H. Hedge's *Prose Writers of Germany* (1848), which contained a translation of Hegel's Introduction to *The Philosophy of History*; Joseph Gostwick's *Outlines of German Literature* (1854), which provided a broad synthesis of Hegel's dialectical method and philosophical claims; and personal conversations with Hegelians such as Amos Bronson Alcott, the transcendentalist philosopher and educator, and W. T. Harris, the editor of *The Journal of Speculative Philosophy*. He was probably drawn to the German philosopher's theory of freedom, according to which the state is coterminous with liberty, and to the philosopher's conceptualization of the nation as an ethical whole. What became especially vital to Whitman, though, was Hegel's dialectical theory of development. As Hegel writes (in Hedge's translation),

> From the consideration of the history of the world itself, we shall come to the result, that [...] it has been the rational and necessary course of the spirit which moves in the world, – a spirit whose nature does indeed ever remain one and the same [...] In this sense, we may say that the history of the world is the exhibition of the process by which spirit comes to the consciousness of that which it really is, – of the significancy of its own nature. And as the seed contains in itself the whole nature of the tree, even to the taste and form of the fruit, so do the first traces of spirit virtually contain the whole of history.[29]

Whitman's appropriation of Hegel's philosophy of history, however, was precisely that: a rewriting of idealist dialectics. For Whitman, democracy rather than *Geist* is that which "contains in itself the whole nature of the tree, even to the taste and form of the fruit." The seed, a figure for latency, comes to occupy the place of simultaneity in Whitman's poetry, and the result is a decidedly more imperialist faith in American hegemony – that future "empire of empires," as he words it in *Democratic Vistas*, "culminating time" itself (*PW*, 2:423).

The Hegelian schema of temporal progression provided Whitman with a way to imaginatively fuse poetry, democracy, and history in the wake of the war. Many of the later poems tend to figure the past as a more or less teleological unfolding, as in "To Thee Old Cause" (1871):

> To thee, old Cause!
> Thou peerless, passionate, good cause!
> Thou stern, remorseless, sweet Idea!
> Deathless throughout the ages, races, lands!
> After a strange, sad war – great war for thee,
> (I think all war through time was really fought, and
>   ever will be really fought, for thee,)
> These chants for thee – the eternal march of thee.
>
> Thou orb of many orbs!
> Thou seething principle! Thou well-kept, latent germ!
> Thou centre!
>
> (LG, 3:628)

Past events, Whitman suggests, are not instances of eternity but sequentially interwoven links in democracy's gradual maturation. According to this poem, the Civil War was a kind of blood sacrifice, a ritualistic offering *en masse* for that "seething principle," or "centre," of human history.

This altered historical sensibility finds its most comprehensive prose voice in *Democratic Vistas* (1867–71), an essay-cum-prophecy in which Whitman redefines his theory of poetry through Hegel's philosophy of history. As in 1855, the poet is still an agent of distillation, but now he is also a dialectician "consistent with the Hegelian formulas" (*PW*, 2:421). In *Democratic Vistas*, Whitman contends that democracy is fully realized only when the poet and the state are folded into one another, thereby creating a "divine, vast, general law" that extends through every facet of society (*PW*, 2:381). And when that happens – first in the United States, and then throughout the globe – democracy will finally take root micropolitically and reshape human character. Of course this grand vision, which pivots on the imperial development the American nation, goes where Hegel himself never did. *The Philosophy of History* famously describes America as "the country of the future," the "world-historical importance" of which "has yet to be revealed." But for Hegel this exceptionalism derives from the New World's *non*-historicity, its definitive removal from time's dialectical oscillations.[30] In Hegel's lectures, this statement is deployed chiefly to justify passing over the Americas in his explication of Spirit's world-historical development. On one level, *Democratic Vistas* and the later *Leaves of Grass* can be read as an extended and eloquent response on Whitman's part to Hegel's qualified statement about America's futurity.

Whitman's later poetry and prose thereby provide us with a spectacular example of transbellum literature's protracted response to the Civil War. As we will see, Douglass, Melville, and Dickinson also approach the war as an event that far exceeds the narrow, four-year span of its execution. The counterhistories in Douglass's lectures, the long cycles of *Battle-Pieces*, *Clarel*, and *Timoleon*, and the erasures in Dickinson's poems all attempt to secure an imaginable temporality for this almost unimaginable conflict. And Whitman's later, Hegelian *Leaves* fully partake in this collective attempt to periodize and emplot this struggle that so manifestly eclipsed the official time of its occurrence. Indeed, it is his newfound faith in dialectics – as a historical idea, political promise, and poetic principle – that enables Whitman to repeatedly refashion *Leaves* in the decades that followed the "real parturition years" (*PW*, 2:724).

This futural turn in Whitman's thought acquires distinct shape in *Leaves*' structural arrangement. In 1855, Whitman's book is an organic collection of poems – all untitled and unclustered – that hook into, extend, and amplify one another's lines and themes, even stretching back to readdress one another's political and philosophical intimations. In the first three editions, the book's own material presentation, from its exterior (green and yellow, like autumn) to its typeface (which twirls across the page, like natural outgrowths), mimics this sense of organic coextensiveness (see Figure 1).

With its poems continuously looping together and moving backwards and forwards in rhythm and theme, *Leaves of Grass* is a decidedly cyclical production prior to *Drum-Taps*. But after the "streams of blood, full of volition, full of joy," this circularity is increasingly supplanted by progression: stanza and section numbers divide and sequence the poems' movements; clusters forge narratives, both collective and self-contained, out of disparate poetic series; and the reader is evermore swept up into time's advancing flow (*LG*, 2:458). In the changes that Whitman makes to *Leaves* in the wake of *Drum-Taps*, we can thus discern a principle of arrangement that rearticulates the phased movement of dialectics. The latter consists, as he argued in 1882, in the generation of unity out of antagonism:

> According to Hegel the whole earth, [...] with its infinite variety, the past, the surroundings of to-day, or what may happen in the future, the contrarieties of material with spiritual, [...] are all, to the eye of the *ensemblist*, but necessary [...] steps or links, in the endless process of Creative thought, which, amid numberless apparent failures and contradictions, is held together by central and never-broken unity – not contradictions or failures

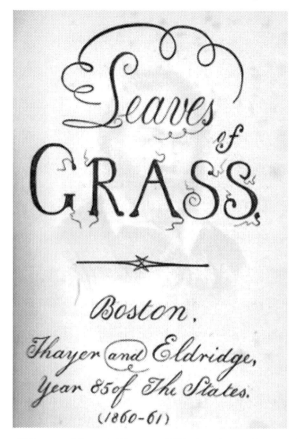

Figure 1. Title page of the 1860 Thayer and Eldridge edition of *Leaves of Grass*.

at all, but radiations of one consistent and eternal purpose; the whole mass of everything steadily, unerringly tending and flowing toward the permanent *utile* and *morale*, as rivers to oceans [... This is] the most thoroughly *American point of view* I know. In my opinion the above formulas of Hegel are an essential and crowning justification of New World democracy in the creative realms of time and space. There is that about them which only the vastness, the multiplicity and the vitality of America would seem able to comprehend, to give scope and illustration to, or to be fit for, or even originate. It is strange to me that they were born in Germany, or in the old world at all. (*PW*, 1:259, 262)

To correct for this strangeness, Whitman translated this philosophy into a formal axiom for *Leaves*. And his massive attempt to reorganize his poetry according to the "*utile* and *morale*" of history leads, among other things, to a careful rewriting and reclustering of his poems.

Emerging, in equal parts, from the waking nightmares of Washington's hospitals and from the ecstatic fantasy of dialectics, Whitman's dream for the war is a dream of absorption. Blood is not spilled, but sacrificed. The Union is not extinguished, but reborn with new splendor. This dream, of course, stands in rather stark contrast to the war that is represented in *Drum-Taps'* early instantiations, and this is why Whitman's subsequent reorganization of that volume is so important. The poems of *Drum-Taps* are not simply scattered by Whitman – they are *dialectically interspersed*.[31] In the 1871-2 edition, the clusters proceed, in paired fashion, from *Leaves* to *Drum-Taps*; from *Leaves* to *Marches Now the War is Over*; from *Leaves* to *Bathed in War's Perfume*; and then back again to *Leaves*. In the 1882 and 1891 editions, *Drum-Taps* is certainly fuller and longer, but it is still balanced out by other poems and clusters – such as "By Blue Ontario's Shore," which describes the United States as the historical realization of "ages, precedents, [that] have long been accumulating" – so as to yield a more sequenced and patterned encounter with the war (*LG*, 1:193). Even considered on its own terms as an independent poetic cluster, *Drum-Taps* reads as a decidedly more narrativized and historically cogent set of poems from 1872 onward. As Cristanne Miller has argued, Whitman's revisions and reorganizations effectively replace "the random order of impressions from the war years" with something else entirely: a narrative, or story, that moves from "early enthusiasm to later lament."[32]

In certain respects, this dialectical recasting of the war reinforces what critics have suggested about Whitman's Hegelian turn: that it is politically and aesthetically compensatory, emerging out of a wish to recover something that has been irretrievably lost. According to David Reynolds, Hegelian dialectics provided Whitman with a philosophical system for resolving the social and political "problems he had formerly tried to resolve in his poetry." "With his poetic 'I' no longer able to absorb and recycle massive amounts of cultural material," Reynolds writes, "he looked to outside systems such as Hegelian philosophy," which imparted a sense of "philosophical consolation."[33] Such accounts of Whitman's Hegelianism have much to support them. Yet I would like to suggest that Whitman also makes use of dialectical time in ways that, instead of pushing him away from late-nineteenth-century political culture, actively reframe that culture as part of a transbellum timescape. What was the Civil War, after all, but a protracted conflict – not a sudden clash, but a long struggle that in certain respects is *still* unresolved? What was *Leaves* but a book that Whitman continuously sought to sublate? And what was Whitman's beloved Union, too, but a dream endlessly delayed?

The Dialectics of Labor

Whitman's transbellum revisions, as well as the political investments that propel them, often crystallize around considerations of work. There is more than a little resemblance, for instance, between the mobile, strong-armed soldiers of *Drum-Taps* and the robust artisans of the early *Leaves*. Whitman's soldiers are essentially workers with guns. This interchangeability plays a crucial role in poems like "A Carol of Harvest, for 1867" (1871):

> A pause – the armies wait;
> A million flush'd, embattled conquerors wait;
> The world, too, waits, then, soft as breaking night, and
>   sure as dawn,
> They melt – they disappear.
> [...]
> Melt, melt away ye armies! disperse ye blue-clad
>   soldiers!
> Resolve ye back again – give up, for good, your deadly
>   arms;
> Other the arms, the fields henceforth for you, or South
>   or North, or East or West,
> With saner wars – sweet wars – life-giving wars.
> [...]
> All till'd and untill'd fields expand before me;
> I see the true arenas of my race – or first or last,
> Man's innocent and strong arenas.
>
> I see the Heroes at other toils;
> I see, well-wielded in their hands, the better weapons.
>   (*LG*, 3:594–5)

These lines locate the war's historicity in a series of metonymic displacements: workers for soldiers; tilling for marching; and "labor-saving implements" for rifles and bayonets (*LG*, 3:596). Whitman's poem thereby enacts the process of symbolic displacement that Elaine Scarry describes as the inevitable result of war, which yields for survivors a "process of perception that allows extreme attributes of the body to be translated into another language, to be broken away from the body and relocated elsewhere at the very moment that the body itself is disowned [and] made to disappear."[34]

In Whitman's lines, this decorporealization unfolds as a transformation of work, which is now geared toward the creation of "products" with the aid of "human-divine inventions" such as "revolving hay-rakes," "steam-power reaping-machines," "the newer saw-mill, the southern cotton-gin, and the / rice-cleanser" (*LG*, 3:596). The war, as Whitman imagines it, is a rupture that will permanently change how labor is organized, both politically and technologically, in modern democracy.

As "A Carol of Harvest" suggests, Whitman's dialectical turn is inextricable from the poet's abiding interest in labor. If there is one thing that is unwavering across the long arc of Whitman's career, from its earliest instantiations to its final moments, it is his sustained engagement with the power, bodies, and desires of workers.[35] As he remarked in 1891, the "working-man and working-woman were to be in my pages from first to last. The ranges of heroism and loftiness with which Greek and feudal poets endow'd their god-like or lordly born characters – indeed prouder and better based and with fuller ranges than those – I was to endow the democratic averages of America" (*PW*, 2:727). In many ways, this focus on workers was inflected and informed by party politics. Like other Free Soil Democrats, Whitman considered labor in general, and white labor in particular, to be democracy's animating force as well the origin of wealth. As he put it in an early essay, "It is to labor that man owes every thing possessed of changeable value. Labor is the talisman that has raised him from the condition of the savage."[36]

Whitman's workerism, however, is not merely an outgrowth of his politics. It is also an aesthetic interest that actively shapes and structures his poetry, from his representations of the body (which, in *Leaves*, is almost always mobile) to his reflections on music (which is frequently tied to working and making). In the early *Leaves*, his poetry of the present fuses many diverse labors into a single, expansive vision. In "A Song for Occupations," Whitman's distended and ubiquitous present draws "house-building," "carving," the "sawing [of] boards," "blacksmithing," and innumerable other forms of work into one another, presenting them as coterminous acts that, in making things at the same moment, make the world (*LG*, 1:93). In the early *Leaves*, simultaneity becomes almost synonymous with democracy itself, and the latter is depicted not as a form of government but as the very act and experience of cooperation. But the Civil War subjected this "ideal dream" to the "practical, vulgar tests" of violence, and the paradise for labor that Whitman hoped would eventually result from the war was subsequently imperiled by economic conditions not at all unlike those of the early twenty-first century (*LG*, 2:522).

The 1870s, the years of Whitman's most strident futural revisions, were marked by massive unemployment, periodic economic recession (including what was previously the United States' longest financial downturn from 1873–9), and an unprecedented centralization of wealth during the Gilded Age.[37]

In fact, the disappearance of the independent artisan – that central figure of Whitman's early poetry – proved to be one of the most enduring legacies of the Union's victory. By 1880, nearly eighty percent of all the manufacturing workers in the United States were part of a vast industrial factory system. Even as early as 1869, the *New York Times* claimed that the artisanal laborer was a relic: "one capitalist employs five men now where he employed one twenty years ago; and […] there is gradually developing at the North a system of slavery as absolute if not as degrading as that which lately prevailed at the South […] A casual observer, walking the streets of a city familiar to him […] cannot fail to notice this fact."[38] This supplanting of artisans with operatives did not go unnoticed by Whitman, who responded to these changes by refashioning the temporal structures of his verse. The Civil War threatened to destroy his vision of a harmonious present, so Whitman shifted this harmony off to the future, reclaiming the still-to-come as the timespace of freedom. In this respect, Whitman's Hegelianism helps him fulfill the promise he first outlined in his pre-*Leaves* notebooks to convene not with "professors and capitalists" but "with drivers and boatmen and men that catch fish or work in the field. [For] I know they are sublime."[39] If this sublimity, once attached to the present in all its splendid variety, disappears from *Leaves*, that is because it is now imaginable only as something that has either been expunged or has not yet arrived.

In fact, I would suggest that the futural turn in Whitman's writing derives from a refusal to accept the troubled present as the sole horizon of political possibility. This investment in deferral proved especially important for Whitman in the 1870s, as the economy collapsed in state after state and the exploited and unemployed began to revolt. The anxiety that underpins his interest in dialectics is evident, for instance, in this brief but remarkable meditation that he penned in 1879, following one of his daily walks through his beloved Manhattan:

> I saw to-day a sight I had never seen before – and it amazed, and made me serious; three quite good-looking American men, of respectable personal presence, two of them young, carrying chiffonier-bags on their shoulders, and the usual long iron hooks in their hands, plodding along, their eyes cast down, spying for scraps, rags, bones, &c [… I am forced to conclude that

underneath] the whole political world, what most presses and perplexes to-day, sending vastest results affecting the future, is not the abstract question of democracy, but of social and economic organization, the treatment of working-people by employers, and all that goes along with it [...] The American Revolution of 1776 was simply a great strike, successful for its immediate object – but whether a real success judged by the scale of the centuries, and the long-striking balance of Time, yet remains to be settled [...] If the United States, like the countries of the Old World, are also to grow vast crops of poor, desperate, dissatisfied, nomadic, miserably-waged populations, such as we see looming upon us of late years – steadily, even if slowly, eating into them like a cancer of lungs or stomach – then our republican experiment, notwithstanding all its surface-successes, is at heart an unhealthy failure. (*PW*, 2:529, 527–28)

These seem to be surprising claims coming from the author of *Leaves of Grass*. Uncertainty and anxiety loom in Whitman's words. Once the sublation "of all the civilization so far known," the United States has metamorphosed into a potentially failed "experiment" (*PW*, 2:415). The political economy of transbellum America may curtail or perhaps even extinguish the principles of that first great strike: this is the nightmare that, Whitman attests, "continually haunts me" – the specter of a dream stamped out (*PW*, 2:368). The gleaners that invite the poet's gaze at the outset (who might very well be Union veterans) are a far cry from the robust artisans of his earlier poems. In 1855 the proud worker's body "balks account." "The expression of a wellmade man," he writes, "strikes through the cotton and flannel; / To see him pass conveys as much as the best poem...perhaps more" (*LG*, 1:122). Now, in the world made by the war, there is still a "divine nimbus" that "attracts with fierce undeniable attraction," but the body has been broken and misused. If the "expression of the wellmade man" manifests in "his walk" and in the "carriage of his neck," these gleaners who shuffle and "plod along" with "their eyes cast down," lack that expression altogether. And this shift is tied to a broader transition from fulfillment to collapse, from prewar harmony to transbellum declension, as the United States – which, he proclaimed in 1855, was "the world's greatest poem" – has either reached its final stanza or become a kind of vast elegy (*PW*, 2:434).

The strikes to which Whitman elliptically refers in his note are the labor revolts of 1877, which commenced with railroad workers in Martinsburg, West Virginia, and then spread from the eastern seaboard to the western territories in the summer of that year. In Baltimore, soon after the revolts began, the state militia was sent south to suppress the strike and working-class citizens descended upon the passing soldiers, throwing rocks and other objects at them. Half of the militia deserted out of sympathy. In

St. Louis, workers halted commerce in the city and challenged the municipal government. In Chicago, workers battled the Illinois National Guard and took over much of the city, and their insurrection ended only when the Secretary of War sent in federal troops. In Pittsburgh, a general strike emerged amongst laborers in the iron mills, glass factories, coal mines, and steel plants. When a militia finally arrived from Philadelphia, the workers already controlled much of the city. As one writer recounted: by the time the troops arrived, "the mob had [...] swollen to an enormous size" and the entire city was "virtually in the hands of [...] laborers and iron-workers, coal-miners, stevedores, and others who are in full sympathy with the strikers." Although these worker revolts were all squelched by the state, they helped spawn a radical labor movement and, in doing so, shifted the fault lines of American political ideology (see Figure 2). As Frances Parkman wrote one year later, "Two enemies, unknown before, have risen like spirits of darkness on our social and political horizon – an ignorant proletariat and a half-taught plutocracy."[40]

The eruption of these conflicts extends Whitman's imaginative engagement with the Civil War far beyond the years of its official occurrence. In *Leaves of Grass*, as in the other transbellum writings we will consider, the war takes shape multilinearly, extending imaginatively across the nineteenth century in a variety of directions. For Whitman, the labor rebellions of the 1870s and 1880s made it painfully clear that the future that the Civil War was supposed to usher in was probably quite far off, and he responds by incorporating both deferral and rebellion into his new dialectical vision.

As he wrote around this same time:

> Not songs of loyalty alone are these,
> But songs of insurrection also;
> For I am the sworn poet of every dauntless rebel, the
> world over

And:

> Courage yet! my brother or my sister!
> Keep on! Liberty is to be subserv'd, whatever occurs;
> That is nothing, that is quell'd by one or two failures,
> or any number of failures, [...]
> Revolt! and still revolt! revolt!
> What we believe in waits latent forever through all
> the continents, and all the islands and archi-
> pelagos of the sea
>
> (*LG*, 1:249–50)[41]

Figure 2. "The Great Strike – The Sixth Maryland Regiment fighting its way through Baltimore," *Harper's Weekly*, August 11, 1877. Library of Congress Prints and Photographs Division.

These lines come from *Songs of Insurrection*, an 1871 cluster that interweaves some of his earlier, pro-rebellion poems (like "France, the 18th Year of These States" and "To a Foil'd European Revolutionaire") with other, newer poems about inheritance and insurgency. Arranged in the aftermath of war, this cluster insists in a surprisingly celebratory tone on the necessity of continued political agitation, and even reclaims insurrectionary violence as both necessary and redemptive:

> Still, though the one I sing,
> (One, yet of contradictions made,) I dedicate to Nationality,
> I leave in him Revolt, (O latent right of insurrection! O
>   quenchless, indispensable fire!)
>
> (*LG*, 3:632)

What Whitman means by revolt here is not agitation in the abstract but something far more situated in a transbellum political scene. As he suggests in a note that he added to the 1871 manuscript: "Not only are These States the born offspring of Revolt against mere overweening authority – but seeing ahead for Them in the future a long, long reign of Peace with all the growths, corruptions and tyrannies & formalisms of Obedience, (accumulating, vast folds, strata, from the rankness of continued prosperity and the more and more insidious grip of capital) I feel to raise a note of caution [...] that the ideas of the following cluster will always be needed, that it may be worth while to keep well up, & vital, such ideas and verses as the following."[42]

This political context helps us to rethink Whitman's taking up of Hegel. His turn to teleology is, among other things, a form of political and poetic reengagment with the Civil War. Rather than concluding, that struggle seemed to be revived by these conflicts over labor, and Hegel's dialectics enable Whitman to hold on to some vision of democracy precisely when it seems to be most implausible. He enlists teleology not to celebrate time's extant harmony but to account for the disharmony of the transbellum present. This sense of dialectical delay propels many of the later poems, like this brief verse from 1881:

> Roaming in Thought
> (*After reading* HEGEL.)
>
> Roaming in thought over the Universe, I saw the little that is Good
>   steadily hastening towards immortality,
> And the vast all that is call'd Evil I saw hastening to merge itself and
>   become lost and dead.
>
> (*LG*, 3:685)

For Whitman, the "vast all" that is evil and "the little that is Good" are not equal forces: even if it is hastening toward extinction, Evil is today larger and greater – and this is no purely metaphysical problem. As "things now exist in the States," he soon wrote, "what is more terrible, more alarming, than the total want of any [...] fusion and mutuality [...] between the comparatively few successful rich, and the great masses of the unsuccessful, the poor? As a mixed political and social question, is not this full of dark significance?" (*PW*, 2:533–534).

These same misgivings find powerful expression at the end his centennial chant, "Song of the Universal" (1876):

> And thou America,
> For the scheme's culmination, its thought and its reality,
> [...]
> In Thy ensemble, whatever else withheld withhold not from us,
> Belief in plan of Thee enclosed in Time and Space,
> Health, peace, salvation universal.
>
> Is it a dream?
> Nay, but the lack of it the dream,
> And failing it life's lore and wealth a dream,
> And all the world a dream.
>
> (*LG*, 3:681–82)

Here we discover a reimagining of freedom in transbellum America as an almost ghostly fantasy. In these lines, an unsteady time scale of hope and desire erupts, and it is a temporality that resembles a dream. Rather than advancing, democracy flees. Rather than realizing itself in some vast sublation, it vanishes into an unknown ether. And we are left with a doubt that would have struck fear in Hegel's heart, a suspicion that history's fated end will perhaps never arrive. Whitman continues:

> In this broad earth of ours,
> Amid the measureless grossness and the slag,
> Enclosed and safe within its central heart,
> Nestles the seed perfection.
> [...]
> For it the mystic evolution,
> Not the right only justified, what we call evil also justified.
>
> (*LG*, 3:679–80)

Despite all the setbacks and failures and excesses of this modern world, a hidden "seed" of democracy, Whitman insists, is already "nestle[d]" away. What propels this evolutionary sense of history, however, is not a naïve belief in amelioration but an anxious awareness of the partialities and imperfections of progress. Whitman returns again to Hegel's metaphor of the seed in order to envision democracy as incomplete. In a transbellum world in which violent antagonisms keep resurging, in which class and racial strife rather than synchronic harmony underpins the nation's polity, and in which the masses "spy" the ground "for scraps, [and] rags, [and] bones," dialectical idealism is, in a way, the only way that freedom still can be envisioned at all.

What Hegel provides for Whitman, then, is a capacious timeframe for democracy, one that, in the midst of continued upheaval, discovers a promise in conflict and failure. As Whitman put it in one of his later lectures, "History, with all its long train of baffling, contradictory events – the tumultuous procession – the dark problem of evil, forming half of the infinite scheme – these are the themes, questions, which have directly [...] to do with any profound consideration of Democracy and finally testing it, as all questions and as underlying all questions." The only figure who truly "advances [...] to light upon these" issues, he adds, is Hegel, "[whom] I rate as Humanity's chiefest teacher and the choicest loved physician of my mind and soul."[43] By way of Hegel, Whitman reimagines history as antagonism, as a process tending toward a sublation that has not yet occurred, and perhaps might never arrive. This understanding of historical time is of course not Hegelian in the strict sense of the word. It is instead a transbellum vision that retains the structure of dialectical anticipation but prizes deferral, improvising on Hegel by imagining the real possibility of nonresolution.

Transbellum Futures

That possibility bears directly on the temporality of the Civil War. In his writings about that conflict, Whitman repeatedly meditates on its pastness. The piebald entries of *Specimen Days* have a preservative function, as though these "specimens" of wartime experience might go uncollected and unremembered if not for Whitman's quick hand. And in many of his new and revised poems, the war's closure repeatedly returns as a kind of intertextual refrain, insisting across the timespace of countless lines that the war has ushered in a new epochal order. But as Whitman addresses the issues of labor and politics in the late nineteenth century, the war's pastness also fades away and *Leaves* constructs a more complex account of that struggle's temporal unfolding. The war's post-1865 durations thereby push Whitman's poetic career, as well as the politico-aesthetic commitments that gave rise to it, into the final years of the nineteenth century. What we encounter across the later editions of *Leaves of Grass* is a timescape that cuts across the war and forges a futural vision that is averted from the very present that it purportedly celebrates. Structured through a potentially limitless deferral, the later *Leaves* unfold as a kind of poetic waiting, or witnessing, that looks askance at the age out of which it emerges, enlisting Hegel to leap far beyond the bounds of the contemporaneous and the war that historically limns it.

This transnational mixture of philosophy and politics permanently alters Whitman's writing. Many of his later compositions, deletions, additions, substitutions, and rearrangements are henceforth predicated on dialectical imminence. And there is, of course, something that is lost in this transition: the rich temporalities of his earlier books. The timescapes of *Drum-Taps* and the early *Leaves* fall away, and in their place there arises an anticipatory poetics, a verse of teleological becoming that carries all the political freight and contradictions that come with this philosophical wish. Nonetheless, I would suggest there is also something gained in this loss, something counterintuitive but nonetheless salutary and sobering. Contained in Whitman's attachment to futurity is a quite radical insistence on freedom's *absence* in the present, as well as a keen awareness of the ways in which the Civil War was reborn as a conflict between bosses and workers.

This transbellum blending of prophecy with critique is especially palpable in a passage that Whitman penned in 1876, not long before the railroad strikes began in West Virginia. At the very end of his *Memoranda during the War*, he writes:

> The old theory of a given country or age, or people, as something isolated and standing by itself – something which only fulfills its luck, eventful or uneventful – or perhaps some meteor, brilliantly flashing on the background or foreground of Time – is indeed no longer advanced among competent minds, as a theory for History – has been supplanted by theories far wider and higher [...] The glory of the Republic of The United States, in my opinion, is to be that, emerging from the light of the Modern [...] it is to cheerfully range itself, and its politics are henceforth to come, under [...] universal laws, and embody them, and carry them out [...] And the real History of the United States – starting from that great convulsive struggle for Unity, triumphantly concluded, and *the South* victorious, after all – is only to be written at the remove of hundreds, perhaps a thousand, years hence.[44]

To be sure, there is something deeply quietist, and perhaps even politically retrograde, about this declaration of future fulfillment out of a "series of [historical] steps." Written on the eve of a compromise between the North and South that would terminate Reconstruction and actually make "the South victorious, after all," Whitman's optimistic, evolutionary interpretation of American democracy seems to be woefully farsighted. However, beyond and between its lines, Whitman's projection is also more than this. Whitman hints that, in a sense, the ideal readers of his verse have not yet even been born. The "weight and form and location" of the "world's greatest poem" are in many respects utterly unavailable to the Americans of the late nineteenth century, who are surrounded by inequality (*LG*, 1:104; *PW*, 2:434). Freedom will arrive only "at the remove of hundreds, perhaps a thousand, years hence": there is a capitulation here, but there is also an insistence on the present's radical inadequacy. This condition of continued deferral positions us, as much as Whitman, in a present that is still ongoing, a transbellum present in which "the light of the Modern" – ostensibly secured by the Union's restoration – has emerged as a fantasy of illumination. The later *Leaves of Grass* thus takes its point of dialectical departure from an event that, in a way, never occurred: the end of the Civil War. And this abiding exploration of a past that never became past is precisely what connects these writers across their later careers.

CHAPTER 2

Frederick Douglass's Revisions

The events of the Civil War, Frederick Douglass was often fond of saying, obeyed a "stern logic." Tottering between stoic acceptance and chastened awe, this phrase repeatedly appears in his wartime essays, letters, and orations.[1] On certain frequencies, it is a surprisingly sanguine locution, implying either that the conflict's final outcome is somehow predetermined or that its spectacular violence is perfectly proportional. For Douglass, however, the war's "logic" had to do primarily with its historicity. He viewed the events of 1861 to 1865 as part of a much longer conflict between freedom and unfreedom that had been waged for centuries by a variety of peoples. The Abolition War (as he preferred to call it) was thus a serialized event that both revived and revised a motley array of other struggles, from the Norman Conquest to the European revolts of 1848.[2]

In many respects, it is altogether fitting that Douglass, who devoted so much of his life to revision, viewed the war in this manner. He channeled his energies into a variety of verbal media (newspapers, oratory, life-writing, fiction, poetry), and often remixed phrases, anecdotes, and ideas that he had either used or encountered elsewhere. He delivered many of his lectures several times, and sometimes dozens of times, over – including one, "Self-Made Men," that he gave on more than fifty occasions over the course of 35 years. He viewed nationality as an experience of shared "compositeness," and the Constitution as an immanently updatable "written document" (SS, 381).[3] And as his autobiographies (which he wrote four different times) beautifully demonstrate, Douglass also revised himself. This man, who was born a slave, also became a fugitive, a freeman, an orator, a traveler, an author, an editor, a statesman, and an ambassador. In fact, Frederick Douglass was not even Frederick Douglass. Born Frederick Augustus Washington Bailey, he took the name Douglass from Nathan Johnson, one of his New Bedford benefactors, who in turn took it from a character in a book.

This revisionary sensibility anchors Douglass's transbellum response to the Civil War. From his earliest wartime speeches to his final autobiographies, Douglass approaches the conflict as a corrective moment in the protracted struggle between freedom and slavery. To elucidate that struggle, he turns to a range of discourses about the origins of worldly change: philosophies of evolution, theories of motion, and histories of religious and political freedom. Yet rather than simply importing these varied ideas, Douglass marshals them into a capacious philosophy of history through which he imaginatively recharts the Civil War.

This chapter traces where that philosophy comes from and how it develops, from his wartime writings through his final autobiography, *The Life and Times of Frederick Douglass* (1881/1892). By reading Douglass across the arc of his transbellum career, the following pages supplement recent scholarship that has challenged Douglass's longstanding reputation as an "antebellum" figure and emphasized his later political, philosophical, and aesthetic investments. Critics have shown us how Douglass used both apocalyptic rhetoric and paternalistic language to respond to the Civil War; how his later trips to Haiti, Egypt, and Rome influenced his ideas about identity; and how his interest in logic and causation led him to embrace empirical science and inductive reasoning.[4] This chapter expands on this criticism by looking at how Douglass plots the Abolition War along a lengthy and discontinuous timeline of historical progress. After the war erupts, he fashions a transbellum account of that conflict, and it is, we shall find, just as expansive, and just as revisionary, as the life story that he retold time and time again.

Let us begin, then, where that account begins: with Douglass, on the edge of war, contemplating a voyage.

Histories of the Irrepressible Conflict

Before the struggle's first shots were fired, Douglass was preparing to temporarily leave the United States. In early 1861, it seemed that American slavery might exist in perpetuity: the Confederate states had successfully seceded and President Lincoln declared that there would be no "bloodshed" unless it was "forced upon the national authority."[5] In response, many abolitionists began to reconsider earlier colonization schemes – including Douglass, who had previously been a staunch opponent of emigration. His friend and fellow New Yorker, James Redpath, was convinced that Haiti was the best possible location for resettlement, and he offered to send Douglass there on "a tour of observation."

For Douglass, it had always been a "dream, fondly indulged" to visit this "theatre of [so] many stirring events and heroic achievements" (*SS*, 442). But he would not set foot upon Haitian soil until decades later. Almost immediately after the violence erupted at Fort Sumter, Douglass scrapped his travel plans and renounced Redpath's colonization efforts. Afterwards, when he explained his decision in *Douglass' Monthly*, he posited that the war against the Confederacy was not simply a struggle over Constitutional authority but a "tremendous revolution" against slavery itself (*SS*, 442). And Douglass repeatedly advanced this claim in his wartime writings. On the eve of emancipation, he declared that the "work before us is nothing less than a radical revolution in all the modes of thought," (*SS*, 522) and in one of his most probing lectures about the conflict he similarly described it as "a gigantic and bloody revolution" in which the United States is "torn and rent asunder," as though by a great "Earthquake":

> Our country is now on fire. No man can now tell what the future will bring forth. The question now is whether this great Republic before it has reached a century from its birth, is to fall in the wake of unhappy Mexico, and become a constant theatre of civil war, or whether it shall become like old Spain, the mother of Mexico, and [...] spend the next seventy years in vainly attempting to regain what it has lost in the space of this one slaveholding rebellion. (*SS*, 495)

As Douglass reflects on the war, his mind slips southward and eastward. Will the United States, he asks, replicate the recent history of Mexico and suffer incessant war? Or will it assume the role of "old Spain" and vainly try to reacquire what "it has lost in the span of this one slaveholding rebellion"? Neither prospect is particularly promising. To the degree that there is any hope, it apparently resides in the war's status as a "revolution," a term that has often been used to organize the chaos of events into a coherent narrative of communal rebirth. Here, in 1862, Douglass draws on "revolution's" sense of patterned history to rein in that most disorderly of things – the violence of the war, which he likens to natural calamities – and locate a historical timeline through which the Abolition War can be plotted.

That timeline, for Douglass, is neither fixed nor uniform. As he argues in his 1864 lecture, "The Mission of the War":

> I know that the acorn involves the oak, but I know also that the commonest accident may destroy its potential character and defeat its natural destiny [...] The saying that revolutions never go backward must [therefore] be taken with limitations. The revolution of 1848 was one of the grandest

that ever dazzled a gazing world [...] Looking on from a distance, the friends of democratic liberty saw in the convulsion the death of kingcraft in Europe and throughout the world [... But] in the twinkling of an eye, the latent forces of despotism rallied [...] and the hopes of democratic liberty were blasted in the moment of their bloom [...] I wish I could say that no such liabilities darken the horizon around us. But the same elements are plainly involved here as there. Though the portents are that we shall flourish, it is too much to say that we cannot fail. (*FDP*, 4:4–5)

Douglass takes up Whitman's favorite metaphor for latency, but for Douglass the seed is a figure for political rebellion's various possibilities: just as the acorn can either produce a great oak or nothing at all, any given revolution can foster "a glorious Republic" or be suppressed. To illustrate this idea, Douglass draws – just as he had in his 1862 speech – upon recent revolutionary history, tying the Abolition War to the European revolts of 1848. Those revolts "shook every throne in Europe" and seemed to inaugurate a rebirth for liberty, but they were soon put down by a series of brutal counterrevolutions. In Italy, the newly established constitutional republic was toppled by Papal forces; in France, the Second Republic was destroyed by an aristocratic coup; and similar reversals occurred in Hungary, Germany, Poland, and Denmark.[6] Is the same thing, Douglass asks, now happening in the United States? Will the Abolition War result in the same chain of events?

Douglass's portrayal of the conflict as a fiery revolution or earthquake, scholars have argued, is steeped in an apocalyptic discourse that was prevalent in Northern wartime writing. Many observers – from soldiers to politicians, preachers, and nurses – framed the struggle as a cataclysm occasioned by God. This millenarian rhetoric crossed racial, regional, and generic lines, appearing in Northern and Southern speeches, African American songs, and in copious sermons, sketches, and poems. In Carolyn Karcher's view, it was this social elasticity that led Douglass to "wholeheartedly embrace" apocalypticism as a way to "bridge the racial gap separating him from white Americans." When Douglass describes the war as a vast convulsion, he does so, Karcher argues, not to inspire fear or justify violence, but to impart a vision of shared experience that "shifts the definition of brotherhood from an intraracial bond between northern and southern whites to a cross-racial bond between white and black opponents of slavery."[7] Douglass thus enlisted apocalyptic rhetoric in the same way that he enlisted many other texts and ideas: by revising from the inside out. Whether he is reflecting on the Fourth of July or the evils of slavery, Douglass tends not to simply endorse or reject a given set of claims but to adopt a practice of immanent critique. In his wartime writings, he frequently deploys the imagery of Northern apocalypticism, but he also reframes that upheaval since what is being destroyed, as though in a massive fire, is not the earth, or some sacred covenant, but slavery itself. As he put it in 1864 (subtly revising a well-known phrase of Byron's): "The blow we strike is not merely to free a country or continent – but the whole world from Slavery – for when slavery falls here – it will fall everywhere. We have no business to mourn over our mission. We are writing the statutes of eternal justice and liberty in the blood of the worst of tyrants as a warning to all after-comers" (*FDP*, 4:8).[8]

Douglass's description of the war's global impact points us toward another way in which his account of the conflict differs from that of the millenarians: for Douglass, the war did not end history – it resequenced it. The struggle's meaning therefore resided less in its annihilative violence than in its textured chronology as a revolution. To elucidate that chronology, he often draws upon two veins of revolutionary thought: a transatlantic discourse that frames revolutions as the *primum movens* of history, and a nationalist discourse that traces freedom back to the revolutionary acts of the founders. The first of these traditions, Reinhart Koselleck has demonstrated, was one of modernity's conceptual innovations. For a long time, revolution referred (as the etymology implies) to a cyclical series; it was only after the secularization of historical time in the seventeenth and eighteenth centuries that revolution came to be associated with a historical transition, an epochal leap forward, as it were, which advances time itself.[9] The rich afterlife of this modern sense of revolution is everywhere evident in nineteenth-century writing, from Marx's political essays ("revolution is the driving force of history") to Emerson's speeches ("Wherever a man comes, there comes a revolution"), Dickinson's poems ("Revolution is the pod"), and Douglass's wartime writings.[10]

Douglass explicitly addresses the other genealogy (that is, the history of the American founding) in many of his commentaries about the war. Part of the reason why apocalypticism inadequately describes Douglass's wartime vision is that he conceived of that struggle as a belated revision of the American Revolution. He often immersed his prose, as Ivy Wilson notes, in "the metalanguage of the nation's founding documents," and during the war he incessantly drew upon the Revolution's terms and categories. The Confederates, he argued, should not be called rebels because that epithet is "too good for slaveholders": "Washington, Jefferson, John Jay, John Adams, Benjamin Franklin, [and] Alexander Hamilton [wore] those appellations, and I hate to see them now worn by wretches who, instead of being rebels against slavery, are actually rebelling against the principles of human liberty and progress."[11] To name these "wretches," Douglass used one of the founders' preferred terms: tyrants. He had always referred to slaveholders as such, but "tyrants" and "tyranny" appear with a marked frequency in his wartime writings. He deploys the epithet, at various moments, to defend the war's violence ("The only penetrable point of a tyrant is the fear of death"), argue for Reconstruction ("the slaveholder [cannot] instantly throw off the sentiments inspired and ground into them by long years of tyranny"), and even construe the event's historical lessons ("Whether the oppressed and despairing bondman […] or the tyrant […] takes the initiative, and strikes the blow […] the result is the same, – society is instructed, or may be").[12]

If the Confederacy could be described through the same terms as the Revolution's enemies, that did not necessarily mean the Revolution was simply preserved through the North's war effort. For Douglass, the Abolition War was a repetition with a difference since it simultaneously restaged the Revolution while correcting for its mistakes and omissions. (Douglass's account thus provides a kind of emancipatory inversion of Melville's poetics of historical repetition, which we will assess in Chapter 3.) In his estimation, the government established by the Revolution was buried "under the frowning battlements of Sumter," and the North was fighting neither for "the dead past" nor "for the Old Union," but "for that which is ten thousand times more important": a mass liberation that has been centuries, and perhaps millennia, in coming (*FDP*, 4:13–14).

Douglass provided his fullest account of the relation between the nation's eighteenth-century founding and its nineteenth-century refounding in his 1862 speech, "The Slaveholders' Rebellion." Delivered on the Fourth of July, "The Slaveholders' Rebellion" is a wartime sequel to his 1852 oration, "What to the Slave is the Fourth of July?" In that earlier speech, he held out the possibility of the Revolution's belated fulfillment by presenting the Constitution and the Declaration of Independence as "glorious liberty document[s]" in which "there is neither warrant, license, nor sanction" of slavery. Read the Constitution's preamble, he implored, and "consider its purposes. Is slavery among them? Is it at the gateway? or is it in the temple? it is neither" (*SS*, 204). Now, 10 years later, Douglass revises his commentary by reading the nation's history against the grain, arguing that "the political current which has swept us on to this rebellion" began not in 1861, with the first military encounters between the Union and the Confederacy, nor in 1850, with the passage of the Fugitive Slave Act, but all the way back in 1820, with the Missouri Compromise. The latter, he explains, hatched a proslavery counterrevolution that has now assumed an armed form. The North's armies are therefore not just putting down some abortive revolt; they are enacting a kind of *counter*-counterrevolution that hews to the Revolution's "grand and all commanding [principles]" by destroying an institution that the Revolution itself left intact (*SS*, 499–500).

For Douglass, the historical progression that ties the Revolutionary War to the Abolition War is transnational and transperiodic. Precisely because the war is a revolution, it is part of the many other rebellions that have punctuated history throughout the globe. In his speeches and essays about the Abolition War, he accordingly folds the latter into a constellation of other struggles that index an underlying trajectory, or "logic," for history.[13] As he explained in 1863, shortly after emancipation was proclaimed, this "mighty event for the bondman" was a still "mightier event" when viewed through the lens of global history:

> [There are certain great acts which,] by their relation to universal principles, properly belong to the whole human family, and Abraham Lincoln's Proclamation of the 1st of January, 1863, is one of those acts. Henceforth that day [. . .] shall stand associated in the minds of men, with all those stately steps of mankind, from the regions of error and oppression, which have lifted them from the trial by poison and fire to the trial by Jury – from the arbitrary will of a despot to the sacred writ of habeas corpus – from abject serfdom to absolute citizenship. It will stand in the history of civilization with Catholic Emancipation, with the British Reform Bill, with the repeal of Corn Laws and with that noble act of Russian liberty, by which twenty millions of servants, against the clamors of haughty tyrants, have been released from servitude.[14]

Lincoln's Proclamation, as Douglass describes it, is a legal act with a specific genealogy, since it was made possible by prior laws that expanded the realm of human freedom by granting "trial by Jury," "habeas corpus," and "absolute citizenship." But Douglass's account is remarkably fluid, both spatially and temporally. To construe American emancipation, he reaches imaginatively across multiple centuries, continents, and oceans, framing this proclamation – as well as the war that gave rise to it – as the result of a protracted global struggle against "error and oppression."

Like Whitman – and, we shall see, like Melville – Douglass views the war not as a discrete interlude between antebellum and postbellum periods, but as a transition-point in a much longer historical process. Despite their considerable differences, these writers share a basic hermeneutic assumption: that the war is a highly sequenced rupture, and history's patterns make that rupture legible. In this regard, the temporalities that emerge across Douglass's essays and orations resemble the timescales of *Leaves of Grass*, *Battle-Pieces*, and *Clarel*, which periodize the war by moving backwards or forwards through time in creative and elliptical ways. These writers' transbellum perspectives all originate in an effort to discern the war's meaning and scope in time's deep patterns. For Douglass, those patterns are conflictual yet emancipatory, and that is why such acts as the Emancipation Proclamation are so important: they are the markers of liberty's punctuated arrival, signs not of a grand design but of history's inherent and almost unlimited revisability.

To emphasize the war's processuality, Douglass often refers to it as "the irrepressible conflict." That phrase originated with William H. Seward, who, in an 1858 speech before the Senate, declared that the political struggle between the North and the South was "an irrepressible conflict between opposing and enduring forces," and the United States would eventually "become entirely a slave-holding nation, or entirely a free-labor nation."[15] Douglass first used the phrase in an 1859 talk about West Indian Emancipation in which he described "the irrepressible conflict" as a struggle of "sentiments, ideas and systems," and then used it repeatedly as the war unfolded (*SS*, 407). After reading Lincoln's First Inaugural Address, he took to the pages of *Douglass' Monthly* to argue that the President's plan to secure "peace between freedom and slavery" was doomed because any attempt to reach such compromises amounts to an "attempt to reverse irreversible law. The 'irrepressible conflict' still proceeds, and must continue till [...] slavery dies" (*SS*, 431). This notion of the irrepressible conflict also plays an important role in an essay that Douglass wrote, just after scrapping his trip to Haiti, to explain why "the freedom of the slave" and the "victory of the Government" were inexorably linked:

> The American people and the Government at Washington may refuse to recognize it for a time; but the "inexorable logic of events" will force it upon them in the end; that the war now being waged in this land is a war for and against slavery; and that it can never be effectually put down till one or the other of these vital forces is completely destroyed. The irrepressible conflict, long confined to words and votes, is now to be carried by bayonets and bullets. (*SS*, 451)

For Douglass, the Abolition War emerged out of another war altogether, one that sometimes takes the form of "words and votes" and at other times is "carried [out] by bayonets and bullets." This idea of a protracted irrepressible conflict, which extends prodigiously across political and military history, thereby reiterates, in a different key, the idea that holds together Douglass's descriptions of the war's "logic" and "revolutionary" character: that historical time is shaped through a series of progressive struggles, of which the current conflict is an integral part.

It is quite befitting that Douglass viewed the Abolition War as bound up, historically and sequentially, with this longer irrepressible conflict. This was a writer for whom reform was not just a political aim but a literary and philosophical act – a writer who edited newspapers for much of his career, and narrated his life story in ways that depict the self as a most fluid and mutable acquisition. It is this commitment of Douglass's to the power of contingency and process – a commitment, in short, to the idea that *everything* is always under revision – that guides his response to the Abolition War, which, across his speeches and essays, manifests as a moment in which history is not expunged or fulfilled, but thoroughly and violently amended.

The Philosophy of Progress

Douglass framed the struggle in this manner to address its most pressing philosophical question: What caused this bloody war? Or to rephrase in Douglass's lexicon: What exactly made the irrepressible struggle irrepressible?

To elucidate the war's causes and effects, Douglass turned to science and philosophy. He was always an insatiable autodidact: his library contained books on fossils, comets, ethnology, sectarianism, human migrations, and the histories of Holland, England, Egypt, Rome, Greece, France, Peru, England, America, and Australia. But Douglass's later writings evince an especially strong interest in theories of force and motion – theories, that is, of how transformation occurs.[16] To the degree that he arrived at a single, cogent idea about it, it amounted to this: that the social world, like the physical world, is perpetually reshaped by invisible forces vying for control – and this is what the Abolition War confirmed. That conflict was irrepressible because slavery and freedom are opposing forces and, as Douglass once put it, "there are certain elective affinities in the moral chemistry of the universe, and the laws controlling them are unceasingly operative and irrepealable [...] No society can long uphold two systems radically different and point blank opposed, like slavery and freedom."[17]

He offered his most thorough explication of these laws in his 1883 speech, " 'It Moves,' Or the Philosophy of Reform." Although it is certainly true that, as David Blight writes, Douglass "never systematically tried to write a philosophy of history," in this speech he got as close as he ever did to doing precisely that.[18] In it, he provides a careful, sustained, and full-throated defense of progress, which he views as the axiom of human history and evolution. If "'It Moves'" belongs to an oratorical genre, it would have to be something like the antijeremiad: it proceeds directly from the idea that the laws of the universe make permanent decline impossible. Before outlining his philosophy, Douglass summarizes what he calls the "misanthropic view of the world":

> It is contended that the balance between good and evil remains, like the sea, fixed, unchangeable, and eternally the same. In support of this disheartening theory, these [misanthropists] turn our eyes towards the East and lead us about among its decayed and wasted civilizations, its ancient cities, its broken monuments, its mouldering temples, [...] and with the gloomy Byron, they inquire, "Where are their greatness and glory now?" I shall not stop to combat this skepticism till I have mentioned another and worse form of unbelief, not the denial that the world is growing better, but the assertion that it is growing worse. Improvement is not only denied, but deterioration is affirmed. According to the advocates of this theory, the men and women of our age are in no respect equal to the ancients, and art, science and philosophy have gained nothing. (*FDP*, 5:128)

To counter such "denial[s] of progress," Douglass considers the raw "nature of man" and advances his version of what had become a set piece in European and American philosophy: an account of man in his original state, stripped of any civilizational trappings.

> He is, upon first blush, less fortunate than all other animals. Nature has prepared nothing for him. He must find his own needed food, raiment and shelter, or the iron hand of nature will smite him with death. But he [... thereby becomes] an object, not only to himself, but to his species, and his species an object to him. Every well formed man finds no rest to his soul while any portion of his species suffers from a recognized evil. The deepest wish of a true man's heart is that good may be augmented and evil, moral and physical, be diminished, and that each generation shall be an improvement on its predecessor. I do not know that I am an evolutionist, but to this extent I am one. I certainly have more patience with those who trace mankind upward from a low condition, even from the lower animals, than with those that start him at a high point of perfection and conduct him to a level with the brutes. [...] Happily for us the world does move, and better still, its movement is an upward movement. Kingdoms, empires, powers, principalities and dominions may appear and disappear; may flourish and decay; but mankind as a whole must ever move onward, and increase

in the perfection of character [...] That the world moves, as affirmed and demonstrated by the Italian mathematician [that is, Galileo], was long since admitted; but movement is not less true of the moral, intellectual and social universe than of the physical. Here, as elsewhere, there are centripetal and centrifugal forces forever at work. Those of the physical world are not more active, certain and effective, than those of the moral world. (*FDP*, 5:129–130)

Douglass advances several related claims here, which he sets up by noting the apparent inadequacy of the human body. At least in terms of the daily "struggle of the fittest," we are woefully ill-equipped: "Nature has prepared nothing for [us]," not food, or shelter, or clothing. These biological deficits nonetheless gave rise to society, since primal man was forced to turn to others, and that created a vast network of interlocking ethical obligations. Douglass then shifts from this Rousseau-like claim about society's charitable origins to a claim about generational and historical movement: if civilization derives from sociability, and in particular from a shared commitment to care, then this tie must be diachronic as well as synchronic. This primal sympathy is what binds people together and pushes the species forward, and that is precisely what is wrong with the idea that "mankind is [in] a downward or retrograde movement": it overlooks the lasting claims of this interpersonal bond (*FDP*, 5:129). To shore up this argument, Douglass then turns, in the concluding sentences, to the troubling fact that supports so many "denial[s] of progress": the continued existence of evil. The world, Douglass grants, is certainly replete with violence and injustice, but these things only lead to progress later on because the universe is governed by "centripetal and centrifugal forces" that are "forever at work," creating unceasing change. (Hence the rationale for the title, " 'It Moves' ": the ambiguous pronoun is quite apropos, since everything moves, and moves onward and upward.)

By emphasizing humanity's universal desire to "augment" good and "diminish" evil, Douglass hews closely to nineteenth-century religious accounts that yoked reform to Providential guidance. However, he contends that this sympathetic impulse derives not from "the clouds" or "the stars," but from "humanity itself":

> It does not appear from the operation of [the world's] laws, or from any trustworthy data, that divine power is *ever* exerted to remove any evil from the world, how great soever it may be. Especially does it never appear to protect the weak against the strong, [...] the oppressed against the oppressor, the slave against his master, [...] or one hostile army against another [...] No power in nature asserts itself to save even innocence from the

consequences of violated law. The babe and the lunatic perish alike when they throw themselves down or by accident fall from a sufficient altitude upon sharp and flinty rocks beneath; for this is the fixed and unalterable penalty for the transgression of the law of gravitation. The law in all directions is imperative and inexorable. (*FDP*, 5:137; emphasis added)

Douglass here refines his earlier claims about sympathy's origins by stressing the earthly absence of divine power. We save each other because, as he writes, "man has neither angels to help him nor devils to hinder him [... He] is to be his own savior or his own destroyer." The only thing that has any true power here on earth is the set of inexorable laws that regulate our physical and moral existence, like "the law of gravitation," which is "fixed and unalterable" for everyone. Through this philosophical account of law and force, Douglass addresses the historical question that has haunted Americans about the Civil War ever since it began: Why did this seeming accident occur? There are, he suggests, no accidents; only transgression of law. The universe's self-actuating laws compel opposing forces – like falling bodies and "flinty rocks," or slavery and freedom – to come into violent contact, and the war was simply one of these moments of collision, a flash-point in this irrepressible conflict that is far "grander than that described by [...] William H. Seward" (*FDP*, 5:130).[19]

Douglass was likely fascinated with these laws and their forms of compulsion because, as Maurice Lee has demonstrated, he was fascinated with chance and probability. During and after the Civil War, Douglass increasingly turned to empirical observation and statistical sociology as explanatory "alternative[s] to Christian theology." This preference for "hard facts" rather than "speculative theories" is evident, for instance, in Douglass's many references to the Abolition War "as a 'school,' 'lesson,' and 'test,'" which suggest that he thought of the conflict as a test-case for causality.[20] The philosophy of "'It Moves'" beautifully extends this interest in probability to reframe the war and assess the historical and moral forces that occasioned it. Even the speech's grandest philosophical claims tend to flow from an inductive logic; hence Douglass's references to "data" and "appearances" immediately prior to his discussion of "violated law."

Douglass's ideas about force and law, however, also draw upon a number of other political, literary, and philosophical developments. In the late nineteenth century, black civil rights depended almost entirely on the government's power to enforce the Civil War and Reconstruction amendments – or as Deak Nabers puts it, "the force of positive law." Realist fiction was also deeply interested in the power of social circumstances to unwittingly structure things like speech, class, and – in the later novels of

Henry James – consciousness itself. That interest was also foregrounded in naturalist prose and poetry, much of which pivoted on the idea that only force mattered. As Frank Norris writes in *The Octopus* (1901), it was "FORCE that brought men into the world, [and] FORCE that crowded them out of it to make way for the succeeding generation."[21]

In "'It Moves,'" Douglass also taps into a variety of scientific discourses. His descriptions of the world's "centripetal and centrifugal" forces draw upon Isaac Newton's *Principia* (1687), which terrestrialized Kepler by tracing motion back to the relationship between matter and force. (A force is centripetal when it propels a body around a given point, and centrifugal when it pushes a body away from that point.) Newton's laws had recently been refined, and in some instances revised, by scientists such as Alexander von Humboldt, Louis Agassiz, John Tyndall, and Michael Faraday, and by mathematicians such as Joseph-Louis Lagrange and Gaspard-Gustave de Coriolis. In the United States, the discoveries of Humboldt, Agassiz, and Faraday in particular were widely circulated and discussed. Humboldt contended in *Kosmos* (1845–62) – his marvelous, five-volume explication of everything – that the universe has a central force, a "centre of gravity lying beyond the confines [of the stars]," which endows every piece of matter, both great and small, with the dual forces of attraction and repulsion. Agassiz's comparative zoological and geological theories hinged on the idea that earth's diversity is the byproduct of forces that are at once immense, unseen, and divinely coordinated. And Faraday, in a number of lectures (six of which were published by Harper & Brothers in 1860), argued that the world is subtended by a multiplicity of forces that, rather than dissipating, are constantly transmuted into other forms (e.g., light into heat, electricity into light), which create "mutually dependent systems." According to Faraday, the ineradicability of force – the impossibility of ever "suspending" or "annihilating" it – is "the highest law in physical science which our faculties permit us to perceive."[22]

Douglass likely encountered these ideas about force both directly and indirectly, through articles, speeches, books, and conversations. Faraday's discoveries were described in a variety of wartime media, appearing in prominent lectures as well as in essays on electricity, meteorology, the economics of slavery, and "the values of accident."[23] Faraday's theories about the world's infinite lines of force also play a pivotal role in two of Ralph Waldo Emerson's wartime orations, which portray the bloody conflict as a struggle between moral forces. "Our Copernican globe," Emerson declared, is really just a great "machine," a colossal "factory or shop of power, with its rotating constellations, times, and tides, bringing now the day of planting then of reaping, then of curing and storing; bringing now water-force, then wind, then caloric, and such magazine of chemicals in its laboratory." Besides "help[ing] man in every" way, these material forces, according to Emerson, also provide us with a model for understanding human society, which is similarly constituted through "a bundle of forces." In our social world, these forces are moral but they have the same properties as their material cousins: they frequently collide with one another; have a broad range of uses; and are infinitely transferable. As Emerson words it, drawing from Faraday: "There is no loss, only transference: when the heat is less here, it is not lost, but more heat is there [...] When the continent sinks, the [...] opposite shore of the ocean, rises."[24]

If Douglass did encounter Emerson's speeches, he would have been especially interested in the conclusion of the second talk:

> I find the survey of these cosmical powers a doctrine of consolation in the dark hours of [the war ...] For the world is a battle ground; every principle is a war-note, and the most quiet and protected life is at any moment exposed to incidents which test your firmness. How then to reconstruct? I say, this time [... do] not lay your cornerstone on a shaking morass: that will let down the superstructure into a bottomless pit, again. Leave slavery out. Since nothing satisfies men but justice, let us have that [...] And speaking in the interest of no man and no party, but as a geometer of his forces, I say, that the smallest beginning, so that it is just, is better and stronger than the largest that is not quite just. This time no compromises, no concealments, no crimes.[25]

Nations, like everything else, Emerson suggests, are subject to the cosmic laws that make the whole world "a battle ground"; and just as the physics of architecture stipulate that "cornerstones" should not be placed on "a shaking morass," the physics of statecraft demand that the reconstructed United States should "leave slavery out." Emerson thereby promotes a view of the war that is quite close to Douglass's in "'It Moves.'" Both writers (or "geometers") discern in the science of force – in its antagonistic perpetuity and invisible compulsions – a lucid model for thinking through the war's causal logic. In certain respects, Douglas's philosophy of progress is a kind of amplified rearticulation of Emerson's theory of force, one that smuggles a transcendentalist (or Faradayian) account of "cosmical laws" into a broad remapping of civilization and its origins.[26]

But Douglass's perspective on the war is more historically oriented than Emerson's. When Douglass enlists theories of force and law in "'It Moves,'" and in many of his other later writings, he does so to philosophically test out the ideas about history that he had wrested from the Abolition War. The sense of complex diachrony stipulated by claims about the continuity of force bears a striking resemblance to the *longue durées* of the irrepressible conflict – a fact surely not lost on Douglass. Douglass's philosophy of progress is also decidedly more "evolutionist" (as he words it) than Emerson's. Given the contents of Douglass's library, it is likely that when he enlists that term he is thinking not only of Charles Darwin (as one might expect) but of Herbert Spencer, the British evolutionary theorist whose *Synthetic Philosophy* first appeared in the 1860s. Spencer's ten-volume study is many things – an ambitious philosophical treatise, a work of scientific speculation, and, in its later phases, a racist tract – but its initial claims revolve around the idea of perpetual motion. "Matter," Spencer maintains, "is indestructible and Motion continuous." Since every force "implies an equal antecedent force" and "cannot disappear without result," forces never truly begin or end; they are instead reborn, over and over, through chains of action and reaction. To illustrate this idea, he gives the example of hearing a shout. When the sound reaches the ears, that acoustic experience occurs only because of a patterned exchange of forces: human muscles use energy to create vibrations in the throat, which are sent "through the ears" and then "impressed" on one's mind and "on surrounding objects." (We have "clear proof" of this, he observes, "when objects are fractured: as windows by the report of a cannon; or a glass vessel by a powerful voice.")[27] Spencer's underlying assertion – which would have been very enticing to Douglass – is that humanity, too, advances through such progressive changes; we are therefore, as a species, not only continuously being transformed, but transformed for the better. Spencer infamously put this grand theory to racist ends, but Douglass remakes it into a robust philosophy of history that is structured around emancipation.

Douglass's ideas about force and transformation were also flavored by his reading of Johann Gottlieb Fichte. Fichte's *The Destination of Man* (1800), which Douglass owned, promotes a theory of perpetual change that overlaps in remarkable ways with Douglass's philosophy of progress. Nature's "undeviating laws," Fichte argues, all point to one idea, which "amounts to this: that to every existence another must be presupposed." Everything in the world – the objects around us, as well as our very identities – are "forms of something [already] formed, modifications of something [already] modified." This vast intercalation of forms, moreover, derives not from Providence, or from what eighteenth-century writers called the great chain of being, but from the unity of Nature itself, which both releases and directs an infinite array of forces that "develop according to their inward laws, and pass through all the forms of which they are capable." That passage, according to Fichte, is both progressive and universal; everyone and everything must "pass through a certain series of changes" in order to expand and become fully realized.[28] One can certainly see why Douglass may have been drawn to *The Destination of Man*: it affirms the naturalness and inevitability of perpetual change, and attributes that change – much as Douglass does with the Abolition War – to the forces that drive the world's myriad transformations.

To account for the war's causality, Douglass thus takes up a heterogeneous array of concepts, theories, and claims about the nature of progressive change. Rather than simply borrowing these various ideas, though, Douglass actively remixes them, channeling them into a philosophy of history capable of construing the war in all of its transbellum complexity. If progress is inscribed in the nature of things, and in matter itself, then the Abolition War did not merely belong to an extended series of revolutions – it also advanced these other struggles and pushed the irrepressible conflict closer to some kind of resolution.

To elucidate this theory of progress, however, Douglass knew he could not remain in the abstract realms of philosophy. He needed to make it concrete – and to do so, he turned to what he was best at: telling (and retelling) a story.

Lincoln in the Sixteenth Century

To bring the airy metaphysics of progress back to earth, Douglass frequently deployed anecdotes. After emancipation, one of his favorite stories (which often provoked laughter) involved a seventeenth-century religious tract. As he related in an 1873 lecture, there is nothing especially new about abolitionism:

> Perhaps the earliest book written of an anti-slavery character only claimed for the negro one thing. It was a book written two hundred years ago by Rev. Dr. Goodwin, of Jamaica written for the purpose of proving that it was not a sin to baptize a negro. (Laughter.) It was a book of two hundred pages [...] The first difficulty that met him was that baptism is an ordinance for a free moral agent for persons who can determine upon their own course of conduct. The negro could not. He was not a free moral agent, and could not decide [...] when he should work, where and how much he should work, and what use was baptism to such a piece of property as that? [...] But it was out of that discussion came the germ of the struggle which gave birth to the freedom you now enjoy. Dr. Goodwin, while he

did not deny a slave was a slave, he insisted upon it, that though a slave he was a man, and in granting him the right of baptism opened the doors by which every other right belonging person to man could be claimed and insisted upon. (*FDP*, 4:365–66)

Although the passage begins as a risible aside about the first antislavery document, it morphs into a much broader account of historical progress. Morgan Godwyn's *The Negro's and Indians' Advocate* (1680) was astonishingly narrow in both scope and ambition, lodging only a single negative claim: that it was *not* a sin "to baptize the negro." Yet this most measured early strike against slavery, Douglass suggests, also inaugurated the abolitionist movement. In this respect, his story about Godwyn is less an anecdote than a brief prehistory of the present, one that addresses the Reconstruction-era debate over black enfranchisement (which revolved around questions of conduct, labor, and self-sufficiency) by way of the seventeenth-century debate over black baptism.[29] As Douglass notes, it was "out of that discussion [that] came the germ of the struggle which gave birth to the freedom you now enjoy."

Douglass repeatedly invoked this ecclesiastic prehistory, referencing Godwyn's little book in lectures, essays, and interviews for more than 20 years after the war. He did so partly because, as Maurice Wallace observes, Douglass was at heart a "bricoleur" who "combined various views," often tying the religious to the secular and the national to the transnational.[30] Douglass also did so to provide his philosophy of progress with an empirical and referenceable history. To that end, he often discussed – sometimes briefly and sometimes at considerable length – a variety of past wars, personages, and struggles. His later writings are utterly replete with accounts of Godwyn, John Brown, Abraham Lincoln, and Galileo Galilei, and historical commentaries on Rome, Egypt, and the abolitionist movement. Nonetheless, Douglass's preferred transbellum prehistory – the narrative to which he attached the most political and philosophical significance – was the story of William the Silent, the laconic rebel who led the Dutch in their sixteenth-century revolution against the Spanish crown.

After reading about that revolution in John Lothrop Motley's *The Rise of the Dutch Republic* (1856), Douglass wrote a speech about William the Silent that he delivered on numerous occasions in the late-1860s and then recycled into several orations and essays. The speech is rarely anthologized or discussed nowadays, but by the end of Douglass's life it was generally considered to be one of his most lasting pieces of writing. An early biographer even called it Douglass's finest production "in point of polish and finish."[31] Here is how it begins:

> War, stern and terrible war, seems to be the inexorable condition exacted for every considerable addition made to the liberties of mankind. The world moves – let us be thankful for it – but it moves only by fighting every inch of its disputed way [… And] among the great wars of nations and parts of nations, waged to obtain a larger measure of liberty [...] there is, perhaps, no one in history more important – certainly not one more remarkable and thrilling in its details – than that of which the Netherlands were the dreary and dismal scene, during the last half of the sixteenth century. Within the narrow limits of that ocean-menaced and dyke-defended country, merely a dot on the map of Europe, apparently by natural conditions fitter for the habitation of amphibious creatures than for men [...] a war was undertaken and carried on for eighty long years, which, when we consider its bearing on civilization [...] was a war, not for that country alone, but for mankind; not for that century alone, but for all time. (*FDP*, 4:187–188)

Douglass's observations here echo the philosophical insights of "'It Moves'": the world progresses only through struggle and each conflict propels civilization forward. In "William the Silent," though, he is primarily interested in progress's deep empirical history. Only a few years after the Abolition War, Douglass is turning back to another "stern and terrible war" to comprehend the meaning of prolonged violence. This is why he describes the Dutch rebellions as a great war not for the Netherlands "but for mankind," and not "for that century alone but for all time": because these revolts and the Abolition War are historically, and even causally, connected.

Americans, he claims, are "in larger measure than" anyone else the "fortunate heirs and possessors of [this war's] beneficent results." Douglass initially frames this inheritance as a shared revolutionary founding – or as he puts it, a "clear and logical" relation between "the war of the Dutch for civil and religious liberty" and "the American war for independence" (*FDP*, 4:189). Both struggles expanded the realm of human liberty and were directed against a tyrant whose "terrible persecution" had destroyed "all hope of relief by peaceful means." But almost immediately after he juxtaposes "these two grand events," Douglass directs his attention to the speech's primary concern: the historical tie between the Dutch rebellions and the Abolition War. Prewar Netherlands, as Douglass describes it, sounds very similar to the prewar United States. The land is "tempest-tossed from end to end by a contest between two [forces]"; "the people are divided"; and the sufferings of the Dutch have been so "long" and "grievous" under the cruel reign of Philip II ("who employed death in every form that could terrify [...] the souls of men") that Douglass says – as he often said of slavery's most heinous aspects – that he has "no words to describe [them]" (*FDP*, 4: 191). He also descries a parallel between the fight for religious liberty and the fight for emancipation – or more accurately, between the belated embrace of these two ideals:

> Though the Dutch were fighting from the first for [...] religious freedom, they did not dare admit that pregnant fact to themselves [...] The fact is the Dutch cowered before the doctrine of the divine right of Kings, while we cowered before the doctrine equally absurd of the divine right of slavery. It is remarkable that when men come across anything in man that is too bad to be called human, they invariably call it divine [...] The Dutch made no progress really against Spanish persecution until they exploded this "divine right" humbug, and we made no progress until we exploded our "divine right" humbug and consented to part with our reverence for slavery, and called on the slaves to assist in the great struggle for national existence as well as for emancipation [...] Both nations were made strong when they discarded these delusions. It is alike instructive and entertaining to observe how gradually and almost imperceptibly these two nations are lifted from one step to another, in the shining pathway of human progress, by the simple logic of events [... and how, only] after years of suffering, after starvation and pestilence, after half the nation had been slain, the Dutch began to [finally] comprehend the true principles for which they were contending, and began to have a conception of what was right and true in the premises. (*FDP*, 4:193–194)

Douglass is drawn to the Dutch rebellions because the sequence of events seems to anticipate that of the Abolition War. In both cases, violence comes in the wake of suffering, but that struggle's true principles manifest only *post festum*. There is certainly a spiritual dimension to this narrative of progress, but Douglass is less invested here in what Reginald F. Davis calls an "anticipation of liberation theology" than in the tangled forces of history. (As he asserted at an 1890 gathering, after hearing a preacher claim that "it was the good Lord" who ended slavery: "the good Lord had a chance to abolish slavery a long time ago" [*FDP*, 5:434].)[32] For Douglass, the antislavery movement and the struggle for religious freedom are bound up with one another in "a relation of historical cause and effect." In short: for the body to be freed, the mind first had to be liberated, and that freeing of the mind only occurred through the violent encounter of opposing forces. Initially, the Dutch rebels possessed no innate "attraction amongst themselves" and could not even "admit" the "pregnant fact" that religious liberty was their cause. It was only the repulsive force, or "external pressure," of the Spanish crown that compelled them to unite and finally "comprehend the true principles for which they were contending." As Douglass nicely summarizes this point elsewhere in the speech: just "as ours was the irrepressible conflict of the nineteenth century, so theirs was the irrepressible conflict of the sixteenth century" (*FDP*, 4:194–195).

Douglass's account of the Dutch revolts is curiously skewed. He over-estimates the number of people tortured and killed during the Inquisition and depicts the rebellions as far more cohesive, both politically and temporally, than they actually were. There was in fact no single war "under-taken and carried on for eighty long years," as Douglass claims; there were instead a discontinuous series of revolts, many of which, in the struggle's early decades, were highly localized and fueled by a variety of social and religious antagonisms. Throughout the conflict, there were also multiple truces and ceasefires, including one at the outset of the seventeenth century that lasted for 12 years. And even after the rebellions went national, many of the southern provinces (which were primarily Catholic) pulled away from the Calvinist north.[33] I would like to suggest, however, that Douglass is not simply getting his history wrong; he is actively revising that history in order to recast the Abolition War through the Dutch conflict and thereby discern the shape of progress across its *longue durée*. (Perhaps that is what Robert Purvis meant when he claimed in his eulogy for Douglass that "William the Silent" will "take rank as a literary effort.")[34] By scaling the Inquisition up, he makes it more closely resemble American slavery (and priests more akin to slaveholders), and by framing the Dutch rebellions as a single revolution, he provides the Abolition War with a precedent and progress with a plottable timeline.

Douglass's revisions also place an added emphasis on biography. After outlining the historical "relation of cause and effect" between these dispa-rate conflicts, Douglass condenses that relation into the exceptional story of a single man: William the Silent (Figure 3). The latter, for Douglass, is not simply the leader of the Dutch revolts; he is the personal embodiment of the war in all of its historical and political totality. William, he explains, was perfectly suited for the crisis: "There was not an element of his charac-ter that could have been spared. He had the sagacity to see, the wisdom to accomplish, the eloquence to persuade, the courage to venture, [...] and [a] dignified reticence." In fact, it was only through William's superlative "statesmanship" that the "angry waves of [...] contention were silenced" and order was rescued from chaos (*FDP*, 4:196).

Figure 3. Dirck Barendsz, *Portrait of William I, Prince of Orange, called William the Silent* (1582–1592). Courtesy of the Rijks Museum in Amsterdam.

In Douglass's description, this Calvinist commander sounds eerily similar to "the first martyr President of the United States" – and that is hardly a coincidence. The idea that "[w]hat Abraham Lincoln was to us, [...] William the Silent was to the struggling cause of religious liberty," is in many respects the animating claim of Douglass's entire speech (*FDP*, 4:196–7). Despite the centuries between them, both of these leaders, he notes, "were loved by their people" ("[t]he countrymen of William soon learned to call him 'Father William,' as we learned to call Abraham

Lincoln 'Father Abraham'") and were eventually destroyed by the very conflict that they so perfectly embodied:

> Like our lamented President, William died by the hand of an assassin; he died uttering a prayer in mitigation of the punishment of his murderer, and if Abraham Lincoln could have uttered a word after the cruel bullet of Booth went crashing through his brain, those who knew him best will not hesitate to believe that his last words would have been in keeping with that which came down from the cross: "Father forgive them, they know not what they do." He had malice toward none, charity to all. The secret power of both men can be found in this very element of their character, [...] in their love for their fellow-men, even though these fellow-men were erring and criminal. Pilgrims pay their vows at the tomb of William the Silent, and while liberty has a home in our land, dusky pilgrims, at least, will find their way to the place where reposes the body of Abraham Lincoln. (*FDP*, 4:197–198)

The biographies of William the Silent and Abraham Lincoln overlap in astonishing ways. Both of these men relished silence; led armies in a great war; and, despite dying "by the hand of an assassin," were known more for their "charity" than for their "malice" (terms that Douglass lifts from Lincoln's Second Inaugural Address). As paradoxical as it seems, the "secret power of both" men resided in their unusual capacity for love. And that strange fusion of love and violence – of unimaginable war on the one hand and an unmitigated, almost Whitmanian affection on the other – is, I would suggest, precisely why Douglass is so fascinated by the relation between these two wildly different, and distant, figures. That seemingly discordant combination of qualities is what made them so well adapted to their given moments. Or to rephrase in Douglass's philosophical language: what connects William the Silent to Abraham Lincoln is the peculiar way in which they incarnated, at the same time, the historical forces behind them *and* the sympathetic impulse upon which all progress is predicated.

By distilling history through biography in this manner, Douglass enlists a hermeneutic that had been popularized in the 1840s and 1850s. Emerson's theory that certain "great men" have a "pictorial or representative quality" which "admit[s] us to the constitution of things" was embraced during the lead-up to the war by many different writers, from Herman Melville, who populated his imaginary ships and islands with various social types, to Margaret Fuller, who demonstrated in *Summer on the Lakes* (1844) and *Woman in the Nineteenth Century* (1845) that there could also be representative women. The self on display in Douglass's prewar autobiographies – "a Representative American man – a type of his countrymen," in the words of James McCune Smith – is also strikingly redolent of the mutable and capacious subjects that one encounters in Thoreau's *Walden* (1854) and Whitman's *Leaves of Grass*.[35] According to the field's prevailing periodization model, this Emersonian investment in representative men is definitively antebellum, but here we find Douglass, in a purportedly post-Emersonian and post-romantic age, enlisting this hermeneutic to construct an elaborate transbellum account of William the Silent and Abraham Lincoln's linked representativeness.

Douglass continued to develop that historical account long after he stopped delivering "William the Silent" on the lyceum circuit. Even as late as 1893, in one of his final speeches, he invoked this story to demonstrate how, in "all such prolonged conflicts," progress can materialize out of "[c]rushing disaster, bitter disappointment, intense suffering, grievous defections and blasted hopes" (*FDP*, 5:508). Pivoting on a theory of representativeness that was supposed to be superseded, Douglass's discussion of William the Silent demonstrates the degree to which transbellum literature exceeds the Civil War, extending compositionally across the nineteenth century and imaginatively across time and space. Douglass's transbellum writings also elucidate just how nonsynchronously this literature unfolds. Rather than deriving from a generic, generational, or epistemic displacement, Douglass's later writings flow from a rich array of revisions that bear directly on the Civil War's complex temporality. In speeches such as "William the Silent" and "'It Moves,'" and in many other transbellum works, the Civil War emerges as the exact opposite of the literary antiperiod it is so often taken to be. It is instead a nexus of revision and experimentation in which, to borrow from Susan Gilman, "multiple times exist simultaneously within and across the same places or coexist as uneven temporalities."[36]

For Douglass, it was particularly important to view progress through multiple times because the late nineteenth century was manifestly a period of political regression. Despite the guarantees of freedom proclaimed by Lincoln and codified by the Reconstruction amendments, many former slaves, especially in the Deep South, discovered that the postbellum world did not differ all that radically from the antebellum world. Slavery was abolished in federal law but the newly acquired liberty of freedmen and freedwomen was severely curtailed by new forms of exploitation on and off the plantation; by the rise of white terrorist organizations such as the Regulators and the Ku Klux Klan; and by voting laws aimed to ensure, as one Virginian put it in 1865, "that the form of slavery," regardless of "what name will be given to it by Yankee ingenuity," will "continue, and that the negroes will have to work harder and fare worse than slaves have ever worked or fared before."[37]

These reversals were accompanied by related changes in Civil War remembrance. Almost as soon as the fighting ceased, emancipationist interpretations of the struggle began to be displaced by narratives that framed the war as a depoliticized tragedy.[38] Most Americans came to remember the war in the manner of Oliver Wendell Holmes, Jr., who characterized it as an existential trial rather than a conflict over slavery. The "generation that carried on the war," he claimed, "has been set apart by its experience," but the only thing that experience proved was the priority of duty over belief. "I do not know what is true," Holmes proclaimed, but "there is one thing I do not doubt": "that the faith is true [...] which sends a soldier to throw away his life in obedience to a blindly accepted duty, in a cause which he little understands, in a plan of campaign of which he has no notion, under tactics of which he does not see the use." In Holmes's formulation, the armed struggle inaugurated by John Brown's zealous insurgency, dubbed by Whitman "the Verteber of Poetry and Art" for "all future America," and described by Douglass as a revolutionary moment in the long irrepressible struggle, is figured as a strangely amoral and apolitical affair. It is not a battle over divergent causes but a tragic quarrel between two equal – and more importantly, equally justified – forces.[39]

Holmes was far from alone. Numerous artists, orators, poets, novelists, historians, and memoirists offered variations on this same story about martial heroism and predestined unity, a story that dislodged the narrative of black freedom from the memory of the United States' most significant conflict. This view of the war is nicely encapsulated by Richard Henry Stoddard's 1888 poem "Decoration Day":

> Such flowers as will to-morrow,
> Be scattered where they lie,
> The blue and gray together,
> Beneath the same sweet sky;
>
> No stain upon their manhood,
> No memory of the Past,
> Except the common valor
> That made us One at last.[40]

These two stanzas cap Stoddard's ode by offering a retrospective fantasy of union, a vision of the Civil War as a struggle that aimed from its very inception at nothing other than national harmony. Commemorated by the laying of flowers before all American soldiers, "the blue and gray together," the war is presented as causeless accident, a "stainless" tragedy that rendered "us" – as was always fated – "One at last."

Douglass's narratives of progress are firmly aligned against such patterns of remembrance. By tracing progress back to humanity's primal origins and abolitionism back to earlier struggles for religious liberty, Douglass promotes an extraordinarily long view of freedom that enables emancipation to be retimed and reframed. In this respect, speeches such as "'It Moves'" and "William the Silent" are an integral part of what Dana Luciano calls Douglass's "countermonumental impulse," which inverts the temporality of nationalist memory by reframing history as an "ever-evolving array" instead of "a single linear narrative." Luciano's illuminating account of Douglass's "trans- and counterhistorical strategy" centers on his 1852 speech, "What to the Slave is the Fourth of July?," but his later speeches and essays about war, evolution, segregation, and civil rights enlist this same strategy to recast freedom as a protracted transbellum attainment.[41] Indeed, if the war was a revision of other revolutions, so too was emancipation, which extended back to the sixteenth century, and beyond that, to the earliest moments of nomadic humanity, when the impulses for care first emerged to make this shelterless world a little more bearable.

The Times of *The Life and Times*

For Douglass, the history of progress was also legible in other biographies – including his own. Prior to the Civil War, he had already written and rewritten his autobiography, publishing *Narrative of the Life of Frederick Douglass, an American Slave,* in 1845, and then, 10 years later, a radically altered and expanded version titled *My Bondage and My Freedom.* After the war, he returned to his own transbellum story as an occasion for thinking about the shape and force of history, issuing *The Life and Times of Frederick Douglass* in 1881, and then again in 1892.

The final two editions of Douglass's story beautifully translate his progressive worldview into a process of autobiographical revision. In the 1881 and 1892 versions, Douglass combines life-writing with philosophy, connecting his personal history of progress to the idea of progress itself. As he declares at one point, "I have lived several lives in one" and discovered in each of them that "the laws of human progress" are "impartial and eternal," and that the universe is structured through "invisible forces" of "moral government" from which "there is no escape."[42] These ideas about force and law, as we have seen, emerged directly out of Douglass's long engagement with the Abolition War and its complex sequentiality. But Douglass also enlisted this philosophy of progress to revise his autobiography – and it is significantly revised: he meticulously altered the syntax, transposing clause after clause until his publisher demanded that he subsidize the cost of the changes; made the narrative more intertextual, filling it out with numerous quotes and, on occasion, entire speeches; and realigned it generically, refashioning his slave narrative into an abolitionist memoir and veteran's autobiography.

Revision, of course, had always played a crucial role in Douglass's life writing. From the 1845 *Narrative* onward, his autobiographies tend to unfold not merely as accounts of his personal experiences but as accounts of what Robert E. Abrams calls Douglass's "complex meditational process of selection, abstraction, omission, and shifting perspective."[43] In *The Life and Times*, that "complex meditational process" revolves almost entirely around the idea of progress. His revisionary practices and progressive philosophy most noticeably converge in the narrative's resequencing. Rather than splitting the book into two symmetrical parts as he had in 1855 ("Life as a Slave" and "Life as a Freeman"), Douglass structures the entire narrative around the progressive unfolding of freedom. The early chapters provide enhanced detail about his acquisition of literacy, and he even inserts new chapters such as "A Child's Reasoning" and "Growing in Knowledge," which, as Nick Bromell points out, deal "specifically with the question of how he, as a slave boy, had learned to think."[44] That initial growth is complemented by the ensuing chapters, which record the public trajectory of Douglass's life as he becomes a well-known orator, presidential interlocutor, and ambassador. Even his escape from slavery and subsequent arrival in the North are reworked so as to frame his experience less in terms of negative liberty ("[I was] homeless, shelterless, breadless, friendless, and moneyless") and more as a sudden temporal expansion ("A new world had opened upon me. If life is more than breath, and the 'quick round of blood,' I lived more in one day than in a year of my slave life" [*LT*, 647]).[45] Slavery and freedom are still – as they always are for Douglass – mixed conditions, but in *The Life and Times* there is more of a progressive arc for the narrative as a whole. In his final retelling of his life's story, Douglass thus presents himself as one of progress's "representative men" whose experiences reveal just how powerful and irrepressible the "invisible forces [...] of moral government" can be (*LT*, 896).

Because of the book's marked emphasis on uplift, scholars have tended to construe *The Life and Times* as Douglass's most traditional, and least subversive, autobiography. In this "philosophically conservative book," several critics have argued, Douglass "retreat[s] from his former pluralist vision" and trades his "sublime black self" for a "self that has become much whiter." Or he replaces the millenarian worldview that anchored his antebellum writing with an almost Darwinian realpolitik. Or, with an "Olympian detachment from the real-world needs and aspirations of the black rank and file in the post-Reconstruction South," Douglass embraces a model of liberal personhood and advocates "the gospel of wealth." Michael Bennett provides an especially powerful version of this reading in *Democratic Discourses*, asserting that the "antebellum Douglass, who was a forceful exponent of economic democracy and radical reform," becomes almost impossible "to recognize as he and others rewrote his story in the more conservative tones befitting a mainstream politician who served as United States Marshal, recorder of deeds, and minister to Haiti." It is this detached and "daunting figure" – "a sort of black Benjamin Franklin," preaching self-respect and perseverance – that Douglass "presents in the final revisions of his autobiography."[46]

The Life and Times, however, largely emerged out of a corrective impulse on Douglass's part. As Robert S. Levine notes, Douglass had been "vilified, by whites and blacks alike, for his involvement" in Republican administrations, his support of American plans to annex Santo Domingo, and his tenure as the president of the Freedman's Savings Bank, which went bankrupt in 1874.[47] *The Life and Times* provides a kind of counterhistory, penned by Douglass himself, of his public life and political affairs. Moreover, the aspect of Douglass's book that is considered to be the most problematic – its robust commitment to the idea of progress – is precisely what makes it such a rich transbellum work. Douglass writes across the Civil War long after it concludes, and in *The Life and Times* he does so by combining the historical ideas he took from that conflict with his practices of revision and self-representation. By framing his life story as a narrative of representative uplift, he rearticulates autobiographically what, in speeches such as "The Slaveholders' Rebellion," " 'It Moves'" and "William the Silent," is a historical subject and philosophical principle. It is also crucial that for Douglass, progress is both processual and nonsynchronous. As he reiterates again and again in his transbellum writings, progress only occurs by way of conflict and reversal; hence his sustained interest in counterrevolutions, the science of motion, theories of evolution, and three-hundred-year-old religious wars.

This complex understanding of progress is articulated in the book's very form. In 1892, Douglass reproduces the first two sections of the 1881 text, in all of its progressive splendor, but adds a third supplement that pushes his autobiography into the present. "Ten years ago," he writes, "I laid aside my pen" with the kind "of relief as might be felt by a weary [...] traveler," but "I have, by my cause, [again] been morally forced into [...] writing." The event that, as he puts it, "forced" and "compelled" him to take up his pen once more was the Supreme Court's decision in *United States v. Stanley* (1883), which revoked the Civil Rights Act of 1875 (*LT*, 938). "The future historian," he asserts, "will turn to the year 1883 to find" the defining moment in the United States' "national deterioration": "Here he will find the Supreme Court of the nation reversing the action of the Government, defeating the manifest purpose of the Constitution, nullifying the Fourteenth Amendment, and placing itself on the side of prejudice, proscription, and persecution" (*LT*, 966). All the progress brought about by the war, and by the many acts and revolutions that preceded it, was imperiled; and Douglass responded, as he so often did, by revising. In the final edition of *The Life and Times*, he added new chapters on Egyptian ethnology, Haitian politics, and American social antagonisms. But it was in the book's structure that Douglass provided his most interesting commentary on the connection between progress and regress. By appending rather than integrating these concluding chapters, Douglass offers a kind of formal version of the argument he had been advancing all along: that progress is nonlinear and the irrepressible conflict is still unresolved.

The historical moment of *The Life and Times* tends to be associated with a very different, and decidedly postbellum, set of literary forms and practices, from the vernacular prose of Mark Twain to the proto-modernist naturalism of Kate Chopin and Jack London. Douglass, however, moves forward by turning back, revising *The Life and Times* by way of the Civil War. Despite its decades-long removal from that conflict, much of *The Life and Times* is devoted to the Civil War: Douglass describes the long lead-up to the struggle (which "illustrated the principle of tension and compression, action and reaction"); his relationship with John Brown (who was "the logical result of slaveholding persecutions"); his colloquies with Abraham Lincoln (whose "patience and silence" remind him of William the Silent, the "soul of the mighty war for religious liberty"); his efforts to recruit black regiments for the Union Army; and his responses to the Emancipation Proclamation, Lincoln's assassination, and Reconstruction (*LT*, 736, 744, 786, 799). These various events, moreover, do not simply slip into the autobiography as occasions for remembrance. According to Douglass, the Abolition War never concluded. In fact, he argues, the "spirit of slavery and rebellion" only *"increased* in power and advanced towards ascendancy" after the military campaigns ended (LT, 789; emphasis added). The "serpent had been wounded but not killed," and the former slaveholders, almost immediately after returning to Congress, used "the fair-seeming name of local self-government" to create a new regime of racial oppression:

> [The whites] were shooting to death just as many of the newly made citizens of the South as was necessary to put the individual States of the Union entirely into their power [...] and they meant now to capture the United States [itself]. The moral difference between those who fought for the Union and liberty, and those who had fought for slavery and the dismemberment of the Union, was fast fading away [...] Insolency born of slave mastery had begun to exhibit itself in the House and Senate of the nation. The recent amendments of the Constitution, adopted to secure the results of the war for the Union, were beginning to be despised and scouted, and the ship of state seemed fast returning to her ancient moorings. (*LT*, 792)

The slaveholders' counterrevolution, it seems, was never entirely suppressed. *The Life and Times* thereby demonstrates, from a transbellum perspective, what is at stake in the idea that progress is processual: it allows the Civil War to be read *forwards* as well as backwards in time and, therefore, as part of the unfolding present.[48]

By yoking the war's past and present, *The Life and Times* simultaneously taps into and distances itself from the genre of Civil War writing with which it has the most in common: the veteran's autobiography. Throughout the later decades of the nineteenth century, many of the war's former soldiers published their remembrances in both article and book form. Some of these memoirs were penned by enlisted men, but the most popular recollections were those of former Union and Confederate generals such as William Tecumseh Sherman, James Longstreet, and Ulysses S. Grant. These veteran autobiographies tend to figure the war through the same deracialized tropes of tragedy and fratricide that are on display in Stoddard's poem and Holmes's speech. This veteran's literature, as Alice Fahs points out, contributed to "the political and cultural project of national reconciliation" by locating the war's "central meaning" in "the shared bravery of white Union and Confederate veterans."[49] This ideological coding of the conflict was also buttressed by a tendency, in many of these memoirs, to bracket the war's political, philosophical, and historical dimensions and focus instead (and often in excruciating detail) on the contest's military movements. Longstreet titled his book *From Manassas*

STATEMENT OF CASUALTIES AND PRISONERS CAPTURED BY THE ARMY IN THE FIELD, CAMPAIGN OF GEORGIA.										
	KILLED.		W'UND'D.		MISSING.			CAPTURED.		
COMMANDS.	Commissioned Officers.	Enlisted Men.	Commissioned Officers.	Enlisted Men.	Commissioned Officers.	Enlisted Men.	Aggregate.	Commissioned Officers.	Enlisted Men.	Aggregate.
Right Wing, Army of the Tennessee, Major-General O. O. Howard commanding	5	35	11	172	. . . .	19	212	34	632	666
Left Wing, Fourteenth and Twentieth Corps, Major-General H. W. Slocum commanding.	2	23	6	112	1	258	402	30	409	439
Cavalry Division, Brigadier-General J. Kilpatrick commanding	3	35	7	120	. . . .	. . . .	120	13	220	233
Total	10	93	21	404	1	277	704	77	1,261	1,338

Figure 4. "Statement of Casualties and Prisoners Captured by the Army in the Field, Campaign of Georgia." From Sherman's *Memoirs* (New York: C.L. Webster, 1892).

to Appomattox (1896) because he sought not "to philosophize upon the war" but to provide a precise chronicle of "the Confederate campaigns in Virginia."[50] In Sherman's *Memoirs* (1875/1886) one encounters far more lists, tables, pictures, maps, transcripts, memoranda, appendixes, and outlines of troop formations than one does discussions of slavery or freedom. (Figure 4 is one of many such tabular reconstructions of the war in Sherman's book.) Douglass, too, fuses his autobiographical self to the war, but in *The Life and Times* that struggle is not a military conflict to be scrupulously recounted, but an integral part of the present and the unsettled, processual history from which it emerged.

In the final chapters of the 1892 edition, Douglass takes a more globalized look at that history as he recounts his recent trips to Europe and North Africa. He dwells in particular on France and Italy, the two countries wherein "the cradle [of] Western Europe and our own country was rocked and developed." As he traverses this land of origins, however, he only discovers grim relics of violence and power: "walled and fortified towns," "old monasteries and castles," "massive walls and gates," "huge iron bolts and heavily barred windows," and "mountain fastnesses." His account of progress's brutal prehistory culminates in this description of a torture chamber, once used in the Inquisition:

> There are [. . .] within these walls [. . .] enough of the ghosts of dead and buried fanaticism, superstition and bigotry to cause a man of modern

times to shudder. Looking into the open and stony mouth of the dungeon into which heretics were hurled and out of which none were allowed to come alive, it required no effort of the imagination to create visions of the Inquisition, to see the terror-stricken faces, the tottering forms, and pleading tears of the accused, and the saintly satisfaction of the inquisitors while ridding the world of the representatives of unbelief and misbelief. It is hard to think that men could from innocent motives thus punish their fellows, but such is, no doubt, the fact [...] They believed [... that] heaven and hell were alike under their control. They believed that they had the keys, and they lived up to their convictions. They could smile when they heard bones crack in the stocks and saw the maiden's flesh torn from her bones. It is only the best things that serve the worst perversions. Many pious souls to-day hate the negro while they think they love the Lord. A difference of religion in the days of this old palace did for a man what a difference of color does for him in some quarters at this day; and though light has not dawned upon the color question as upon freedom of thought, it is to be hoped that it soon will. (*LT*, 993)

If this is where "civilization" was "cradle[d]," then progress is no linear thing. In fact, as Douglass plumbs the depths of this torture chamber, he becomes less interested in dividing the past from the present than in teasing out the abiding relation between them. He even suggests, in a rather Hawthornian way, that torture has not disappeared – it has simply been transformed: people are still tormented, but race has supplanted religion as the irrational cause for persecution. The inquisitors, as Douglass describes them, are hard to distinguish from slaveholders: they flay flesh; thrive on fear; believe everything is "in their control"; and because of their blinding hate, are impervious to "pleading tears." In this dusty torture chamber, we thereby discover – yet again – an abiding connection between the past wars for religious liberty and the recent wars for political freedom, as Douglass revives the timeline he earlier constructed in speeches such as "William the Silent," "'It Moves,'" and "The Slaveholders' Rebellion."

That timeline, as we have seen, tied the revolution of 1861–5 to the Spanish Inquisition, the American Revolution, the Dutch wars for independence, and to many other acts, struggles, and movements. By repeatedly retiming the war, Douglass thus fashioned a counterhistory for emancipation, an alternative chronology through which to measure freedom's progress – or lack thereof. And that sustained effort at periodization made his career just as interperiodic as the Abolition War about which he so often wrote ... and wrote, and wrote again.

CHAPTER 3

Herman Melville's Civil Wars

Although he never delivered wartime orations like Douglass, or volunteered in the hospitals like Whitman, Herman Melville also found the Civil War to be a pivotal event in his literary career. Prior to the outbreak of violence, he was among the most prolific of American prose writers. In the span of just 11 years he had written nine novels, a volume of short stories, and numerous lectures, essays, and reviews. But by the time the Southern states seceded from the Union, the author who had penned some of the most probing and exquisite fiction in the nineteenth century – including, most famously, *Moby-Dick* (1851) – was far more interested in poetry. In the mid to late 1850s he plunged into verse, studying the major and minor works of Milton, Dante, Schiller, Heine, Arnold, and Keats, among others. He published his first two books of poetry – *Battle-Pieces and Aspects of the War* and *Clarel: A Poem and Pilgrimage in the Holy Land* – in 1866 and 1876. Then, in his remaining years, he composed two more books of verse – *John Marr and Other Sailors* (1888) and *Timoleon* (1891) – and a simple ballad that eventually morphed into a stunning novella (*Billy Budd*).[1]

This later phase of Melville's career has proven to be quite the loose fish. Ever since Raymond Weaver, in the first biography of the author (1921), described the period after 1857 as a period of "whisper[s]," "recoil," and "sedulous isolation," critics have tended to construe Melville's later works as the result of a reversal, decline, or withdrawal. Melville, it has been alleged, comes to accept the power of the state and decides to "make peace with his pen." Or after "failing" as an author and a lecturer, he "withdrew from public life" and renounced the "adventurous freedom" of his earlier writings. Or after "quarreling with fiction," he takes up a private genre that allows him to "attend only to his own voice without obligation to serve either the eternal verities or the populace." Or after suffering an "inner conflict," he abandons the democratic egalitarianism of his youth, and his later writing evolves out of this political chastening.[2]

This declension narrative has had a long afterlife, influencing how and why Melville is read, because it dovetails rather seamlessly with the periodization crafted during the first generations of American literary studies. The story of a postwar Melville who has renounced his subversive art and retreated into poetry is the story of a prewar author out of time and out of place, now writing in the midst of a literary era to which he does not truly belong. Melville's purported unbelonging particularizes the epochal shift that the terms antebellum and postbellum stipulate, both conceptually (that is, as a sudden periodic displacement) and generically (that is, as a transition from romance to realism). This narrative has also been reinforced by what has often gone unsaid, unread, or left out. Despite the fact that Melville devoted nearly 30 years and a majority of his career to poetry, his stories of the 1850s still garner the most critical attention and anthology space. And that overidentification of Melville's career with these particular narratives is hardly coincidental: these are the texts that Melville composed during that brief but marvelous window of time that F.O. Matthiessen, in 1941, identified as the microperiod of the American Renaissance. The question, "What should we make of Melville's poetry?," is therefore a question not only about a particular career, but about the sequencing of American literary history and the periodic status of the Civil War.

In recent years, this old story about Melville's antebellum climax and postbellum recoiling has been challenged by a chorus of critics. Deak Nabers, Eliza Richards, and Michael Warner have elucidated Melville's intricate negotiations with the rhetorics of law, journalism, and war. Dennis Berthold, Lawrence Buell, and Timothy Marr have underscored his poetry's profound investments in global movements and frames of experience. And Peter Coviello, Samuel Otter, and Elizabeth Renker have examined the formal and generic complexity that makes Melville's poetry so wonderfully strange and enthralling.[3] Melville the poet, these critics have argued, is no less creative or subversive than Melville the novelist. After the war, he is not a lonely Ishmael cast out from the world that bore him, but a fiercely committed writer who, like many other nineteenth-century Americans, understood poetry first and foremost as a medium of political and rhetorical engagement.

Melville migrated into poetry for a host of reasons. He probably did so in part because he increasingly preferred writing for "the people" to writing for "the public" (to use Lemsford's distinction in *White-Jacket*). In the mid nineteenth century, poems were highly popular and widely circulated literary vehicles, which likely appealed to Melville, who once described himself as an advocate of "unconditional democracy in all things." (He may have had this bond between poetry and democracy in mind when he wrote, in *Weeds and Wildings*, that in the realm of verse – which is "accessible and familiar" to every one – "we are [all] communists.")[4] Melville's poetic turn also evolved out of his long-standing interest in inside versus outside narratives – a division that is increasingly muddled in the fiction of the 1850s, and then structurally foregrounded in his verse, from the multi-perspectival lyrics of *Battle-Pieces* to the proliferating dialogues of *Clarel*. And several other ambitions, anxieties, and engagements probably inspired Melville to take up poetry, including (among other things) a dual interest in shielding his writing from the instrumental logic of industrial modernity and aligning himself, instead, with forms of thought and expression that reached back to the deepest recesses of history.

Yet whatever caused Melville to remake himself into a poet, the fact is that when he did so, he often wrote – and kept writing – about the Civil War. This is most explicitly addressed in *Battle-Pieces*, but the sense of history cultivated in that volume – a sense that "civil war" is a cyclical event that assumes a variety of forms – also animates many of his later works. There is a reason why his later books are full of countless internecine conflicts, from the ancient fratricide restaged in *Timoleon* to the psychic struggles *Clarel*'s characters, and it is not simply that the Civil War was an important subject for Melville to which he repeatedly returned – although it certainly was, and he certainly did. Rather, across these volumes, Melville's poetry tends to be structured around questions that the Civil War conjured up but left profoundly unresolved: questions about the shape of history, the relationship between war and art, and the legacies of violence. Melville often addresses these questions in very different ways – by transporting the Civil War out to the ocean, for instance, or finding its roots in the Holy Land – but these books are tied together by a sustained inquiry into the war's historical, philosophical, and aesthetic complexities. The following pages accordingly provide an account not of the origins of Melville's poetic career, but of the Civil War-related ideas and investments that subtend that career. And that transbellum engagement, we shall find, unfolds through a distinct pattern, as Melville moves from the relatively tight historical logic of *Battle-Pieces* to a more figurative, and even cosmic, rendering of the war in *Clarel* and *Timoleon*.

Battle-Pieces and the Shape of History

Battle-Pieces begins with a meditation on time and movement. Before addressing the war's myriad battles and the historical cycles that gave rise to them, Melville focuses on John Brown, whose dead body swings, pendulum-like, in the opening poem:

> *Hanging from the beam,*
>   *Slowly swaying (such the law),*
> *Gaunt the shadow on your green,*
>   *Shenandoah!*
> *The cut is on the crown*
> *(Lo, John Brown),*
> *And the stabs shall heal no more.*
>
> *Hidden in the cap*
>   *Is the anguish none can draw;*
> *So your future veils its face,*
>   *Shenandoah!*
> *But the streaming beard is shown*
> *(Weird John Brown),*
> *The meteor of the war.*
>
>   (*BP*, 5)

Melville's Brown is the most ambiguous of human augurs. He is, it seems, the very embodiment of the future, both poetically (by prefacing the volume) and historically (by initiating a chronology of the war and foreshadowing its violence), yet he is presented by way of artistic disavowal: his mien and affect, like Shenandoah's fate, exceed representation. Melville titled this poem "The Portent" in part because "Weird John Brown," whose symbolic instability is reinforced by his purely parenthetical presence, propels the reader's historical vision forward to Virginia's coming battles and, more generally, to the nation's own psychic traumas ("the stabs shall heal no more"). Writing, as Hennig Cohen puts it, not in the "white heat generated by immediacy" but in "the cool calculation which the passage of time makes possible," Melville is crafting, out of these italicized words that literally lean forward, a history that projects as much as it recalls.[5] Melville's Brown also portends a future that has in a sense already occurred. The "future veils its face" not simply because this abolitionist's martyrdom has disabled fictions of national harmony, but because the future can be read only in its antecedents. And this is the thrust of Melville's retelling of the war: violence's events do not expire; they instead create patterns of change that extend through the present and beyond.

Battle-Pieces consequently turns back, again and again, to the war's historical precedents: the Crusades, ancient Roman coups, and France's revolutions and rebellions. This temporal movement goes by different names – in "Lee in the Capitol," it is "Fate" that drives the North and South to arms, and in the prose Supplement "Destiny" is what shapes human events – but these formulations all emphasize history's reiterative nature (*BP*, 163, 182). Melville's poetic vision, as Helen Vendler observes, is not directed "upward, like Dickinson's," nor "in a democratic horizontal, like Whitman's"; it is instead pitched downward to "the sea, or to the fiery hell at the core of the earth."[6] A large part of this downward gaze is temporal: to glimpse that which lies beneath, Melville turns to the deep time of history. In "Misgivings (1860)" –

> Nature's dark side is heeded now –
> [. . .]
> With shouts the torrents down the gorges go,
> And storms are formed behind the storm we feel:
> The hemlock shakes in the rafter, the oak in the driving keel.
> (*BP*, 7)

– he portrays the war not only as a deep structural disturbance, but one with a specific historical antecedent. As he writes in the footnote to "The Conflict of Convictions": "The gloomy lull of the early part of the winter of 1860–1, seeming big with final disaster to our institutions, affected some minds that believed them to constitute one of the great hopes of mankind, much as the eclipse which came over the promise of the first French Revolution affected kindred natures, throwing them for the time into doubts and misgivings universal" (*BP*, 173). Melville's suggestion here is that the American Civil War somehow correlates with the Jacobin phase of the French Revolution. Whether the implication is that the coming war may imperil America's democratic institutions in the way that the Reign of Terror liquidated France's aristocracy, or that the South's secession involves a belated counterrevolution, a warped reiteration of the Founding, the point is that Melville is actively searching history for codes and patterns. Moreover, as Melville well knew – and would again reflect on in *Clarel* – the French Revolution was but a string of connected revolts: there is no 1789 without 1830, 1848, and 1871, and vice versa. Blanqui doubles Robespierre. Thiers resurrects, and reembodies, Barras. Melville does not hate revolution but, unlike Douglass, he is deeply troubled by its cyclicality.

Melville returns to France again, this time via New York, in "The House-Top: A Night Piece." Situated midway in the volume and set during the 1863 draft riots that rocked Manhattan for close to a week, the poem is the imagined soliloquy of an upper-class observer – Stanton Garner identifies him, more specifically, as a member of the city's conservative Urban League Club[7] – who, while standing on his rooftop and removed from the fray, waxes philosophic as "The Town is taken by its rats":

> All is hushed near by.
> Yet fitfully from far breaks the mixed surf
> Of muffled sound, the Atheist roar of riot.
> Yonder, where parching Sirius set in drought,
> Balefully glares red Arson – there – and there.
> The Town is taken by its rats – ship-rats
> And rats of the wharves. All civil charms
> And priestly spells which late held hearts in awe –
> Fear-bound, subjected to a better sway
> Than sway of self; these like a dream dissolve,
> And man rebounds whole aeons back in nature.
>
> (*BP*, 64)

The poem's speaker coolly reflects on the sight and sound of the city's working-class multitude. Refusing to be drafted into a war that in mid 1863 seemed unwinnable and from which the rich were exempt (paying a three hundred dollar fee exempted one from service), these rioters looted stores, burned homes, attacked police, cracked heads against lampposts, and lynched random African Americans in the streets, eventually killing nineteen people. Eric Foner notes that it was "the largest civil insurrection in American history apart from the South's rebellion itself."[8] Like the riots, though, the poem does not simply end with the masses' uprising. "Hail to the low dull rumble" of armed repression, the speaker proclaims:

> Wise Draco comes, deep in the midnight roll
> Of black artillery; he comes, though late;
> In code corroborating Calvin's creed
> And cynic tyrannies of honest kings;
> He comes, nor parlies; and the Town, redeemed,
> Gives thanks devout; nor, being thankful, heeds
> The grimy slur on the Republic's faith implied,
> Which holds that Man is naturally good,
> And – more – is Nature's Roman, never to be scourged.

Paul's conception of man ("Nature's Roman, never to be scourged") is, for Melville's genteel witness, disconfirmed by the necessity of violence. One of the more remarkable things about the poem, and about this stanza in particular, is what it leaves unsaid: it mentions none of the carnage of that week, not the rioters' destruction of the Colored Orphan Asylum and the city's docks, not their roasting of men over slow fires, not the federal troops' use of bayonets and howitzers to kill somewhere between two hundred and one thousand New Yorkers, not even the clandestine disappearing of the rioters' bodies afterwards. "The House-Top" instead abstracts the events of the uprising via allusion and figuration.

Melville explains his allusive representation of the riot in his footnote, which transports the reader from nineteenth-century New York to fourteenth-century France: "'I do not write the horrible and inconceivable atrocities committed,' says Froissart, in alluding to the remarkable sedition in France during his time. The like may be hinted of some proceedings of the draft-rioters" (*BP*, 175). *Froissart's Chronicle* (1400), which Melville references here, narrates the principal battles in and between England and France from 1322 to 1400. Of particular interest is the chapter about the 1358 peasant rebellion (or *jacquerie*) outside of Paris from which this quote is drawn. As Froissart relates, numerous peasants, discontent with their lot, began banding together and destroying the property of the rich:

> Wherever they went their numbers grew [...] And those evil men, who had come together without leaders or arms, pillaged and burned everything and violated and killed all the ladies and girls without mercy, like mad dogs. Their barbarous acts were worse than anything that ever took place between Christians and Saracens. Never did men commit such vile deeds. They were such that no living creature ought to see, or even imagine or think of, and the men who committed the most were admired and had the highest places among them. I could never bring myself to write down the horrible and shameful things which they did to the ladies. But, among other brutal excesses, they killed a knight, put him on a spit, and turned him at the fire and roasted him before the lady and her children. After about a dozen of them had violated the lady, they tried to force her and the children to eat the knight's flesh before putting them cruelly to death.[9]

Froissart's account of wartime cannibalism puts an entirely different twist on the claim in "The House-Top" that, in the draft riots, and perhaps in periods of great upheaval more generally (such as the Civil War), society's "civil charms" dissolve "like a dream." The poem's reference thus points us, by way of the war, to history's underlying patterns of disintegration and collapse: lynching free blacks and dock workers in mid nineteenth-century Manhattan is inseparable from – because it repeats, in another time and another form – a failed peasant revolution in mid fourteenth-century France. But the scope of historical reiteration does not end for Melville with the dissolution of boundaries between inside and outside, between civilization and its other. Like Melville's upper-class observer, Froissart concludes not with rebellion but with its Draconian suppression:

> When the gentry [...] saw their houses destroyed and their friends killed, they [...] began to kill those evil men and to cut them to pieces without mercy. Sometimes they hanged them on the trees under which they found them. Similarly the King of Navarre put an end to more than three thousand of them in one day [...] When they were asked why they did these things, they replied that they did not know; it was because they saw others doing them and they copied them. They thought that by such means they could destroy all the nobles and gentry in the world, so that there would be no more of them.[10]

Each attempt to reappropriate the commons, Melville realizes, provokes a corresponding and more violent reaction from the propertied class. History's principle is supersession. The gentry may now wield rifles, but modern rebellions, like their medieval antecedents, bring "the midnight roll" of "black artillery" just the same.

Melville's conception of historical repetition not only deepens the volume's chronology of the war; it also resituates that war along a transbellum timeline wherein rebellion and reprisal cyclically and traumatically succeed one another. That timeline has many of the same nodes as Frederick Douglass's – ancient Rome, medieval Europe, nineteenth-century France – but in *Battle-Pieces* history is tilted toward regress rather than progress. Consider "The Frenzy in the Wake," the second poem of a diptych about Sherman's march. The lament of Melville's Southern observer –

> With burning woods our skies are brass,
>   The pillars of dust are seen;
> The live-long day their cavalry pass –
>   No crossing the road between.
>   We were sore deceived – an awful host!
>   They move like a roaring wind.
>   Have we gamed and lost? but even despair
>   Shall never our hate rescind.
>
> (BP, 98)

– finds its historical analogue in the Roman Civil War. "Plutarch," writes Melville, "relates that in a military council held by Pompey and the chiefs of that party which stood for the Commonwealth, it was decided that under no plea should any city be sacked that was subject to the people of

Rome. There was this difference, however, between the Roman civil conflict and the American one. The war of Pompey and Caesar divided the Roman people promiscuously; that of the North and South ran a frontier line between what for the time were distinct communities or nations" (*BP*, 177). Sherman's scorched earth campaign, which turned churches and courthouses into "pillars of dust" and covered the skies with ash (imagery that also haunts *Clarel*), thus becomes a more brutal repetition of Julius Caesar's subjugation of Pompey. This historical linkage joins Roman and American applications of violence to the aleatory grounds of legal authority, and it supports Edgar Dryden's perceptive claim that *Battle-Pieces* tends to present the Civil War as "an example of a conflict, periodically reenacted, [. . .] in the long sequence of events that are the history of the Western world. Hence reading the signs and omens of the present is a matter of identifying patterns of recurrence that reveal the coercive force of history."[11]

Melville's comparison also posits an important internal difference between the two scenes of devastation: because of its more totalizing regional divisions, the American struggle allows for even greater bloodshed. The war is part of a long temporal sequence, but that sequence has nothing to do with mere resemblances, parallels, or easily exchangeable events. Rather, Melville is fascinated, both aesthetically and politically, with a kind of repetition that manifests in echoes and rebirths. Melville's poetry, from *Battle-Pieces* to *Timoleon*, hinges on what Gilles Deleuze calls "complex repetition," which, instead of simply replicating something, repeats "an 'unrepeatable'": it does not "add a second and third time to the first, but carr[ies] the first time to the 'nth' power."[12] *Battle-Pieces* forges a transbellum chain of connection out of disparate events – joining Manhattan rioters, Unionists, and Secessionists with rebellious peasants, medieval knights, and Roman generals – but this chain's links are also strangely set apart, even traumatically severed, since time's events are for Melville not wholly congruous instants but related moments of undoing in a vast historical cycle.[13]

To represent that cycle, Melville's poems often oscillate between retrospection and anticipation. Consider "The Apparition (A Retrospect)," a poem partly based on the 1864 Battle of the Crater, where Northern miners placed dynamite beneath Confederate troops:

> Convulsions came; and, where the field
>   Long slept in pastoral green,
> A goblin-mountain was upheaved

(Sure the scared sense was all deceived),
   Marl-glen and slag-ravine.

The unreserved of Ill was there,
   The clinkers in her last retreat;
But, ere the eye could take it in,
Or mind could comprehension win,
   It sunk! – and at our feet.

So, then, Solidity's a crust –
   The core of fire below;
All may go well for many a year,
But who can think without a fear
   Of horrors that happen so?
                              (*BP*, 116)

William Shurr rightly calls this poem "the most concise statement of Melville's philosophy to be found anywhere in his writings."[14] The poem's brutal implication is that a true chronometer would measure not progression but regression, and would point with disillusioned hands toward the manifold convulsions that constitute the modern world. The poem's ideas about time are also rearticulated in its form since, in each of these stanzas, or mounds of verse, the poem's own structural "Solidity" is exploded. Metrically, each stanza attempts to contain a trimetric line (beginning with "A goblin-mountain was upheaved") within its tetrameter, but this containment never succeeds: the trimeter keeps returning as an irrepressible metrical "core." In its rhyme scheme the poem thus seems to deploy or repeat the ballad form, but with a difference: the typical quatrain and *abcb* rhyme pattern are disrupted, in each stanza, by an extra, uncontainable c-line. Establishing a link between psychic and temporal instability (by joining, collectively, deception and "comprehension" to the guarantee of historical disorder), these c-lines offer an excess that the poem cannot assimilate and which obliges, at the verse's end, not a "statement" but a pained question: "But who can think without a fear / Of horrors that happen so?" Oscillating between pressure and release, the poem rearticulates in its form the philosophy of history so powerfully enunciated in the poem's content, reiterating in rhyme and meter the idea that the present is a succession of convulsions and time itself is a long chain of cataclysms.[15]

This bond between repetition and destruction becomes most vivid in Melville's poems about the sea. In *Battle-Pieces*, the war's ships, sailors, and bodies of waters become violent expressions of history's cyclicality. In

"The Stone Fleet," an "old sailor" laments the sinking of ancient whalers, now "serv[ing] the Obsolete" in Port Royal:

> I have a feeling for those ships,
>   Each worn and ancient one,
> With great bluff bows, and broad in the beam:
>   Ay, it was unkindly done.
>   But so they serve the Obsolete –
>   Even so, Stone Fleet!
> [...]
> To scuttle them – a pirate deed –
>   Sack them, and dismast;
> They sunk so slow, they died so hard,
>   But gurgling dropped at last.
>   Their ghosts in gales repeat
>   *Woe's us, Stone Fleet!*
>   (*BP*, 21, 22)

The age of wood, Melville realizes, is giving birth to an age of iron and steel. In each stanza, the sinking of these wooden ships – all drowning like sailors tossed overboard – is repeated in a concluding couplet, which returns like the voices of the dead. For Melville's old sailor, these whalers are almost animate: they have "bones" and "wrinkles"; they wear "shawls" and "fans"; they breathe and "gurgle"; and they can even die (*BP*, 21–2). But these "worn and ancient ships" are not simply destroyed: they are replaced by ironclads, those heavy metallic wonders of wartime engineering. Obsolescence thereby gives way to emergence – or as Melville puts it in the concluding stanza (figuring history, yet again, by way of the sea), "the waters [inevitably] pass" and the "currents will have their way" (*BP*, 22).

These deceased ships find a counterpart in "The Temeraire," Melville's poem about Horatio Nelson's decommissioned man-of-war. This gorgeous ship, which once "fought so often and [so] well," is now but a relic:

> The fighting Temeraire,
>   Built of a thousand trees,
> Lunging out her lightnings,
>   And beetling o'er the seas –
> [...]
> But Trafalgar' is over now,
>   The quarter-deck undone;
> The carved and castled navies fire
>   Their evening-gun.
> O, Titan Temeraire,

> Your stern-lights fade away;
> Your bulwarks to the years must yield,
> And heart-of-oak decay.
>
> (*BP*, 41–2)

Melville's depictions of decay in these poems, as Timothy Sweet has demonstrated, challenge the representational claims of pastoral organicism.[16] The Civil War not only breaches "Nature's dark side" but also threatens to undo nature altogether by unleashing mechanized production (*BP*, 7). Melville, however, is less interested in simply mourning the preindustrial world of wood than he is in bringing it into striking, and at times unnerving, juxtaposition with the world of iron that replaces it. Nelson's superannuated warship, for instance, is hauled back to shore by its nautical obverse, a small, ugly, and decidedly inglorious tugboat:

> A pigmy steam-tug tows you,
>   Gigantic, to the shore –
> Dismantled of your guns and spars,
>   And sweeping wings of war.
> The rivets clinch the iron-clads,
>   Men learn a deadlier lore;
> But Fame has nailed your battle-flags –
>   Your ghost it sails before:
> O, the navies old and oaken,
>   O, the Temeraire no more!
>
> (*BP*, 42–3)

With its contained rhymes (*abba*) – the same scheme that Tennyson uses to such great, elegiac effect in *In Memoriam* (1849) – the poem attempts to seize onto something that is either fleeing or already gone. The historical transition upon which the poem turns is partially illuminated in Melville's footnote: "The *Temeraire*, that storied ship of the old English fleet, and the subject of the well-known painting by Turner, commends itself to the mind seeking for some one craft to stand for the poetic ideal of those great historic wooden war-ships, whose gradual displacement is lamented by none more than by regularly educated navy officers, and of all nations" (*BP*, 174).

The oil painting to which Melville is referring, J.M.W. Turner's *The Fighting "Temeraire" Tugged to Her Last Berth to be Broken Up* (1838) (see Figure 5), likewise contrasts the retiring "Titan" with a "pigmy steam-tug." Turner's painting – which Melville saw on his 1849 trip to London – associates the anachronistic man-of-war with the setting sun both spatially (by centering the point-of-view between the two objects)

Figure 5. Joseph Mallord William Turner, *The Fighting "Temeraire" Tugged to
Her Last Berth to be Broken Up* (1838).
Courtesy of The National Gallery, London.

and chromatically (the sun and the ship abound in yellows, whites, and
oranges whereas the iron tugboat, though illuminated by the light, seems
trapped in its own blackness). Like Turner, Melville is interested in the
Temeraire's symbolic capacity as a "poetic ideal," but for Melville the displacement this scene announces is both broader and narrower than the
one Turner identifies. The temporal anamorphosis of Melville's poem,
through which an episode in England in 1838 is woven into the historical fabric of the American Civil War, reinforces an internal differentia-
tion within Melville's repetition of Turner's scene.[17] The statement "But
Trafalgar is over now" not only declares the termination of a single past
event but also announces, as the poem's subtitle implies, the death of an
epoch: "*(Supposed to have been suggested to an Englishman of the old order
by the fight of the Monitor and Merrimac.)*" The displacement encapsulated by the *Temeraire*'s retirement is thereby restaged and intensified in
the 1862 battle between Northern and Southern ironclads, those grim
agents of mechanism and industry. But as Melville's other representations
of temporal change reveal, this instance of historical supersession – the

Figure 6. James F. Gibson, "Deck and Turret of the U.S.S. *Monitor*" (1862).
Library of Congress Prints and Photographs Division.

birth of iron out of the womb of wood – is at once synchronic and diachronic: the solidity of the world of *Temeraires* has been broken up by
the world of *Merrimacs* and *Monitors*, but the latter will also in due time
obsolesce (see Figure 6).

In the book's sea-poems, such displacements also bear directly on the
methods of war. For Melville, the destruction of antiquated ships signals
a change in the modes of destruction itself. "A utilitarian View of the
Monitor's Fight" construes the first encounter between ironclads, in 1861,
as both augur and instance of a widespread replacement of "passion" with
"crank, / Pivot, and screw, / And calculations of caloric":

> Hail to victory without the gaud
> Of glory; zeal that needs no fans
> Of banners; plain mechanic power
> Plied cogently in War now placed –
> Where War belongs –
> Among the trades and artisans.
> (*BP*, 44)

The phrase "plain mechanic power" wonderfully names, at once, the motive-force of mechanized warfare and the catalyst of these sailors' metamorphosis into all-too-modern laborers, now but operatives on factory-like ships. That cruel power is also "plied" in "In the Turret," Melville's poem about John Worden, the Union commander who attacked the *Virginia* while "walled" in the *Monitor's* "armored tower"; and in "Battle for the Bay," which recounts how, off the coast of Alabama, in 1864, the Union fleet's "rapid broadsides" (which made "a din / Like hammers round a boiler forged") sank the Confederacy's prized ironclads, thereby repeating with a difference the dismantling of those wooden ships now serving "the Obsolete" (*BP*, 40, 81, 83, 21). In these sea-poems, Melville thus conjures up the terrifying possibility that animates *Battle-Pieces* and, we shall see, much of his later poetry: that the Civil War, instead of occurring within history, *is* history – and we are all swept up in its waves.

Civil Wars after *Battle-Pieces*

That possibility haunted Melville long after these war-poems were first published. Like each of these other transbellum writers, he conceived of the Civil War as an event that was far more temporally and geographically unbounded than it is often taken to be. Instead of commencing in 1861 and concluding in 1865, and instead of occurring exclusively in the United States, the Civil War, in Melville's imagination, repeats itself across time and space, at once evincing and enacting history's violent cyclicality.

Although that multilinear upheaval is most amply represented in *Battle-Pieces*, its "core of fire" also erupts across Melville's later works. Many of the poems in *John Marr and Other Sailors* (1888) are strikingly redolent of "In the Turret," "The Fighting Temeraire," and Melville's other Civil War sea-pieces. *John Marr* focuses almost entirely on the sailors who were replaced by operatives (and many of them are veterans). After an invocation for mariners who once battled "foemen looming through the spray," the volume opens with the lyric reflections of Bridegroom Dick, who describes the "red dance of death" conducted in 1862, when the Confederacy's *Virginia* "stilettoed" the Union's wooden-walled *Cumberland*:

> Like a sword-fish's blade in leviathan waylaid,
> The tusk was left infixed in the fast-foundering wreck.
> There, dungeoned in the cockpit, the wounded go down,
> And the chaplain with them. But the surges uplift

The prone dead from deck, and for moment they drift
Washed with the swimmers, and the spent swimmers drown.
Nine fathom did she sink, – erect, though hid from light
Save her colors unsurrendered and spars that kept the height.

(*PP*, 205)

Once more, Melville turns to the sea, and as this wooden ship sinks beneath the waves, so does the whole historical world that it represents. This loss is also registered in ways that are quite familiar for readers of *Battle-Pieces*: the poem mixes the animate with the inanimate (the *Cumberland* is like a "leviathan waylaid"); emphasizes the experience of drowning (much like "The Stone Fleet"); and pivots on the complexities of sight and perspective ("erect, though hid from light / Save her colors unsurrendered"). Yet Melville is writing at more than a 20 year remove from the conflict that seems so immediate, and so palpable, in this description.

The Civil War also finds its way, circuitously and elliptically, into some of Melville's later, unpublished manuscripts. "Iris (1865)," a poem that Melville penned in the 1870s, focuses on the world's "loveliest invader," a Southern belle who enchants three Union colonels and thereby transforms these "disenslavers" into men who "embrace a chain" for themselves. *At the Hostelry*, which features a series of expansive dialogues about art and the picturesque, begins with a description of the Risorgimento that makes Italy sound strikingly redolent of the United States: after being held "long in chains," "Italia [was] disenthralled," but only by being "cut up" and "divided." In fact, Melville adds – echoing his earlier poems, "The Canticle" and "America" – it was only out of this violence that "disunited" Italy was remade into a single, cogent, national "unit."[18] And similar traces and loose resonances of the Civil War can be found in *Billy Budd*, which, despite being set during an interstate war, takes place almost entirely on a single ship. *Billy Budd*, in fact, tends to be far less interested in the stark disparities encapsulated by the conflict between monarchical England and Revolutionary France than in the meaning and consequences of various *internal* divisions: the psychic struggles of Claggart; the mutinies that loom in the background, stoking both hope and fear onboard the *Bellipotent*; and Captain Vere's brutal legal philosophy, which divorces the intent and effect of a single act. None of these works, of course, is primarily *about* the Civil War, but that conflict does retain a lasting presence in Melville's writing long after the fall of Richmond.

To what, then, should we attribute the Civil War's incredible persistence across Melville's works? One could certainly interpret it as a thematic reprisal or nostalgic return: Melville, that is, routinely turns back to the war because it either elicits or compels revisiting. That possibility is strengthened by the fact that when Melville wrote about something, he almost never stopped writing about it. His obsession with obsession; his uses of the body as a metaphor; his fascination with in-betweenness (whether sexual, psychological, or aesthetic); and his Pauline interest in the "mystery of iniquity" all extend across the entirety of his oeuvre, from *Typee* through *Billy Budd*. Melville also tends to revisit certain scenes, over and over again, that are symbolically surcharged and typologically significant – like the sinking of a ship, or the experience of seeing the strange or exotic for the very first time. The Civil War almost certainly becomes one of these scenes. The issues around which it revolved for Melville – whether violence was natural or unnatural; whether *anything*, whether a nation or a single human mind, can be undivided; and whether unfreedom could indeed give way to freedom – fascinated him before, during, and for a long time after the war itself. The Civil War, in effect, crystallized what Melville had been interested in all along, so it was altogether fitting that he subsequently drew, fluidly and generatively, from this event for the rest of his life.

But in other crucial respects, Melville does not really return to the Civil War at all. If, as he suggests in *Battle-Pieces*, the war cycles on and on without end, mimicking the movement of history itself, then it is not a conflict that he (or anyone else) can revisit *post festum*. It is instead – and this is indeed the general thrust of Melville's later allusions – a serial upheaval that bridges the past, the present, and the future. Melville invokes and explores the war in his later years for a variety of reasons – because his style depends on acts of retrieval, because he was just as interested as Whitman and Douglass in late-nineteenth-century political events – but one of the foremost reasons has to do with the war's historicity. From *Battle-Pieces* onward, Melville approaches that struggle as an instantiation of historical time more generally, a symbolic exemplum through which the sequential structure of human events becomes at least partially legible and knowable. The Civil War thereby functions as both a continuous and a discontinuous upheaval across the timespace of Melville's own career, providing, in its myriad repetitions, a through-line for the transbellum conception of history that buttresses many of his writings.

The war's lasting importance to Melville is perhaps most fully registered in *Clarel*. Published a decade after *Battle-Pieces*, this epic poem is usually considered to be a very different kind of book than its war-born predecessor. It is set in the Holy Land, features only a few American characters, and addresses matters of faith instead of matters of war. Nonetheless, there is a great deal of continuity in these books' temporal structures and historical visions. Consider the following meditation, of *Clarel*'s narrator, on the history of Jerusalem:

> Days fleet. They rove the storied ground –
> Tread many a site that rues the ban
> Where serial wrecks on wrecks confound
> Era and monument and man;
> Or rather, in stratifying way
> Bed and impact and overlay.
> The Hospitalers' cloisters shamed
> Crumble in ruin unreclaimed
> On shivered Fatimite palaces
> Reared upon crash of Herod's sway –
> In turn built on the Maccabees,
> And on King David's glory, they;
> And David on antiquities
> Of Jebusites and Ornan's floor,
> And hunters' camps of ages long before.
> So Glenroy's tiers of beaches be –
> Abandoned margins of the Glacial Sea.[19]

On this "storied ground," we seem to be quite far removed from the world of the Civil War. There are no ironclads or draft riots here; only ancient knights and crumbling temples. However, as these lines move back through time, we encounter a very *Battle-Pieces*-like cycle of destruction and displacement. Those first European crusaders (the "Hospitalers"), Melville observes, constructed their cloisters directly on top of Muslim (or "Fatimite") palaces. And those, in turn, were "reared upon the crash" of Herod's Temple. Which was built on Solomon's. Which was erected all the way back in the eleventh century BCE.[20] The history of Jerusalem, it would seem, is just as violent, layered, and relic-filled as the history of the earth. Despite the patent shift in Melville's subject matter, the historical viewpoint that frames this passage is, at its core, the historical viewpoint of *Battle-Pieces*, which presents the Civil War as part of a long series of "wrecks on wrecks." These lines, like many others in *Clarel*, also gesture toward the idea that strings together *Verses Inscriptive and Memorial*: that these wrecks either exceed memorialization or only find it, partially and provisionally, in the upheaved earth. Jerusalem's obliterated monuments and littered stones may not be part of the American Civil War, but they are undoubtedly a part of Melville's rich, transbellum response to it.

That response is even more capacious and wide-ranging in *Clarel* than it is in *Battle-Pieces*. Over the course of the poem's 150-plus cantos, Melville addresses a mind-bending array of phenomena: the art and politics of the European Renaissance; the deep histories of Italy, France, and the Middle East; the millennia-long development of Jewish culture; the connections between the world's religions; the possible fates of socialism and democracy; the geological evolution of the earth; and the biological evolution of the human species. *Clarel* is no less philosophically speculative or cosmically inclined than Edgar Allan Poe's *Eureka*, Whitman's "Song of Myself," or Melville's own *Moby-Dick*. The poem's stunning range, however, does not tend to fragment it. *Clarel* is a very tightly woven poem, and one of the things that holds it together, fusing many of the dialogues and meditations, is the view of time on display in Melville's reflections on Jerusalem's "storied ground." Whether the poem is addressing the history of the Reformation, the legacies of the French Revolution, or the fates of various religious relics, one thing remains fairly constant: the sense that history is a repeating cycle of destruction and creation. Some characters, such as Derwent, view this cycle as a benevolent process of change that both liberalizes and liberates, while other characters, such as Mortmain, view it as a process of decline and decay, but the underlying idea remains: that history is constituted through successive, internal antagonisms.

That historical idea, as we have seen, is for Melville inexorably connected to the Civil War. But *Clarel* reveals just how blurred and coextensive Melville's ideas about history and his ideas about the war subsequently became. Indeed, this is the crucial difference between *Battle-Pieces* and the books that follow it. Melville's later works tend to reverse the interpretive flow enacted in *Battle-Pieces*, which imports a variety of visual, historical, and literary registers to process the Civil War. Afterwards, the war itself tends to resonate outwards, inflecting a wide array of other ideas and impressions. Or to put this another way: the Civil War functions in Melville's later works much in the same way that, according to Christopher Freeburg, blackness functions in his earlier works – as a figure that is simultaneously concrete *and* abstract. Melville's racial representations, Freeburg argues, almost always explore blackness as both a form of embodied particularity and a metaphorical state in which truth cannot be fully seen or mastered.[21] The Civil War, I would suggest, is treated in a similar fashion in Melville's later books. It is at once a specific set of events that occurred in the United States in the 1860s; a repeated sequence of upheavals that is both transnational and transhistorical; *and* a highly malleable metaphor for internal conflict more generally.

Clarel enlists all three of these Civil War resonances – sometimes within the span of a single canto. Here, for instance, is how the poem introduces Ungar, a former Confederate soldier:

> Behooveth it to hint in brief
> The rankling thing in Ungar's grief;
> For bravest grieve. – That evil day,
> Black in the New World's calendar –
> The dolorous winter ere the war;
> True Bridge of Sighs – so yet 'twill be
> Esteemed in riper history –
> Sad arch between contrasted eras;
> The span of fate; that evil day
> When the cadets from rival zones,
> Tradition's generous adherers,
> Their country's pick and flower of sons,
> Abrupt were called upon to act –
> For life or death, nor brook delay –
> Touching construction of a pact,
> A paper pact, with points abstruse
> As theologic ones – profuse
> In matter for an honest doubt;
> And which, in end, a stubborn knot
> Some cut but with the sword; that day
> With its decision, yet could sway
> Ungar, and plunging thoughts excite.
>   (4.5.72–93)

The "rankling thing" that underlies Ungar's grief is, of course, the American Civil War: the "rival zones" are the North and the South, and the all-too-ambiguous "paper pact" is the Constitution. To draw out this connection, Melville figuratively condenses the history of the New World into a calendrical cycle in which the Civil War is but one black winter day. This tidy metaphor, however, begins to unravel almost as soon as it is invoked. If the war was an "evil day," it has evidently not ended for Ungar, who is still "swayed" by its violence. Ungar is many respects a latter-day Ahab: his life revolves around a formative, traumatic event; his grief has given way to hate; and he worships something that he cannot see (the "Parsee of a sun gone out" [4.5.53]). After the war, Melville explains, Ungar took to "reading and revery," but this contemplation – much like Ahab's – only "confirmed" his pain, "and made it take a flight / Beyond experience and the reign of self" (4.5.94–97).[22] He now sees civil wars everywhere he looks: in the annals of theology, in capitalist development, and even in innocuous landscapes. (At one point, the pilgrims come across a pasture that has been split up, and the very act of "halving the land" makes Ungar think of the "*North and the South!*" – despite the fact that it is divided along an east/west axis [4.9.66, 81].) The Civil War may have been a particular moment in American history when Northerners and Southerners went to battle against one another, but for Ungar it is also a psychic and metaphysical struggle that is still very much ongoing.

This passage – as well as the canto in which it appears – is also quite "abstruse" about when and where this war actually took place. Melville's lines about the origins of Ungar's grief are bookended, on both sides, by reflections that frame the war as a repeated global event. Right before this passage, Rolfe suggests that "the hemispheres are counterparts," and the canto concludes with a lyric from Ungar that internationalizes his war-born grief by invoking a worldwide "surge / Reactionary" (4.5.63, 182–3). Here, and throughout the poem, Melville strongly suggests that the American Civil War is simply one of many other civil wars brought about by the flawed "construction of a pact." That is a large part of the reason why *Clarel* frequently refers to the Crusades, the French Revolution, the European revolts of 1848, the Mexican War of Reform, the Italian Wars of Independence, the February Revolution, the Paris Commune, the American Civil War, and other similar upheavals: these struggles all index the same thing – a long historical cycle of internal violence and displacement. Whenever they are mentioned, these civil wars even tend to bleed into one another. When the Dominican monk, for instance, laments that –

> Rome is the Protestant to-day:
> The Red Republic slinging flame
> In Europe – she's your Scarlet Dame.
> Rome stands; but who may tell the end?
> Relapse barbaric may impend,
> Dismission into ages blind –
>
> (2.25.106–112)

– he somehow fuses the brief (and quickly exploded) solidity of Parisian communism, in 1871, with the post-Risorgimento state of Italy *and* the millennia-long history of conflict between Rome and the "barbarians." Ungar's grief, *Clarel* repeatedly suggests, is hardly Ungar's alone; political history throughout the globe is, in a way, but the history of the Civil War writ large.

That history also bears on matters of faith. One of the poem's main ideas, which extends through almost all of the characters' dialogues, is that religion and politics are almost epistemologically identical: both require belief; are enacted through rituals; and are rooted in written pacts that are often no less ambiguous, or tantalizing, than Moby Dick's hieroglyphic skin. As Melville notes, the debated "points" that spawned the war were not simply "abstruse"'; they were "abstruse / As *theologic* ones."²³ And religious history, too, is replete with internal schisms and bloody wars – a fact that leads Clarel, and many of the other characters, to wonder: "Was feud the heritage He left" (1.6.41)? That woeful inheritance seems to be precisely what Melville finds in Jerusalem's embedded rocks, which testify to the numerous times this sacred city was destroyed and then rebuilt, then destroyed and rebuilt again, by a variety of peoples, from the ancient Canaanites to the Egyptians, Babylonians, Philistines, Assyrians, Persians, Macedonians, Seleucids, Romans, Christians, and Muslims.

Although those countless wars were fueled by stark differences in religious belief, *Clarel* also suggests – and this is one of the poem's most haunting ideas – that those differences might derive from internal divisions in the cosmos itself. When the pilgrims, for instance, travel to Saint Catherine's Monastery to see the purported site of the Burning Bush, their reveries, Melville writes, unfolded "At variance, yet entangled too – / Like wrestlers," thus recalling

> Abel and Cain –
> Ormuzd involved with Ahriman
> In deadly lock. Were those gods gone?
> Or under other names lived on?
> The theme they started. 'Twas averred
> That, in old Gnostic pages blurred,
> Jehovah was construed to be
> Author of evil, yea, its god;
> And Christ divine his contrary:
> A god was held against a god,
> But Christ revered alone.
>   (3.5.33–44)

Perhaps the pilgrims view the bush in such radically different ways, these lines speculate, because divinity itself is structured through immanent conflict. The Gnostic idea invoked here – that Jehovah is the god of evil and Jesus is "his contrary" – reiterates, theologically, what Melville has been asserting all along, from *Battle-Pieces* through *Clarel*: that everything, maybe even the divine, is part of a long cycle of civil war.

Many of these Civil War figures and allusions recall the poems of that earlier volume. *Clarel's* theological recasting of the war is anticipated, in a way, by "The Conflict of Convictions" and "The Fall of Richmond," which describe God's deafening silence and noninvolvement. The war's geological dimensions, which take shape across *Clarel's* meditations on rocks and monuments, also inflect poems such as "The Apparition," "Look-Out Mountain," and "America," which linger on the earth's physical divisions and violent history. And the war's historical cognates, which *Clarel* repeatedly invokes, also frame and inform poems like "Misgivings," "The House-Top," and "The Frenzy in the Wake," which fold numerous earlier struggles – from the internecine wars of ancient Rome to the peasant revolts of medieval France – into Melville's vision of the Civil War. In *Battle-Pieces*, however, Melville tends to draw upon these various exempla in order to elucidate the war's historicity. In *Clarel* – and, we shall see, in *Timoleon* – that relation is inverted, as the Civil War migrates out into other times and places, and into even more immaterial realms.

Transbellum *Timoleon*

Melville saved his most figurative treatments of the Civil War for last. *Timoleon, Etc.* (1891), his final published book, focuses not on religious strife or warring ships, but on Greek statues, French paintings, and Melville's prior experiences in Polynesia and the Mediterranean. Yet it is precisely through this referential shift that *Timoleon* extends Melville's earlier volumes, largely by reimagining the civil wars that cycle through them.

Sometimes that reimagining takes a familiar form, as in the opening poem's account of Timoleon's decision to have his brother-turned-tyrant, Timophanes, assassinated. Set in 394 BCE, the poem seems to shuttle us back to a classical past that is now accessible only in misty fables and faded monuments. We discover at the outset, though, that Melville continues to be fascinated with history's patterns:

> If more than once, as annals tell,
> Through blood without compunction spilt,
> An egotist arch rule has snatched,
>   And stamped the seizure with his sabre's hilt,
> And, legalized by lawyers, stood;
> Shall the good heart whose patriot fire
> Leaps to a deed of startling note,
>   Do it, then flinch? Shall good in weak expire?
>   (*PP*, 253)

Timoleon killed his brother eons ago, but "annals tell" us that it has happened "more than once": it is a repeated, symbolic act; one fratricide among many. The poem is also a kind of repetition for Melville, who draws upon his earlier wartime rhetoric and conceptual frames to describe Timoleon's bloody deed. The latter, in Melville's recounting, is almost Lincoln-like: "the loyal son" – a "patriot true" – is compelled to end his brother's "crimes," and in doing so becomes the "saviour of the state" (*PP*, 255, 258). Timophanes's crimes, however, are only crimes of conscience, since his rule had been "legalized by lawyers." Indeed, because it was both morally justified and, strictly speaking, against the law, Timoleon's fratri-cidal violence revives many of the ethical and juridical questions that endow *Battle-Pieces* with much of its philosophical architecture, from "Dupont's Round Fight" to "The Fall of Richmond," the conclusion of which ("But God is in Heaven, and Grant in the Town, / And Right through might is Law" [*BP*, 99]) is echoed in the poem's summation of Timophanes's death ("And Right in Corinth reassumes its place" [*PP*, 256]). *Timoleon* thus com-mences by carving out yet another node in Melville's transbellum timeline.

In *Timoleon*, however, these battles tend to be absorbed into much broader philosophical considerations. Whereas *Clarel* represents the war in three different ways – as a historical referent, transhistorical sequence, and figurative struggle – *Timoleon* is primarily interested in the war's met-aphoric resonances. Throughout the volume, Melville stages an extended poetic inquiry into the metaphysics of internal conflict, from the famil-ial violence of "Timoleon" to the "unlike things" that "meet and mate" in "Art" (*PP*, 280). The war-born sense of history that structures much of *Battle-Pieces* and *Clarel* also provides *Timoleon* with a temporal frame-work, but in Melville's final book of poems that cyclicality is far more metaphysical in its scope and origins:

> *   *   *   *
>
> Found a family, build a state,
> The pledged event is still the same:
> Matter in end will never abate
> His ancient brutal claim.
>
> *   *   *   *
>
> Indolence is heaven's ally here,
> And energy the child of hell:
> The Good Man pouring from his pitcher clear
> But brims the poisoned well.
>
> (*PP*, 284)

Everything that is made is eventually unmade but what secures that destruction, Melville suggests, is not fate, or evil, but matter itself. The very thing that makes families and states possible also makes their dissolution both imminent and internal. This poem, "Fragments of a Lost Gnostic Poem of the 12ᵗʰ Century," thereby offers a new twist on Melville's earlier intimations, in *Battle-Pieces*, that all "Solidity's a crust," and in *Clarel*, that the civil wars on earth might be a divine inheritance. This is certainly not a poem about the Civil War, but it *is* a poem, like many others in *Timoleon*, that grows out of Melville's protracted response to that struggle and the questions about time, conflict, and causality that it provoked.

The manner in which Melville approaches those questions in *Timoleon* is partly attributable to his discovery, in the late-1880s and early-1890s, of Arthur Schopenhauer and his self-styled philosophical "pessimism." Toward the end of his life, Melville devoted a great deal of his time to reading and studying the German philosopher: he owned, read, and marked up the margins of *Counsels and Maxims*, *Studies of Pessimism*, *Religion: A Dialogue*, *The Wisdom of Life*, and all three volumes of *The World as Will and Idea*.²⁴ Melville likely read Schopenhauer with such care not because the philosopher presented him with new ideas, but because Schopenhauer provided a cogent metaphysical system for many of the ideas that already anchored Melville's transbellum writing. In Schopenhauer's books – which Melville read several decades after they first appeared – he found thrilling echoes and eerie anticipations of his own views on the cyclicality of time and experience ("[do] not believe with the vulgar that time may produce something actually new and significant" or "that it itself as a whole has beginning and end"); the inexorability of suffering ("pleasure is only the negation of pain" and "pain is the [only] positive element in life"); and the importance of poetry and art ("in the apprehension of Art we are raised out of our bondage, [by] contemplating objects [...] free of any taint of the will").²⁵

The philosophy that is delineated in *The World as Will and Idea*, and in Schopenhauer's supplemental essays, has a fairly clear ideational architecture. The premise, from which everything else flows, is that the only thing that truly binds us – the sole experience that is wholly and utterly universal – is suffering. "It is absurd," Schopenhauer observes, "to look upon the enormous amount of pain that abounds everywhere in the world, and originates in needs and necessities inseparable from life itself, as serving no purpose at all and the result of mere chance." Although each "separate misfortune" seems to be either exceptional or accidental, "misfortunate in general is the rule": it is the fabric out of which the universe is made. In reframing suffering as a positive rather than a negative force, Schopenhauer extends an array of other religio-philosophical accounts of cosmic creation, from the Buddhist idea that the world was hatched from an "inexplicable disturbance" in "the crystal clearness" of the "state of Nirvana," to the Gnostic idea that Jehovah created "this world of misery and affliction *animi causa* and *de gaité de coeur*." But Schopenhauer traces this suffering back to a different and far more earthly cause: the incessant and antagonistic unfolding of the will. Volition, he argues, is not – as it is often reputed to be – a discrete and distinctly human capacity, but the "foundation of all being," an egotistic drive for affirmation that "is part and parcel of every creature, and the permanent element of everything."[26]

According to Schopenhauer, the will assumes a wide range of objective and subjective forms. He identifies it with the seeking of happiness, with experiences of pleasure, and with an array of other acts and desires. The will is for Schopenhauer what atoms are for Democritus: the basic substratum of existence itself. Even matter, in all of its spectacular variety, he claims (echoing Melville's "Fragments of a Lost Gnostic Poem"), is but will's objective expression ("what objectively is matter is subjectively will"); and so, too, is the human body, which "is just the visibility [...] of our will." Yet if that is true, and all the phenomena around us are but manifestations "of the will at some one of its grades," then history itself is simply the star-crossed history of the will – and Melville's marginalia suggest that he was especially intrigued by this grand, revisionary claim.[27] He scored Schopenhauer's suggestion that "an undiminished eternity is always open for the return of any event or work that was nipped in the bud" (thus making "true loss" and "true gain" impossible in "this world of phenomena"), and took note of his anti-Hegelian commentary on time and repetition:

> the Hegelian pseudo-philosophy, everywhere so pernicious and stupefying to the mind [... errs in construing] the phenomenon for the inner being of the world [...] In truth, only [...] the incidents of our *inner* life, since they concern the will, have true reality, and are actual events; because the will alone is the thing in itself. In every microcosm lies the whole macrocosm [... All] external events are mere configurations of the phenomenal world, and have therefore directly neither reality nor significance, but only indirectly through their relation to the wills of the individuals. The endeavor to explain and interpret them directly is accordingly like the endeavor to see in the forms of the clouds groups of men and animals. What history narrates is in fact only the long, heavy, and confused dream of humanity [...] A true philosophy of history [therefore ...] does not consist in raising the

temporal ends of men to eternal and absolute ends, and then with art and imagination constructing their progress through all complications; but in the insight that not only in its development, but in its very nature, history is mendacious; for [...] it pretends always to relate something different, while from beginning to end it repeats always the same thing under different names and in a different dress. The true philosophy of history consists in the insight that in all these endless changes [...] have always before us only the same, even, unchanging nature, which to-day acts in the same way as yesterday and always; thus it ought to recognise the identical in all events, of ancient as of modern times, of the east as of the west.[28]

In Schopenhauer's view, the very thing that Hegel construes as the essence of history – its diachronic structure and sequential logic – is almost entirely illusory, since the will is the universe's *prima causa* and the only real events are internal rather than external. The major instances of change that Hegel takes to be indications of history's shape and movement – wars, assassinations, abdications, and so forth – are therefore only expressions of the will, which continuously repeats itself "under different names and in a different dress." Schopenhauer thereby reframes history as a series of endless changes that *appear* to be different but, in fact, are just contiguous manifestations of the will asserting itself across time.

Melville draws from many of these ideas in *Timoleon*, approaching issues of temporality, repetition, and internal conflict by way of a more or less Schopenhauerian metaphysics. The American Civil War is completely gone as a discrete historical referent, but even in its metaphorical afterlife it continues to shape Melville's writing, particularly when he meditates on the internecine struggles of the will. Those meditations veer from a wish for will-less annulment (in "Buddha") to reflections on the "Pantheist energy of will" (in "Venice") and the prospect of terror's cessation (in "The New Zealot to the Sun"), but throughout these poems Melville is keenly interested in the meaning and aesthetics of the will's myriad machinations (*PP*, 291). *Timoleon* thereby offers a subtle and largely indirect philosophical reconsideration of the Civil War, which is figuratively recast into a variety of metaphysical conflicts and processes. And that recasting derives in part from Melville's reading of Schopenhauer, who describes all suffering – even the suffering of war – as simply "crossed volition," since "even the pain of the body when it is injured or destroyed is as such only possible through the fact that the body is nothing but the will itself become object."[29] The civil wars that fill out *Battle-Pieces* and *Clarel* thus become, in *Timoleon*, indexes not of progress or regress but of the will's irrepressible returns.

That sense of ongoing metaphysical struggle certainly bears more than a little resemblance to Douglass's ideas about continuous motion. (Schopenhauer even writes, in *Studies in Pessimism*, that "the whole foundation on which our existence rests" is "the form of constant motion," which provides us with "no possibility of ever attaining the rest for which we are always striving.")[30] But whereas Douglass construes the constancy of change as both historically progressive and scientifically grounded, for Melville it is uniformly repetitive and metaphysical in origin. The volume's opening poem, for instance, focuses not simply on an act of fratricide but on the "crossed volition" that gave rise to it.[31] The concluding stanzas praise Timoleon for his deed ("Justice in long arrears is thine: / Not slayer of thy brother, no, / But [...] Jove's soldier, man divine") only because it was willed not by Timoleon himself, but by the gods whose "mandate call[ed], / Or seem[ed] to call, peremptory from the skies" (*PP*, 258, 256). When Timoleon "sobs the predetermined word," it is, for him, a will-less act. Here, and throughout *Timoleon*, the war – or more accurately, the type of internal conflict that it embodied for Melville – is philosophically reframed and poetically reconstituted.

Although the metaphysical particulars of that reframing owe a great deal to Schopenhauer, it is also very much in keeping with a long-standing practice of Melville's. Of the many investments and techniques that take shape across his career, perhaps none is more important, or more lasting, than his exploration of meaning's multiplicity. Melville continuously draws attention to things that simultaneously oblige interpretation and ensure that those interpretations both proliferate and diverge: Queequeg's tattooed skin, Bartleby's perplexing yes-no, Moby Dick's "mystical" color, Babo's silence, Billy Budd's stutter.[32] During the era of poststructuralism, this dimension of his writing was often considered to be a meditation on language's inherent and irresolvable ambiguity, but Melville, I think, has a very different literary and philosophical concern: the tendency of physical phenomena to become metaphysical phenomena. That is precisely what happens to the ritual practices in *Typee*, which become bound up with questions about identity; to the islands in *Mardi*, which occasion all kinds of political allegories; and to the whales in *Moby-Dick*, which become elusive metaphors for sublimity, agency, and other immaterial ideas. And that is also what happens to the Civil War in Melville's later poems, which fold this event, as well as its many historical cognates, into polymorphous instances of psychic tension and release, from the abiding, fratricidal "fealty" of "The Enthusiast" to the strange calmness that comes "after long wars" in "Herba Santa" (*PP*, 279, 288).

For Melville, these considerations regarding will, time, and conflict also pose questions about aesthetics. If nearly everything around us either originates in or expresses the will, then might art, too, simply expand the world's suffering? That is precisely what seems to be suggested in "The Ravaged Villa":

> In shards the sylvan vases lie,
>   Their links of dance undone,
> And brambles wither by the brim,
>   Choked fountain of the sun!
> The spider in the laurel spins,
>   The weed exiles the flower;
> And, flung to kiln, Apollo's bust
>   Makes lime for Mammon's tower.
>   (*PP*, 266)

This poem immediately follows "The Night-March," in which an army obeys the "mandate" of its unseen commander (*PP*, 265). That order may very well be the destruction of this village, which is figured as an aesthetic event – or, at least, as an event with aesthetic consequences: "sylvan vases" are destroyed; cobwebs form over laurel wreaths; weeds replace flowers; and "Apollo's bust" is melted down. These lines thereby offer a dark inversion of Keats's "Ode on a Grecian Urn" (1820), which describes Attic pottery as an ideal figure for art's immunity to time and circumstance. As Keats puts it, such artworks are humanity's "sylvan historians," expressing a "flower tale more sweetly than our rhyme": that art "shalt [always] remain, in midst of other woe."[33]

In "The Ravaged Villa," only that will-borne woe endures. But in other parts of *Timoleon* – indeed, throughout most of the volume – art does acquire a lasting power. In "The Parthenon," Melville evokes the abiding beauty of that ancient, half-destroyed temple:

> Estranged in site,
> Aerial gleaming, warmly white,
> You look a sun-cloud motionless
> In noon of day divine;
> Your beauty charmed enhancement takes
> In Art's long after-shine.
>   (*PP*, 302)

For Melville, the Parthenon (see Figure 7) retains its aesthetic power not because it is timeless (as Keats would have it) but because its subtle design – its gorgeous frieze and perfect lines, which represent "Art's meridian" (*PP*, 303) – can still be glimpsed in spite of the very decay

Figure 7. Frederic Edwin Church, *The Parthenon* (1871).
Courtesy of the Metropolitan Museum of Art. Bequest of Maria DeWitt Jesup,
from the collection of her husband, Morris K. Jesup, 1914.

that continues, ever so slowly, to destroy it. The sense of art cultivated in these lines also inflects "The Bench of Boors," which lingers on Teniers's seventeenth-century paintings of "beery losels" seeking solace from pain; "The Attic Landscape," which revels in Greece's "linear charm" and "sculptural grace"; and "In a Garret," which expresses a potent desire "to grapple from Art's deep / One dripping trophy" (*PP*, 278, 300, 275).[34]

These parts of *Timoleon* seem to reiterate Schopenhauer's idea that art can momentarily suspend the will and cultivate forms of experience that are utterly free from its incessant pull. Traces of this idea can be felt in "The Garden of Metrodorus," "Buddha," and several other poems – but it is here, more than anywhere else, that Melville also departs from Schopenhauer. In *Timoleon* art is bound up with, rather than removed from, the struggles of the will; hence the fate of Apollo's bust, and the Parthenon's "after-shine." This aesthetic theory is nicely encapsulated by the poem titled (appropriately enough) "Art":

> In placid hours well pleased we dream
> Of many a brave unbodied scheme.
> But form to lend, pulsed life create,
> What unlike things must meet and mate:
> A flame to melt – a wind to freeze;

> Sad patience – joyous energies;
> Humility – yet pride and scorn;
> Instinct and study; love and hate;
> Audacity – reverence. These must mate,
> And fuse with Jacob's mystic heart,
> To wrestle with the angel – Art.
>
> (*PP*, 280)

If, as these lines suggest, art acquires its "pulsed life" only through the fusion of "unlike things," then Melville's poem is an instantiation of the very aesthetic principle that it so gracefully articulates. "Art" is a mélange of disparate strands of aesthetic theory. The segue from nature to the affects – likening a melted "flame" and frozen "wind" to the "meeting" of contrasting emotions – recalls Samuel Taylor Coleridge's conception of art as a "mediatress between, and reconciler of nature and man" which transfuses the passions into various objects of contemplation and "stamps them into unity." By locating art's origins in the affects, the poem also draws upon Matthew Arnold's idea (which he wrested from Greek art) that poetry should be rooted in the "human affections" that "subsist permanently," from antiquity through modernity. Melville's "Art" also echoes, both verbally and conceptually, Emerson's poem "Initial, Daemonic and Celestial Love" (1847), which describes the "pure realm" wherein everything is transmuted into a single "form," a "region"

> Where unlike things are like;
> Where good and ill,
> And joy and moan,
> Melt into one.[35]

And in describing art as the fruit of pleasant dreaming in "placid hours," Melville also subtly invokes Schopenhauer's theory that art is our only respite from the will's incessant manifestations – a kind of "sunbeam" which cuts through life's "storm, [and is] quite unaffected by it."[36] All of these assorted aesthetic claims "meet and mate" in Melville's sonnet, revealing the latter to be far more intertextual and philosophical than it seems, at first, to be.

But Melville does not simply combine these various ideas. Each of the poem's sources – from Arnold's account of art's antique foundations to Coleridge's claims about art's contemplativeness – advance an idea that is conspicuously absent in the poem itself: that art *transcends* conflict. The opening lines conjure up a view of aesthetic placidity, but as the poem unfolds we discover that art is in fact constituted through, rather than liberated from, antagonism. Whereas for Emerson the "unlike things are like," for Melville they merely "mate" (and therefore retain their original forms) and only come together in a place we cannot see or know (a "mystic heart"). And the poem concludes by likening the artist to Jacob, the bookish son of Isaac who, in *Genesis*, grapples with an angel and is rechristened Israel (in Hebrew: "Struggled with God"). Art, in short, is an ongoing act of "wrestling" with the divine. It is a medium rather than a renunciation of strife.

Melville thereby folds the question of art – what it is, what it does, and how it is made – into the broader inquiry into internal conflict that sustains so much of his literary career. That inquiry assumes a wide array of forms, from the historical visions of *Battle-Pieces* to the religious and metaphysical discord of *Clarel* and *Timoleon*, but they all grow out of Melville's sustained interest in the meaning and origins of internecine struggle, which he increasingly takes up as a loose and multiresonant figure. And in that respect, Melville's late works are closely aligned with those of our final transbellum writer, Emily Dickinson, who – we shall see – also approaches the war as a conflict best understood by way of metaphor.

CHAPTER 4

Emily Dickinson's Erasures

In the spring of 1862, when Whitman was composing some of the poems that eventually evolved into *Drum-Taps*, Douglass was delivering lecture after lecture about this bloody revolution, and Melville was poring over wartime periodicals, Emily Dickinson mailed an unsolicited letter to Thomas Wentworth Higginson, an abolitionist (and soon to be Captain in the Union Army) who had recently published an essay for aspiring writers in the *Atlantic Monthly*. Evidently, it piqued Dickinson's interest. After reading it, she mailed him some of her poems and asked: "Mr. Higginson, – Are you too deeply occupied to say if my verse is alive?" Although we do not have Higginson's reply, we do have Dickinson's follow-up letter and it contains some of her most intriguing comments about her poetry and her literary career. After thanking him for his feedback ("the surgery [...] was not so painful as I supposed"), she addresses – or seems to address – one of the questions that Higginson apparently posed:

> You asked how old I was? I made no verse – but one or two – until this winter – Sir – I had a terror – since September – I could tell to none – and so I sing, as the Boy does by the Burying Ground – because I am afraid[1]

These lines conduct a rhetorical dance. In his initial reply, Higginson presumably inquired about Dickinson's age and she responds by redirecting the inquiry. Instead of discussing the chronology of her body, she discusses the chronology of her poems – and the latter is curiously skewed. In fact, by this winter she had already composed nearly three hundred poems and had spent the past two years assiduously constructing those splendid booklets that we now call her fascicles. Dickinson's account of her authorial development, however, is not so much erroneous as it is imaginative: she is locating an origin-point for her mature poetic self, and that moment coincides with the war's first winter of devastating battles. That indeed might have been the "terror" that made her "sing," a possibility supported not only by the arc of her career (since she wrote more than half of her poems in the midst of "Battle's – horrid Bowl") but also by the contents of those war-born poems, many of which pivot on the imagining of death and the relationship between violence, transgression, and insight (F 524).

For much of the twentieth century, the bellum context of Dickinson's verse was construed as a matter of coincidence. As Thomas Johnson suggested in 1958, Dickinson was the opposite of Whitman, who "projected himself into the world" and made the nation "the [continuous] substance of his thought in prose and verse." For Dickinson, who "did not live in history and held no view of it, past or current," the war was merely "an annoyance." Numerous scholars echoed this idea, asserting that Dickinson was too inwardly focused to pay close attention to the country's bloodiest conflict. Most notably, this reading of Dickinson as a private poet aloof from the struggle anchored two of the foundational studies of Civil War literature: Daniel Aaron's *The Unwritten War* (1973) and Edmund Wilson's *Patriotic Gore* (1962). In *The Unwritten War*, Dickinson appears only in a four-page annex at the end of the book, and in *Patriotic Gore* Wilson briefly mentions her poetry only to explain why it does not count as wartime writing. "[T]here is no point," according to Wilson, "in describing her poetry here"; although the "years of the Civil War were for Miss Dickinson especially productive, [...] she never, so far as I know, refers to the war in her poetry." Christopher Benfey has recently argued, in this same vein, that Dickinson was utterly "immune to the war fever around her" and that the critics who have "combed her verse for mention of the Civil War" have so far failed to demonstrate that her remarkable wartime output was anything other than an accident of history.[2]

Those critics to whom Benfey refers have nonetheless done far more than "combed" through her poems and letters "for mention of the Civil War" (as if that momentous conflict could only possibly be smuggled into literature by way of explicit references). In the 1980s, a wave of revisionary scholarship spearheaded by Shira Wolosky, Karen Dandurand, and Barton Levi St. Armand revealed Dickinson to be deeply and passionately engaged with the language, events, and ideas of the war. In 1864, she even mailed several of her wartime poems to New York-area periodicals, including *Drum Beat*, a pro-Union newspaper and fundraising vehicle. Dickinson, as Wolosky put it, was not some detached "librarian, remaining indoors in order to sort her reading and sift her emotions into little packets reminiscent of a card catalog. Her language instead records the converging crises in metaphysics and culture that came to a head in the Civil War."[3]

The remarkable variety of these bellum entanglements have been further elucidated in recent years by critics such as Faith Barrett, Benjamin Friedlander, and Eliza Richards, who have resituated Dickinson's poems in relation to popular wartime rhetorics, reading practices, and political ideologies. Collectively, this criticism has shattered the view that Dickinson was somehow extraneous to the war and demonstrated just how foundational that struggle was to Dickinson's conception of poetry itself.[4]

One of the most stunning implications of this scholarship – indeed, the periodizing insight that flows from Dickinson's wartime entanglements – is that she is not really an antebellum writer. She herself traced the birth of her poetic career to the early 1860s; many of her finest poems and defining ideas originate in the conflict that ostensibly closed the antebellum era; and she continued to write – often about the same philosophical and aesthetic dilemmas involved in that bloody struggle – for more than two decades after 1865. Despite all this, and despite the splendid scholarship on Dickinson's Civil War engagements, she is still frequently considered to be a definitively antebellum writer. Critical studies often place her poems within distinct prewar contexts: antebellum hymn practices; antebellum horticulture; antebellum rhetoric; antebellum epistolary traditions; antebellum uses of dress and clothing.[5] And this same periodizing framework is redeployed in each of the major anthologies. Both the *Heath* and the *Bedford* anthologies present Dickinson as writer of the 1850s. Only in the *Norton* does she make an appearance as a postwar writer, but even here she is included at the very beginning of the post-1865 volume and without a section heading – as though she were an inexplicable holdover from the pre-1865 installment.

A large part of the reason why she continues to be read as an antebellum author is that such a periodization was a precondition for her belated induction into the American Renaissance. When Matthiessen nationalized the New England Renaissance, he deemed Dickinson to be too much of a literary relic to have participated in this literary movement. Rather than contributing to the autochthonous fashioning of new American expressive forms, Dickinson's poems, in Matthiessen's view, are "authentically in the [older] metaphysical tradition" of the Puritans. (Matthiessen, of course, was drawing on a long line of interpretation. In the 1890s, the first reviewers of Dickinson's poems tended to read them as remnants of a bygone era and superseded culture.)[6] When critics in the following decades reclaimed Dickinson as an integral part of the American Renaissance, they underscored the remarkable overlaps between her writings and those of her male contemporaries – a shared interest in surfaces and depths, the complexities of vision, and linguistic and experiential limits – while preserving the microperiodization of Matthiessen's original account. Dickinson's ostensible antebellumness thus emerged as a kind of corollary of her canonization: to be included in the Renaissance, her poems needed to be separated from their actual moments of composition and merged into a narrative about American literature's pre-modernist wave-cycles.

Yet as we have seen, there is a great deal of transbellum writing that proceeds through the Civil War and periodizes itself within its imaginative worlds. Dickinson, who writes about the war across much of the late nineteenth century, is an exemplary case of this multiperiodicity. I shall also argue, however, that she tends to figure the war in three different ways from what most critics have suggested. First, instead of trafficking in direct representations of the Civil War's issues and events, her poems frequently depict it as a vast destruction that is unmoored from chronology itself, whether political or theological. This is why so many of her Civil War poems are shot through with moments of erasure: for Dickinson, such fading away is the struggle's defining temporality. Second, precisely because Dickinson addresses the war figuratively – as an occasion for meditating on the unperiodizability of pain, for instance, or the violence of nature – I suggest that some of her most interesting and incisive Civil War poems are not the ones explicitly about the conflict. Many of her poems about wind, poetry, and song are also, on certain frequencies, meditations on the war and the aesthetic dilemmas that it posed. Third, I contend that her literary response to the war, instead of concluding in 1865, continues to unfold through the 1870s and 1880s, and is therefore just as protracted as the transbellum responses of Whitman, Douglass, and Melville.

Civil War Annulments

Like many of her contemporaries, Dickinson witnessed the Civil War from afar. She read about it almost daily in local newspapers (such as the *Springfield Republican* and *Amherst Record*), national periodicals (such as *Harper's*, *Scribner's*, and the *Atlantic Monthly*), and in the letters that she frequently exchanged with family and friends. Her war was imaginatively fashioned out of the bloody disarray of reports, rumors, stories, images, and poems; and Dickinson was keenly, even obsessively, aware of this fact. As she put it in another letter to Higginson, "War feels to me an oblique place": it is less an event than a site, a "place" elsewhere that can only be indirectly apprehended.[7]

This obliqueness fills out Dickinson's wartime verse. The poems populated by soldiers, armies, and surgeries tend to focus on boundaries (both spatial and psychic), episodes of deafness and blindness, and various communicative failures that underscore the poems' distance from the very conflict that occasions them. When Dickinson claims (as she often does) to receive "report[s]" from "the South" – "A News express to Me – / A spicy Charge" (F 780) – these missives frequently impart an acute sense of separation. As she writes in poem 883,

A South Wind – has a pathos
Of individual Voice –
As One detect on Landings
An Emigrant's address –

A Hint of Ports – and Peoples –
And much not understood –
The fairer – for the farness –
And for the foreignhood –

The North and South are linked through an exquisite pattern of circulating winds, but this interconnection yields neither intimacy nor knowledge. Like someone listening to an "Emigrant's" speech at a port, the Northerner *feels* the "South Wind" – a figure here for the war, and perhaps for poetry itself – but cannot translate that sensation into any kind of rational understanding. The embattled regions, it seems, can hear each other but do not even share the same language; and Dickinson, instead of shuddering at this impasse, embraces it. Her wartime poems suggest repeatedly that the war cannot be fully deciphered. In many instances, it cannot even be spoken about – except by the dead, who cannot speak.

To represent this almost unrepresentable war, Dickinson shuttles between a dazzling array of viewpoints, registering the conflict at various moments from the perspective of a mourner, a neighbor, a carcass, a foreigner, a loaded gun, an emptied gun, a floating spirit, and a flower. This cacophony of perspectives, Tyler Hoffman and Eliza Richards have argued, derives from Dickinson's intricate understanding of her "mediated relationship to the war." She represents the Civil War by way of disparate positions and frameworks because she is intent, as Hoffman puts it, on "turn[ing] the limits of her [civilian] condition to rhetorical advantage." For Richards, Dickinson's fractured viewpoints must be traced back to the poet's deep skepticism regarding the possibility of ever "fully know[ing] the experience of another." During the Civil War, as Dickinson became painfully aware that her experience of the conflict was, like that of so many other Northerners, inescapably mediated, that skepticism was probably magnified. The proliferating points of view in her war poems repeatedly reveal the astounding differences "between civilians' vicarious experience of the war, gained through newspaper reports and pictorial representations, and soldiers' direct, physical, and largely unimaginable experience of combat," and Dickinson, instead of eliding this experiential gap, foregrounds it in her verse.[8]

These readings provide us with a compelling account of how and why Dickinson repeatedly shifts between positions and identities in her wartime poetry. I am less interested, however, in the sheer perspectival variety of Dickinson's poems than I am in the temporal and aesthetic effects of that variety. As these points of view multiply across the fascicles, it becomes nearly impossible to record and locate the war. Dickinson's perspectives produce motley timeframes, from the raw synchrony of grief ("Occupied with Shot / Gammuts of Eternities / Are as they were not –" [F 833]) to the belatedness of victory (which always "comes late" [F 195]) and the sensations of suspense, regret, and death, all of which disclose the myriad, non-linear ways in which the war is apprehended. Or to put this another way: experience is so unextractable and unexchangeable in Dickinson's poems because the war's obliqueness inheres as much in its historical illegibility as it does in its mediated printedness. It is, in both its details and its totality, an almost completely untimeable upheaval.

For Dickinson, the Civil War is not part of a long process of destruction or emancipation but a radical annulment that eludes history itself. As she writes in 1863,

> If any sink, assure that this, now standing –
> Failed like Themselves – and conscious that it rose –
> Grew by the Fact, and not the Understanding
> How Weakness passed – or Force – arose –
>
> Tell that the Worst, is easy in a Moment –
> Dread, but the Whizzing, before the Ball –
> When the Ball enters, enters Silence –
> Dying – annuls the power to kill –
>
> (F 616)

These lines transport us to the bloodstained battlefields, but the violence that occurs here has very little to do with the political and theological frameworks that prompted that violence in the first place. Dickinson describes this death (perhaps of an anonymous soldier) as an event unavailable to "the Understanding" and therefore marked by absence.

Once the bullet enters the body, it only yields a kind of stunned mute-ness. "Dying – annuls the power to kill –": it begets nothing, neither vic-tory nor sacrifice. It simply effaces the terrible power to murder another human being.

Such annulment, Dickinson repeatedly implies, is not merely an effect of the Civil War; it is the latter's central dynamic. Across her poems, the war manifests as a mass repealing that is exceedingly difficult, if not impossible, to record. War simply destroys, and its erasures outstrip all of our earthly chronometrics. Even the very deaths that purportedly endow that war with meaning are, for Dickinson, instances of release or disap-pearance. As she puts it in a poem from 1862,

> The Feet, mechanical, go round –
> A Wooden way
> Of Ground, or Air, or Ought –
> Regardless grown,
> A Quartz contentment, like a stone –
>
> This is the Hour of Lead –
> Remembered, if outlived,
> As Freezing persons, recollect the Snow –
> First – Chill – then Stupor – then the letting go –
> (F 372)

To draw out death's sensation – its "formal feeling," as it were – Dickinson enlists the punctuated regularity of the clock ("the Hour of Lead" in which the "feet, mechanical, go round"), the deep time of the earth (encapsu-lated by "Quartz" and "stone"), and the language of weather and the sea-sons ("Freezing" in the winter), yet the final lines of the poem strongly suggest that such meager temporal registers can only partially account for this death. The latter's untimability is likewise underscored by the poem's meter, which switches irregularly between beats. The only person who can recollect this experience, and thereby make these timescales converge, is gone forever. Unlike the "brave men" of Lincoln's "Gettysburg Address" who "hallow" the ground with their sacrifice, or the dead of *Drum-Taps* who transfer their experiences to Whitman, or the soldiers of Douglass's later lectures who fought for the "grandest declaration of human rights the world ever heard," these men's souls have simply absconded.[9] "The Hour of Lead" is succeeded by nothing. There is just a letting go, a dash, and then blankness.

A similar erasure occurs in a poem that Dickinson penned in 1865 – prompted, perhaps, by the death of a young soldier:

How the Waters closed above Him
We shall never know –
How He stretched His anguish to us
That – is covered too –

Spreads the Pond Her Base of Lilies
Bold above the Boy
Whose unclaimed Hat and Jacket
Sum the History –

(F 941)

There is of course nothing immediately war-related about this poem. But Dickinson's poetic response to the war – much like Melville's in *Clarel* and *Timoleon* – requires us to conceive of that struggle not simply as a martial affair but as a complex array of ideas, discourses, and images.[10] And this forgotten boy – who, as he sinks to the bottom of the pond, also sinks away from any narrative framework that could possibly justify his death – is a counterpart to many of the other figures who populate Dickinson's wartime poems. There is neither victory nor defeat in this poem; nor God, nor Union. There is History with a capital "H," but it emerges in the final line as an ironic addendum, signaling loss rather than remembrance. Even that powerful vehicle of poetic memory, rhyme, is almost completely absent here (with the single exception of "Bold" and "Boy" in line 6). Since this boy's "unclaimed Hat and Jacket" are the only artifacts left from the amorphous event that has claimed him, they are just as lost to "History" as they are to their original owner.

This does not mean, of course, that Dickinson altogether eschews concrete representations of the war. She might have composed "The Black Berry – wears a Thorn in his side –" (F 548) in response to Higginson's 1863 reports about commanding a black regiment in South Carolina's Sea Islands, and "As the Starved Maelstrom laps the Navies" (F 1064), a poem about constraint and release, in response to the Emancipation Proclamation. Other poems, such as "The name – of it – is 'Autumn' –" (F 465) and "It feels a shame to be Alive – " (F 524), draw some of their imagery and language from specific military engagements, like the battles at Antietam and Ball's Bluff. For Dickinson, the war also acquired a terrifying concreteness in the spring of 1862, when Frazar Stearns, the son of Amherst College's president, was killed in the Battle of New Bern.[11] As she wrote her cousins shortly afterwards,

> [I must] tell you of brave Frazer – "killed at Newbern," darlings. His big heart shot away by a "minie ball." I had read of those – I didn't think that Frazer would carry one to Eden with him [...] He fell by the side

of Professor Clark, his superior officer – lived ten minutes in a soldier's arms, asked twice for water – murmured just, "My God!" and passed! [...] Nobody here could look on Frazer – not even his father. The doctors would not allow it.[12]

Such losses, which came so close to home, seem to have found their way into numerous poems, such as "When I was small, a Woman died –" (F 518), which describes a boy "clipt" by bullets, and "Victory comes late –" (F 195), a meditation on the utter unavailability of victory to the dead, whose "freezing lips" are "[t]oo rapt with frost / to take" its kiss.

There are risks, however, in placing too much emphasis on the historical particularity of Dickinson's poems. If her Civil War poems are Civil War poems only because they were written between 1861 and 1865, and because they draw their imagery from specific events that occurred during that 4 year span, then we are left, once again, with the specious idea that the war was merely an interregnum in American literary history, a sudden break yielding a minor literature that commences and concludes with the war itself. Such a definition of Civil War literature blinds us to the heterogeneous ways in which writers reimagined the conflict, either in part or in whole, by creating alternative worlds and timescapes, many of which extend – like Dickinson's poems – far beyond the war's chronological end-points.[13]

Moreover, even in her most situated and localized poems, the Civil War is often marked less by its historicity – which is almost completely indiscernible in Dickinson's lines – than by the woe and grief that its violence occasions. That affective focus is a large part of the reason why, for Dickinson, the war outstrips history. Grief is the most unruly of affects: its non-linear durations, lapses, and returns bear little resemblance to the tidy chronologies of newspapers, governments, and creeds.[14] And in many of Dickinson's wartime poems, that struggle only becomes legible by way of self-periodizing affects such as pain:

> Pain – has an Element of Blank –
> It cannot recollect
> When it begun – Or if there were
> A time when it was not –
>
> It has no Future – but itself –
> It's Infinite contain
> It's Past – enlightened to perceive
> New Periods – Of Pain.
>
> (F 760)

This poem is a startling meditation on pain's untimeliness. When it surges, pain breaks down those narrow measurements through which we carve up our daily lives and arrange our temporal worlds. Because of this focus on the gap between pain and measurement – or more accurately, between the disorderly temporalities of pain (whether physical or psychic) and the orderly forms of public time – "Pain – has an Element of Blank" could certainly be categorized as one of Dickinson's many metaphysical poems. But for Dickinson, writing in 1863, the most violent year of the Civil War, these lines about pain and periodicity likely had a more immediate resonance. Bounded epochal periods depend on psychic states that are either suspended or remixed by war. To the degree that the conflict's primary byproduct is not Unionism but pain – and to Dickinson, this very much seemed to be the case – the war itself constitutes a kind of unperiodizable event, an infinite "Blank" that, instead of beginning or ending, continuously gives way to "New Periods" of loss.

These war poems therefore put considerable pressure not only on Dickinson's long-standing reception as an antebellum poet, but also on the periodization model that has catalyzed that reception. Her poetic responses to the war unmoor her, and us, from *any* stable historical order, and we find ourselves absorbed instead into moments of unsummable history. In Dickinson's "Hour[s] of Lead" and "Periods – of Pain," the antebellum/postbellum divide which anchors so many courses, anthologies, and monographs fades away, as if it too has been obliterated by battle's "Infinite contain" (F 760). To even make such a distinction between antebellum and postbellum eras requires segmenting historical time into progressive epochal sequences, and no chronology could be more alien to Dickinson. As she writes in 1865, when the postbellum period ostensibly emerges out of diplomatic peace,

> Peace is a fiction of our Faith –
> The Bells a Winter Night
> Bearing the Neighbor out of Sound
> That never did alight.
>
> (F 971)

The 1865 partition that continues to divide nineteenth-century literary history is no less a "fiction of our Faith" than this winter "Peace" heralded by the bells. Such a moment of miraculous periodic succession may have been a singular and identifiable event in the annals of warfare, but in Dickinson's fascicles – as in *Leaves of Grass*, and *Timoleon*, and Douglass's writings – it is a transition that, in many respects, "never did alight," and we are left instead in a multilinear timescape that, to the degree that it can be named at all, can only be called transbellum.

The patternless destruction imaginatively enacted in Dickinson's poems likely derives from her entanglements with wartime print culture. In the periodicals that she read, Dickinson came across countless letters, speeches, histories, essays, and autobiographical accounts that attempted to make the war historically legible. In many of these texts, calendrical time is enlisted as a bulwark against the war's informational chaos. Dates repeatedly appear in titles, subheadings, and section breaks, thereby transforming the war's heterogeneous events into a series of streamlined narratives. Reading the *Springfield Republican*, *Harper's Weekly*, or *Putnam's Monthly*, for example, demanded a continuous calendrical emplotment of the day's, week's, or month's events. Higginson himself reflected on the importance of such day-by-day transcriptions in some of his articles in the *Atlantic*, which Dickinson almost certainly read. Diurnal meditations, he stressed, were absolutely necessary "during a civil war" in which "events succeed each other so rapidly" that they were almost immediately erased as soon as they occurred.[15] The war was also calendrically tabulated in a variety of other almanacs and collections, such as Richard Fisher's *Chronological History of the Civil War in America* (1863) (see Figure 8), which recorded the war by providing a brief historical synopsis for each passing day.

Popular writers tried to make the war's history accessible in a variety of other ways as well. Most periodicals supplemented their battle reportage with long articles on related historical subjects: Shay's Rebellion; the War of 1812; the Italian Risorgimento; the global history of slavery; the evolution of warfare; the Roman civil wars.[16] In many of these accounts, the main interest was not the past as such but the complex web of historical relations that provided the Civil War with order and meaning. To elucidate that meaning, writers also considered the struggle's possible futures. This anticipatory impulse famously propels Nathaniel Hawthorne's essay, "Chiefly about War Matters" (1862), which frames the war – and the invention of the ironclad in particular – as the birth-moment of a utilitarian future:

> [The ironclad I saw] could not be called a vessel at all; it was a machine, [...] destined, along with others of the same breed, to annihilate whole navies and batter down old supremacies. The wooden walls of Old England cease to exist and a whole history of naval renown reaches its period, now that the Monitor comes smoking into view [...] There will be other battles,

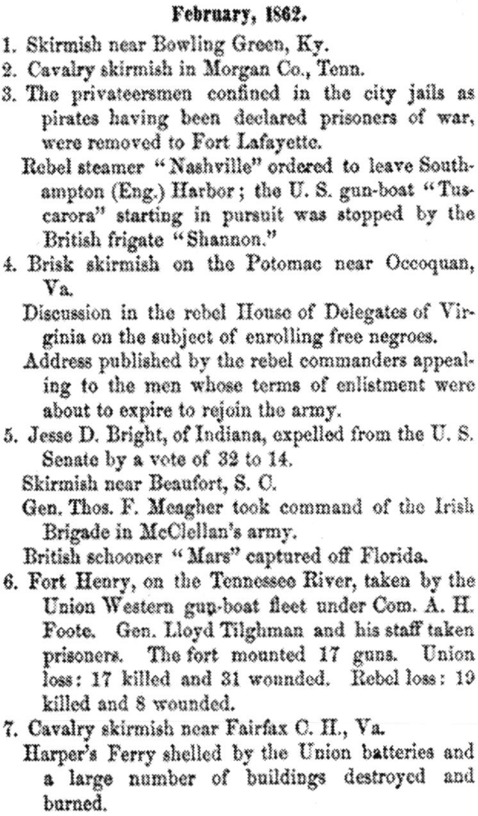

February, 1862.

1. Skirmish near Bowling Green, Ky.
2. Cavalry skirmish in Morgan Co., Tenn.
3. The privateersmen confined in the city jails as pirates having been declared prisoners of war, were removed to Fort Lafayette.

   Rebel steamer "Nashville" ordered to leave Southampton (Eng.) Harbor; the U. S. gun-boat "Tuscarora" starting in pursuit was stopped by the British frigate "Shannon."
4. Brisk skirmish on the Potomac near Occoquan, Va.

   Discussion in the rebel House of Delegates of Virginia on the subject of enrolling free negroes.

   Address published by the rebel commanders appealing to the men whose terms of enlistment were about to expire to rejoin the army.
5. Jesse D. Bright, of Indiana, expelled from the U. S. Senate by a vote of 32 to 14.

   Skirmish near Beaufort, S. C.

   Gen. Thos. F. Meagher took command of the Irish Brigade in McClellan's army.

   British schooner "Mars" captured off Florida.
6. Fort Henry, on the Tennessee River, taken by the Union Western gun-boat fleet under Com. A. H. Foote. Gen. Lloyd Tilghman and his staff taken prisoners. The fort mounted 17 guns. Union loss: 17 killed and 31 wounded. Rebel loss: 19 killed and 8 wounded.
7. Cavalry skirmish near Fairfax C. H., Va.

   Harper's Ferry shelled by the Union batteries and a large number of buildings destroyed and burned.

Figure 8. Page from Richard S. Fisher's *Chronological History of the Civil War in America* (New York: Johnson and Ward, 1863).

but no more such tests of seamanship and manhood as the battles of the past; and, moreover, the Millennium is certainly approaching, because human strife is to be transferred from the heart and personality of man into cunning contrivances of machinery, which by and by will fight out our wars with only the clank and smash of iron, strewing the field with broken engines, but damaging no one's little finger except by accident.[17]

For Hawthorne, as for Melville, the ironclad represents a rupture in time itself ("the Millennium is certainly approaching"). It is the symbol of an emerging age of unburdened mechanization, an epoch in which everything will be governed by engines instead of "the heart and personality of man." Melville, as we have seen, imaginatively yokes this rise of machinery to an array of other violent displacements, and by doing so rearticulates one of the most tantalizing and widespread ideas about the war (to which Whitman and Douglass are drawn as well): that its events are eloquent ciphers of history itself.

These protracted efforts to time the war point to one of the central features of Civil War literature: that it is self-periodizing from the very outset. Rather than emerging in some lull between antebellum and postbellum eras, this literature mobilizes a variety of timescapes in order to imaginatively map and remap the Civil War. The first histories of the conflict, it is important to recall, were written not after it concluded but shortly after it began. Evert Duyckinck's *History of the War for the Union*, Orville Victor's *Comprehensive History of the Southern Rebellion*, Jennett Frost's *The Rebellion in the United States*, and Edward Pollard's *The Southern History of the War* were all published in 1862, and they were quickly followed up by such chronicles as John Abbott's *History of the Civil War in America* (1863) and Elliot Storke's *The Great American Rebellion* (1863).[18] The violence that consumed the nation was exactingly recorded as it occurred and then almost immediately assimilated into various compendiums, histories, and chronicles. Perhaps the most famous documentary books about the war, Frank Moore's *The Rebellion Record*, were printed mostly during the war itself (volumes one through nine appeared between 1862 and 1865) and featured, on the cover page, a wartime endorsement from none other than Abraham Lincoln. Yet Moore's "contemporary" *Record* was not even the most voluminous archive. That honor belongs to the War Department's meticulous documentary records, which, upon their release later in the nineteenth century, overflowed into 70 separate books.[19]

These myriad attempts at documenting the war as it transpired all depend on a historical hermeneutics of which Dickinson is deeply suspicious. From Higginson's beautiful diaries to Douglass's speeches, these texts all suppose that the war's historicity is somehow immanently communicated through either its chain of events or through its symbols, signs, and personages. Indeed if, as scholars have argued, the prewar United States was shot through with discordant timeframes and narratives of historical belonging, that temporal "pluralization" was likely *accelerated* by the war, as Americans sought out stories and scales of reference capable of making the war make sense.[20] Most of the transbellum literature we have examined so far originates in this war-born drive for historicization, yet this diachronic coding of the conflict is precisely what does *not* happen in Dickinson's poems. The latter tend to suggest that the war is something like a repealing of history itself, an annulment that can certainly be felt but not transcribed or remembered. To read the war as a cogent historical event – or to retroactively periodize literature based on that cogency – one must acquire an unmediated view of the conflict that simply does not exist in Dickinson's verse.

Rather than claiming that Dickinson was a critic of wartime ideologies *tout court* – an argument that, as Faith Barrett notes, "flattens the complexity and range both of popular responses to these ideologies and of Dickinson's own response to them" – I am suggesting that Dickinson was skeptical about the senses of historical time often stipulated by such ideologies.[21] In her poems, the war, instead of materializing into some finely ordered historical pattern, simply melts everything away:

> A still – Volcano – Life –
> That flickered in the night –
> When it was dark enough to do
> Without erasing sight –
>
> A quiet – Earthquake style –
> Too subtle to suspect
> By natures this side Naples –
> The North cannot detect
>
> The solemn – Torrid – Symbol –
> The lips that never lie –
> Whose hissing Corals part – and shut –
> And Cities – ooze away –
>
> (F 517)

Like other wartime writers, Dickinson uses the volcano here as a figure of violent surprise. Dickinson is nonetheless far less interested in progress or regress than she is in sheer dissolution. When these "Corals part," we are left with nothing with which to record this destruction – no archives, or calendars, or books. The only thing that remains is a terrifying image of heated destruction exacted in the blackest moments of the night. The reference to Naples in line seven likely comes from an article that Dickinson had read in the *Atlantic*, which tied an 1857 earthquake in southern Italy to an array of electrical storms: "'At Salerno, the walls of the houses were rent from top to bottom. Numerous villages were half destroyed.' Were these coincidences of extraordinary auroras with extraordinary commotions in the physical condition of our globe merely accidental? or are these phenomena due to a common cause?" There is indeed a "common cause," the anonymous *Atlantic* contributor suggests, and it is the Humboldtian "terrestrial magnetism" of the earth: as electrical currents flow between the north and the south, "the equilibrium between the positive electricity of the vapors and the negative electricity of the earth" is sometimes disrupted, and these convulsions produce a geological "discharge," often accompanied by a brilliant light "of a purple or reddish-violent color."[22] Dickinson draws upon this article's language and imagery to meditate on the war, but the eruption that occurs in "A Still Volcano – Life –" discloses something very different from the intricately patterned – and therefore, potentially predictable – havoc that is explicated in the *Atlantic* essay. Dickinson's discharge is a repealing rather than a repetition. It is a form of destruction that liquidates everything. And as the final dash seems to suggest, these cities are still oozing away.

Dickinson in the Winds of War

Similar eruptions occur throughout the poems that she wrote during the war, from "My life had stood – a Loaded Gun –" (which focuses on the speaker's "Vesuvian face" [F 764]) to "Dare you see a Soul at the 'White Heat'?" (which likens poetic creation to a volcanic "Blaze" [F 401]). However, Dickinson's most frequently used figure for representing the war, in all of its superlative destructiveness and extra-historicity, is the wind. The latter blows repeatedly in her wartime poems, manifesting as both a harbinger of change and an agent of destruction. Sometimes entire poems – even entire fascicles – unfold as meditations on this "transitive fellow" whose "martial ways" cannot be tracked or measured (F 494, F 1164). At other moments, the wind enters more surreptitiously, as in this 1862 poem:

> They dropped like Flakes –
> They dropped like stars –
> Like Petals from a Rose –
> When suddenly across the June
> A Wind with fingers – goes –
>
> They perished in the seamless Grass –
> No eye could find the place –
> But God can summon every face
> On his Repeallless – List.
>
> (F 545)

This poem is almost always included as an example of Dickinson's Civil War verse, and one can certainly see why: it familiarizes the unfamiliar by likening the war's industrial-scale harvesting of bodies to more natural and peaceful instances of change, like the dropping of "Petals from a Rose." These petals, however, do not fall on their own accord: they are removed and scattered by the June wind, which makes things "drop" and then hides them from view. No one can locate what has fallen and "perished" because the wind's flurries are self-erasing.

The wind, of course, always plurisignifies in Dickinson's poems. It is frequently a figure for nature itself, for unexpected change, or for song and poetry. Yet as Dickinson writes across the Civil War, the latter also gets swept up into the wind's symbolic dimensions. This figurative relation between the wind and the war surfaces, for instance, in poem 1044:

> Revolution is the Pod
> Systems rattle from
> When the Winds of Will are stirred
> Excellent is Bloom
>
> But except it's Russett Base
> Every Summer be
> The entomber of itself,
> So of Liberty –
>
> Left inactive on the Stalk
> All it's Purple fled
> Revolution shakes it for
> Test if it be dead –

In this plant-poem (a kind of subgenre in its own right in the fascicles) Dickinson flirts with a more teleological reading of the war, intimating that "Liberty" is not a fixed inheritance but something that must occasionally be reclaimed. This description of freedom's seedlike latencies is, in this respect, not far removed from the philosophy of history that Whitman hatches in the *Songs of Insurrection*. Dickinson's idea of revolution, however, is complicated by the fact that the poem enlists two distinct temporal frameworks: the regenerative cycle of the plant and the punctuated history of political rebellion.[23] The only thing that momentarily brings these diverging temporalities together is the wind, since Revolution's "Pod" must burst and then be shaken off the stalk. In fact, without "the Winds of Will" – which could blow at any time and in any direction – the purple flees and the pod withers. This interplay between necessity, contingency, and repetition even extends into Dickinson's rhymes, which are absent in the first stanza, "Bloom" in lines six and eight, and then return – like Revolution itself, as both word and act – in the concluding stanza.

By figuratively linking the war to the wind, Dickinson connects her own verse to many other Civil War poems that linger on the weather. From William E. Pabor's "Emancipation" (1862), which associates the wind with the eradication of slavery ("Wind of the mountain and wind of the plain, / Bear on your bosom the Grand Proclamation!"), to Henry Timrod's "Ethnogenesis" (1862), which describes the wind as a Confederate partisan ("The winds in our defence / Shall seem to blow"), poems from both the North and the South frequently described the struggle as a storm. This atmospheric focus is largely attributable, Eliza Richards contends, to the development of modern meteorology and the accompanying realization that the weather was a global and circulatory system. By the 1860s, many Americans understood that "what is [happening] elsewhere will eventually arrive here, perhaps in altered form," and writers construed this interconnection as an example of the "complex, ever-shifting relation" between "proximity and distance" in this internecine conflict.[24] For Melville, this flux bears directly on the shape of history, which is punctuated by innumerable returns and altered forms. In "The Conflict of Convictions (1860–1)," the strong surge of historical "Necessity" is figuratively doubled by "a wind in purpose strong" that spins "against the way it drives," and in "Frenzy in the Wake," Sherman's march – which leaves behind vast "pillars of dust" as the South's forests and houses are burned – is likened to a "roaring wind" (*BP*, 10, 98). The latter for Melville is not simply a patterned force, but one whose destructive circulations mimic the movement of history writ large.

For Dickinson, too, the wind often approximates the war's temporality, but in her poems it is almost always directionless, as though history itself has been uprooted. As she writes in 1868,

> The Wind took up the Northern Things
> And piled them in the South –
> Then gave the East unto the West
> And opening his mouth
> The Four Divisions of the Earth
> Did make as to devour
> While everything to corners slunk
> Behind the awful power –
>
> The Wind unto his Chamber went
> And nature ventured out –
> Her subjects scattered into place
> Her systems ranged about

Again the smoke from Dwellings rose
The Day abroad was heard
How intimate, a Tempest past
The Transport of the Bird –
(F 1152)

Reflecting on what the war has wrought, Dickinson describes the conflict as a terrible storm that has nearly swallowed up the earth. If this poem is indeed occasioned by the war, as the first two lines seem to suggest, that conflict is apparently unanchored from any sense of necessity. This is not even a natural occurrence: the bellicose "Wind" is at war here with "nature," which "ventures out" only *after* the former has returned to "his Chamber" – a shift formally redoubled in the movement from an octet to two quatrains, as if the structure of the first stanza is split apart and then "scattered into place." In this poem, as in so many others, the wind's annihilative force approximates the war's extra-historical destruction.

Dickinson enlists the wind, in part, because its uncertain movements underscore the epistemological and phenomenological dilemmas that always fascinated her. One may very well realize that the wind is the result of a complex array of atmospheric systems, but none of those patterned dynamics can be experienced. When the wind blows, it simply feels like a raw force. It therefore exemplifies one of Dickinson's most often repeated poetic claims: that there is a radical, and perhaps unbridgeable, difference between feeling and knowledge. For civilians during the Civil War, who could only access the conflict imaginatively, this difference was an inextricable part of wartime experience. However, there are also other, more aesthetic reasons why Dickinson so frequently takes up the wind. The latter, after all, is formed out of the same invisible substance that animates poetry. It is only through the intake and release of breaths that verse acquires a vocal life: poems depend no less than petals or pods on the air. (Some of this conceptual heritage is recorded in our language: *afflatus*, in its Latin origins, refers to "blowing" or "breathing on"; and to *inspire* means both to "move or influence the intellect or emotions" and to "draw air into the lungs."[25])

This connection between poetry and wind interested many of the writers whom Dickinson read. Percy Bysshe Shelley – whose *Poetical Works* (1853) was housed in the Dickinson family library – repeatedly invokes the wind as a figure for worldly change. In "Mutability" (1816), the wind's "varying blast[s]" model the impermanence that structures everyday life, and in "Ode to the West Wind" (1820) the wind shakes "the earth's decaying leaves" and "cleaves" the Atlantic "into chasms," epitomizing poetry's transformative force. John Keats – the first writer named by Dickinson when Higginson asked her about her favorite poets – similarly associates the wind with change and loss. When Clymene hears the "shifting wind" in "Hyperion" (1819), she hears only "songs of misery" and the natural "music of our woes," and when Pan hears "the lovely sighing of the wind" in "I Stood Tip-Toe upon a Little Hill" (1816), this sound "full of sweet desolation" and "balmy pain" makes him weep. This same Romantic wind also struck lyres on Dickinson's side of the Atlantic. In *Walden*, Henry David Thoreau describes the "morning wind" as coextensive with the earth's "living poetry": when it "blows, the poem of creation is uninterrupted." In his essays and poems, Emerson similarly traces poetry back to the earth, locating its origins in the wind that "converts all trees to wind-harps." In fact, when Emerson stages his awakening to nature in "Musketaquid" – which first appeared in *Poems* (1847), a book that Dickinson owned and loved – it is occasioned by a submission to the wind's gusts along the river: "For still / I am a willow of the wilderness, / Loving the wind that bent me."[26]

By the time that Dickinson writes her war poems, the wind therefore had a long history as a figure for poetic inspiration; and that troubling confluence between destruction and creation emerges in her poetry as an immanent aesthetic concern. Her poems figure the war via the wind because that conflict's extra-historicity conjured up the possibility that it might also be, at the same time, extra-poetic. Not coincidentally, many of Dickinson's most well-known war poems are part of sequences that connect that internecine struggle to broader reflections on poetry and art. "They dropped like Flakes –" (F 545) and "The Black Berry – wears a Thorn in his side –" (F 548), which critics have described as exemplary specimens of Dickinson's Civil War verse, are immediately followed by several poems about poems: "I measure every Grief I meet" (F 550), "Conjecturing a Climate" (F 551), and "When Diamonds are a Legend" (F 553). In each of these texts, Dickinson meditates on the conditions, capacities, and limitations of what she terms "My Art," asking whether it can indeed – as wartime poetry must – make grief exchangeable or describe a region that can only be imaginatively conjectured. Dickinson's 1863 poem about the erotic dimensions of captivity and violence, "My Life had stood – a Loaded Gun –" (F 764), is likewise bound up, both ideationally and structurally, with the two poems that succeed it: "The Sunrise runs for Both –" (F 765), which reflects, Hawthorne-like, on the connections wrought by sunlight and moonlight, and "No Bobolink – reverse His Singing" (F 766), which describes "Music" as the "Only Anodyne" for loss.

Even that most famous of Dickinson's wartime poems, "The name – of it – is 'Autumn' –," was composed as part of a sequence:

> The name – of it – is "Autumn" –
> The hue – of it – is Blood –
> An Artery – opon the Hill –
> A Vein – along the Road –
>
> Great globules – in the Alleys –
> And Oh, the Shower of Stain –
> When Winds – upset the Basin –
> And spill the Scarlet Rain –
>
> It sprinkles Bonnets – far below –
> It gathers ruddy Pools –
> Then – eddies like a Rose – away –
> Opon Vermillion Wheels –
>
> [...]
>
> I dwell in Possibility –
> A fairer House than Prose –
> More numerous of Windows –
> Superior – for Doors –
>
> Of Chambers as the Cedars –
> Impregnable of eye –
> And for an everlasting Roof
> The Gambrels of the Sky –
>
> Of Visitors – the fairest –
> For Occupation – This –
> The spreading wide my narrow Hands
> To gather Paradise –
>
> [...]
>
> Whole Gulfs – of Red, and Fleets – of Red –
> And Crews – of solid Blood –
> Did place about the West – Tonight –
> As 'twere specific Ground –
>
> And They – appointed Creatures –
> In Authorized Arrays –
> Due – promptly – as a Drama –
> That bows – and disappears –
>
> (F 465, 466, 468)

The first poem commences as an exercise in naming. Bracketed by quotes and dashes, the word "Autumn" nonetheless fails to describe what follows, as the landscape morphs into a kind of body that has been ripped apart. The hills are stained with blood; the fields are covered in twisted veins; and this anti-pastoral violence even has a chemical afterlife, as the blood evaporates into the clouds and then returns in the form of purple rain. If the name of this awful scene is Autumn, then either Autumn is either a very different thing than we ever imagined or this bloody change – replete with the gushing arteries and "Shower of Stain" – exceeds the visual and linguistic frameworks provided by the seasons. (Dickinson, Tyler Hoffman observes, might be playing with the "phonetic correspondence of the words 'autumn' and 'Antietam' – which begin with the neighboring vowels /ae/ and /e/, respectively, and end in the identical syllable.") This poem accordingly belongs to that group, or subgenre, of Dickinson poems in which "the point of definition," as Sharon Cameron puts it, is not to elucidate a given word but to "reveal the speaker's knowledge of its inadequacy" and thereby come "to terms with a discrepancy between what one believes and what one feels."[27] That meditative labor through which one seeks to bridge knowledge and feeling is in certain respects the special province of poetry, and that is precisely what the second poem (F 466) suggests. The world's myriad discrepancies, whether between language and reality or between history and sensation, are best apprehended not in the "House of Prose" but in poetry, which is more "numerous of Windows" and "Superior – for Doors –." For Dickinson, that generic difference has to do with poetry's particular fields of vision: line, rhyme, and meter create new vantage-points and angles for reflection. (Hence the emphasis on positionality and sight, as well as the reference to poetry's "Gambrels" – double-sloped roofs that have twice the number of sides and angles as their triangular counterparts.) Pivoting from this insight, Dickinson then returns, in poem 468, to the violence she initially described in "The name – of it – is 'Autumn' –," but here we are transported to the sea, where blood is spilled in "Gulfs," and "Fleets," and "Crews." This "Drama – / That bows – and disappears –" is thus the same drama we already witnessed, but glimpsed now through an entirely different door or window.[28]

The sequentiality of these poems underscores one of the most important claims of recent Dickinson scholarship: that she is a wide-ranging writer who experimented with a variety of poetic genres and compositional practices. One practice of which she was especially fond involved taking up a single impression, act, or idea and then writing several interconnected poems about it – much like Whitman does with his annexes and clusters. Although Dickinson is often remembered for her dashes and elisions, many of her poems, as Cameron argues in *Choosing Not Choosing*, are "contiguous," generating "scenes and subjects" that "unfold between and among the [individual] poems as well as within them." That contiguity, Alexandra Socarides has demonstrated, tends to take the form not of fascicle-long sequences but of "more loosely-tied together [...] pairs" and poetic constellations.[29] This clustering is at once a basic structural feature of the fascicles and a crucial part of her response to the Civil War. Because that struggle so radically divided experience from chronology, Dickinson sought to foster alternative ways of registering – or viewing – that conflict, and she did so not by summarizing its unsummable history, but by "spreading wide [her] narrow Hands" and showing just how disorderly and destructive this event was.

These considerations regarding the war's variety, aesthetics, and extra-historicity often dovetail in Dickinson's descriptions of the wind, since the very gusts that scatter the petals, "upset the Basin – / And spill the Scarlet Rain –" are also figures for poetry itself. Consider the wind that blows in poem 334:

> Of all the Sounds dispatched abroad
> There's not a Charge to me
> Like that old measure in the Boughs –
> That Phraseless Melody –
> The Wind does – working like a Hand –
> Whose fingers comb the Sky –
> Then quiver down, with tufts of tune
> Permitted Gods – and me –

The wind's "fingers" return in these lines, but instead of scattering pods or bodies, they conduct a symphony. As the breeze rushes through "the Sky – / Then quiver[s] down," it yields a kind of felt music, a gorgeous "measure" or "tune." Since this stringless, self-generated "Melody" provides an ideal "Charge" that verse alone can hope to approximate, this poem is a beautiful example of Dickinson's many poems about poetry. However, when it is read as part of the sequence of poems that precede and follow it, it becomes clear that "Of all the Sounds dispatched abroad" is also, at the same time, a meditation on Civil War song. This "Fleshless Chant" is surrounded by poems about the proximity between pain and pleasure. Some of these poems, such as "Of Bronze – and Blaze –" (F 319) and "After great pain, a formal feeling comes –"

(F 372), locate this intertwining in the conflict itself, which makes victories out of a bloody harvest of death, while others, such as "I can wade Grief –" (F 312) and "There's a certain Slant of light" (F 320), depict this collusion as coextensive with poetry, which depends no less than warfare on "the look of Death" and other "imperial affliction[s] / Sent us of the Air –."

Poetry, Dickinson intimates again and again, puts what is otherwise "phraseless" into language. It is therefore all the more necessary in the midst of a war that has annihilated everything. As she wrote in 1865,

> Crisis is a Hair
> Toward which forces creep
> Past which – forces retrograde
> If it come in sleep
>
> To suspend the Breath
> Is the most we can
> (F 1067)

If this is true, then poetry is a vital form of suspension. Precisely by "traversing" as it "halts" and then curling "in[to] Capricorn – / Denying that it was," poetry enables a momentary escape, an imaginative transport that carries one not *away* from the destruction but *into* its erasures (F 291). The war thus limns these poems, but with each stolen breath that conflict's historicity fades away and we are left with a "Crisis" that is utterly unperiodizable "this side [of] Naples" (F 517).

Transbellum Lyrics

Although the Civil War spanned the most prolific phase of Dickinson's career, that terror which made her sing did not suddenly vanish when peace was sealed at Appomattox. In fact, from 1865 until her death in 1886, she composed more than 560 new poems, and many of these later verses revolve around the same questions about the aesthetics of destruction that so haunted Dickinson during the war.

Despite their ostensibly postbellum status, many of these poems actively draw upon the war in order to evoke, describe, or recast other battles, from the avian warfare of "His Bill is locked – his Eye estranged" (F 1126) to the spiritual conflicts of "There's the Battle of Burgoyne –" (F 1316) and the metaphoric skirmishes of "My Wars are laid away in Books –" (F 1579) and "Their Barricade against the Sky" (F 1505). In "'Tis

Seasons since the Dimpled War," Dickinson enlists the language of internecine violence to recount a fight between friends:

> 'Tis Seasons since the Dimpled War
> In which we each were Conqueror
> And each of us were slain
> And Centuries 'twill be and more
> Another Massacre before
> So modest and so vain –
> Without a Formula we fought
> Each was to each the Pink Redoubt –
>   (F 1551)

This poem recalls a falling out, a war conducted under the guise of smiles and false modesty. The "we" or "us" to whom Dickinson refers may very well be that elusive subject of the Master letters, whoever he was, or Susan Dickinson, Emily's beloved sister-in-law. Arguing for the latter possibility, Martha Nell Smith writes that "Dickinson seemed aware that such love may well call for defenses and for each woman to be a fortress [that is, a 'Pink Redoubt'] for the other."[30] Regardless of the particular occasion for these lines, their language is patently that of armed combat. The relationship does not simply falter – it's a "Massacre." "Dimple" is also one of those words, like "bomb" and "volcano," that Dickinson began to use quite frequently during the war; and throughout her later poems "pink" tends to carry a connotation of transgression. (In poem 1776, for instance, a slumbering volcano hatches "projects pink," and in 1657, pinkness is something that nature devours.) By joining bloodshed with blushing, " 'Tis Seasons" becomes a poem of – and perhaps even about – the Civil War, intimating that the North and South were both "conquerors" in an irrational fratricide whose absent "Formula" cannot be found in the "Seasons" or "Centuries" that encircle it.

Such poems subvert the narrative that we have long inherited about these transbellum authors: that their imaginative engagement with the world concludes after the Civil War. In Dickinson's case, her postwar career is often framed as an extended creative decline. Dickinson "wrote less and less after Appomattox," scholars have argued, because the antebellum world to which she belonged, the world of Romanticism and New England Puritanism, had been destroyed.[31] Several critics – such as Paula Bennett, who has divulged Dickinson's connections to late-nineteenth-century magazine poetry, and Cristanne Miller, who has examined Dickinson's postwar poetics of memory – have struggled mightily against this fiction of decline. But American literary studies is institutionally, pedagogically, and professionally structured in ways that make it nearly impossible for such counter-narratives to gain broad intellectual traction.[32] The partitioning of the nineteenth century into antebellum and postbellum halves creates a furious feedback loop: courses in American literature tend to begin or end at 1865, scholars are hired or recruited in part to fill these curricular needs, and publishers use the same temporal fencing in their histories and anthologies, thereby granting these periodic categories, which are deeply at odds with the modes of periodization actually hatched within these literatures, a self-perpetuating sense of naturalness.

When it comes to Dickinson, this story of decline hinges on two things: her diminished poetic output after 1865 and her gradual abandonment of her fascicle-system. These dual changes, Ralph Franklin argues, are symptoms of Dickinson's postwar "entropy": "Most of the poems of these 20 years survive on scraps of discarded household paper – incoming letters, abandoned envelops, advertising flyers, wrapping paper [...] Step by step, she had abandoned the system established in 1858."[33] While it is certainly true that Dickinson wrote fewer poems in her later years, the ratios of her literary production are to my mind less important than the astonishing duration of that production. This "antebellum" poet continued to write for nearly 20 years after the war and fashioned hundreds of new poems into the 1880s. Her turn away from the fascicles that had consumed her waking life during the 1860s is therefore not a turn away from her earlier poetry but a shift within her long career, a transition that grows directly out of her transbellum response to the Civil War and its annihilative gusts.

When Dickinson writes about the war after the war, as it were, the past and the present often flow into one another:

> My Triumph lasted till the Drums
> Had left the Dead alone
> And then I dropped my Victory
> And chastened stole along
> To where the finished Faces
> Conclusion turned on me
> And then I hated Glory
> And wished myself were They.
>
> What is to be is best descried
> When it has also been –
> Could Prospect taste of Retrospect

The Tyrannies of Men
Were Tenderer, diviner
The Transitive toward –
A Bayonet's contrition
Is nothing to the Dead –
(F 1212)

Critics have praised this meditation on the cruel erasures of "Triumph" for its relatively direct treatment of the war. This poem situates itself not simply in the midst of the struggle but on the battlefield itself, as the speaker steals along the rows of the dead and then reflects on the awful power of the bayonet. As Shira Wolosky notes, as these lines unfold they stamp out "any consoling or atoning value to victory, in distress for the 'finished Faces'" that the war has irreversibly destroyed.[34] Nevertheless, Dickinson penned this poem about 6 years after the Civil War had officially ended. So while it is certainly true that the poem challenges the war's political lexicon by disclosing what is omitted or repressed by such words as "Glory," "Victory," and "Triumph," it is equally true that the poem is imaginatively engaged with a conflict that, according to the field's long-established chronologies, had already ceased more than half a decade ago. Situated between prospect and retrospect, "My Triumph lasted till the Drums" is a transbellum poem that weaves the war's multilinearity into its very timescape. That interperiodicity is most keenly felt in the second stanza, which offers the promise of a grand lesson – that grief may make us "Tenderer" or men less tyrannical – only to brutally retract it in the concluding lines: "A Bayonet's contrition / Is nothing to the Dead –." If such contrition means nothing, then the poem leaves us only with the intransitive "Dead," for whom distinctions between the past and the present do not matter.

Here, and throughout Dickinson's later poems, the war acquires an array of afterlives that extend across and beyond the nineteenth century. For Dickinson, as for each of these transbellum writers, the Civil War resists periodic closure. The extent to which that pink event exceeds the calendrical years of its occurrence is most fully registered, however, not in the thematic or philosophical engagements of her later poems, but in their form and genre. As she continues to write through the 1870s and 1880s, Dickinson tends to alter the structure of her poems, both formally (by shortening the poetic line and stanza) and materially (by leaving behind the fascicles and composing more poems individually). Many of these later poems are markedly briefer than their earlier analogues:

No Passenger was known to flee –
That lodged a Night in memory –
That wily – subterranean Inn
Contrives that none go out again –
(F 1451)

[...]
One note from One Bird
Is better than a Million Word –
A scabbard has – but one sword
(F 1478)

These poems, which Dickinson wrote in 1877 and 1878, are exceedingly familiar in terms of their ideational content. This is still the same poet who has always been interested in birds, passengers, and the proximity between unlike things (joy and pain, words and weapons, coming and going). Nonetheless, there is a surprising breeziness to these poems, an almost epigrammatic quality that is more than a little at odds with many of Dickinson's well-known, earlier productions. One of the main things that poems such as "Safe in their Alabaster Chambers –" (F 124), "Split the Lark – and you'll find the Music –" (F 905), and "After great pain, a formal feeling comes –" (F 372) have in common is their almost an *anti*-epigrammatic quality. Their enjambments, dashes, and rearticulations – all of which are a crucial part of Dickinson's wartime poetic – overload particular words and phrases with ambiguity. They also tend to enlist an even stanza structure (either two or four quartets) that allows her various claims and impressions to turn back on themselves and find some alternative viewpoint (or window, as it were). In contrast, many of her later poems, like the ones listed above, either forego or forestall such rearticulation almost altogether.

What interests me about Dickinson's later poems is the possibility that the very things that mark them as formally different – their truncated lines and more autonomous stanzas – may in fact derive from a generic reorientation of her verse. If, as Virginia Jackson has argued, Dickinson experimented with many of the assorted genres that anchored poetry before its late-nineteenth-century "lyricization," it is entirely plausible – and given Dickinson's abiding interest in popular writing, perhaps even likely – that her poetry becomes increasingly lyricized in her later years.[35] Indeed if the lyric becomes the prevailing mode of poetic reading and interpretation in the decades that span the war and the early twentieth century, the most interesting question, to my mind, is how Dickinson herself negotiated the lyricization of poetry in her later verse. That negotiation plays a crucial role in poems like 1647 –

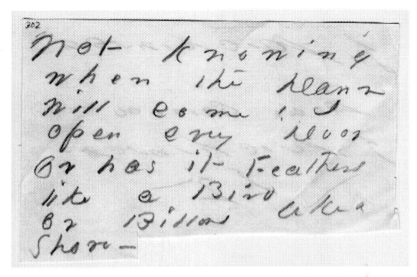

Figure 9. Manuscript for "Not knowing when the Dawn will come" (F 1647).
Courtesy of Amherst College Archives and Special Collections.

> Not knowing when the Dawn will come,
> I open every Door,
> Or has it Feathers, like a Bird,
> Or Billows, like a Shore –

– in which the sense of time, mode of address, and ideational movement are markedly, and quite self-reflexively, lyrical. There is no redoubling here: a single impression about the coming dawn simply unfolds, or "Billows" outward. This poem was also written not as part of a long cluster or fascicle sequence, but as an individual text, and Dickinson used this more particularized compositional method quite frequently in her later years, precisely when the lyric was progressively swallowing up the other genres of American poetry (see Figure 9).

Although many of Dickinson's later poems are not lyrics, many of them do actively draw upon the lyric's conventions. Her later poems (whatever we wish to call them) are keenly interested in the tension between evanescence and preservation that troubles so much lyric poetry, particularly in its Romantic instantiations. From Shelley's "Ozymandias" (1818) to Wordsworth's "Lucy Poems" (1798–1801), Romantic lyrics often take shape through a kind of double movement, at once recording and contesting the sudden erasure of an impression, experience, or idea. According to Theodor Adorno, this dialectical impulse is what makes the lyric political, since it preserves something that has not yet been subsumed by the forces of modernization and gestures toward a possible future in which universality is no longer inhibited by individual experience.[36] Dickinson's later poems, however, have less in common with the lyrics of Goethe and Rilke that Adorno celebrates than with the British and American lyrics that Anne-Lise François elucidates in *Open Secrets: The Literature of Uncounted Experience* (2008). In François's reading, the lyric pivots on "recessive actions" and "gestures of self-cancelling revelation" which present history as a kind of "passing out of existence, a trailing off or lapse, rather than as a concretization or production of significance."[37] This erasure of history – which may have been precisely what troubled Whitman about the literariness of *Leaves of Grass* ("No one will get at my verses who insists upon viewing them as a literary performance" [*PW*, 2:731]) – finds its most eloquent expression in Dickinson's poems, which are shot through with countless moments of lyric dematerialization: "Fate" bolts "the Door [...] behind us," but instead of undergoing some transformation or acquiring some insight, we simply "accost no more –" (F 1546). Or the "universe" itself is "borne [...] / Entirely away" (F 1567) Or, as Dickinson puts it in poem 1548 (and this is the text in its entirety): "All things swept sole away / This – is immensity –."

For Dickinson, the war conjured up aesthetic and epistemological dilemmas regarding the opacity of experience and the confluence between destruction and creation that did not spontaneously evaporate in 1865. If the war was so cataclysmic that it could not be recorded or remembered, then even poetry was not safe. Language, like bodies, might very well be swept away. As the conflict unfolded, Dickinson tended to address that dilemma by allowing her poems to be taken up by the "Winds of Will," but her later poems are more autonomous. Many of them are written independently and not circulated at all (or very selectively), as if they were designed to be shielded from the wind. In one of these poems, Dickinson reflects, by way of a bird, on the nature of her own late verse:

> After all Birds have been investigated and laid aside –
> Nature imparts the little Blue-Bird – assured
> Her conscientious Voice will soar unmoved
> Above ostensible Vicissitude.
>
> First at March – competing with the Wind –
> Her panting note exalts us – like a friend –
> Last to adhere when Summer cleaves away –
> Elegy of Integrity.
>
> (F 1383)

Modeling the capacity for song with its "conscientious Voice," this bird, like its Keatsian and Shelleyan cousins, is a figure for poetry itself. Unlike those nightingales and skylarks, however, this "little Blue-Bird" is untimely: she releases "her panting note" before all the other birds *and* is the last to sing before the "Summer cleaves away." For Dickinson, writing in the late-1870s, this blue-bird's final note – held until the very last moment, until integrity is no longer possible – must have seemed to resemble her own late style; and what that style enables, at least until it dissipates, is "adherence." To merely "adhere," of course, seems like a small thing. But as every reader of Dickinson knows, scales can flip and sizes can be remarkably fluid: daisies can contain the cosmos, and butterflies can embody aesthetics itself. After the hours of lead, in which countless men "perished in the seamless grass," to adhere at all is a glorious act – a "specific Grace" if ever there was one (F 545, 1238).

In this respect, it is altogether fitting that many of Dickinson's final poems focus not on the loose wind but on things that stay: stones; the sea; ruins; mosses; trees; and the earth itself. Transformations continue to be staged throughout these poems, but Dickinson now is increasingly interested in moments – however fleeting and however tenuous – of stability. In one of her 1882 poems, she likens that stability to the forgotten permanence of a tiny rock:

> How happy is the little Stone
> That rambles in the Road alone,
> And does'nt care about Careers
> And Exigencies never fears –
> Whose Coat of elemental Brown
> A passing Universe put on,
> And independent as the sun,
> Associates or glows alone,
> Fulfilling absolute Decree
> In casual simplicity –
>   (F 1570)

Years ago, Dickinson described her poems as "pearl[s]" shaped through "Gem Tactics" (F 282). That movement from "paste" to "pearl" ends with this "little Stone," which "glows alone" and fulfills its own "Decree." This rambling rock is a beautiful and apt figure for Dickinson's own late poems, which draw upon the lyric not to enlist its promise of imaginative transport but to shield certain experiences when everything else has been swept away.

Dickinson's late poems are thus expressions not of resistance, but of elusive preservation. This safeguarding impulse, Cristanne Miller suggests, is likewise reflected in the public afterlives of these poems – or more accurately, the lack thereof. "Everything we know about her mode of composition and copying," Miller remarks, indicates "that at least through 1865 the poet typically copied poems to retain or circulate fairly soon after writing them," but after the war "she largely stopped making fair copies, preserving poems instead primarily on scraps of paper that include fragments and drafts." The war, in short, disillusions Dickinson of the idea that poetry should be made public: the war's suffering – and more importantly, the inexorable distance and unfathomability of that suffering – led her to opt for preservation rather than circulation.[38] That choice, I am arguing, takes shape both formally and generically in the later poems, as Dickinson turns increasingly to the lyric to slip beneath the pink winds.

Although these poems are both structurally and materially distinct from many of their earlier predecessors, they derive not from a single moment of departure or reversal, but from a long process of transbellum composition. If, as Dickinson once wrote, "'Nothing' is the force / That renovates the World –" (F 1611), that same creative destruction anchors her own poetic career, which began with a wail by the "Burying Ground" and continued across the nineteenth century. The Civil War thereby manifests in her poems as a pluridimensional event – a rupture, yes, but one that cannot be adequately timed or chronicled. These poems accordingly belong not to an antebellum, or postbellum, or even a Civil War period, but to that temporal borderland I have been calling transbellum, this multiperiod in which authors responded to the Civil War's myriad *durées* by continuing to write and revise.

Up until the very end of their careers, these transbellum writers carried the Civil War into other stretches, scales, and instances of time. When "strong Necessity / Surge[d], and heap[ed] Time's strand with wrecks," they picked up the pieces and they wove them into chronologies, both splendid and strange, which reframed the conflict (*BP*, 9). As we have seen, those chronologies are nothing if not unruly. Instead of advancing along a straight line, they loop, or slide, or fade away, taking us far beyond the antebellum and postbellum eras. Yet despite their varied structures, these chronologies all point toward the same idea: that the Civil War eclipsed the years in which it officially occurred, and continued to unfold long after 1865. Or perhaps it never ended at all – in which case, the transbellum names a present that is still unfolding, and a war that is still unresolved.

Coda
Other Nineteenth Centuries

Of course, many things do conclude, however partially or belatedly. And one thing that seems to have run its course is the idea that American literature is either encompassed or defined by the United States' territorial boundaries. The practices of reprinting, the global evolution of genres, the promiscuous circulation of bodies, stories, and ideas – in short, the very phenomena that constitute literary and cultural history – reveal spatial experience to be remarkably aleatory and imaginative. This does not mean that national borders do not matter, or that their power can simply be critiqued away. But it does mean that in spite of the longstanding tendency to categorize texts by way of the state, literature often passes through and beyond the boundaries that ostensibly contain it, either by leaping imaginatively into other places and other times or by bringing the outside in and creating new textures of feeling and relation. The fact that, as Paul Giles puts it, "the interrelation between American literature and geography, far from being [...] natural, involves contested terrain," has inspired numerous scholars to rechart American literature through new, alternative geographies.[1] The latter are incredibly rich and varied – some stretch eastward across the Atlantic, or southward through the Caribbean and Latin America, while others focus on diasporas, archipelagoes, or the planet itself – but these transnational perspectives are bound together by a single claim: that to remap American literature, we must redraw that literature's spatial configurations and locate borderlands of intercultural exchange.

The preceding chapters push that claim in a very different direction by asking: What if there are temporal as well as spatial borderlands? What if everything we have learned about boundaries – their fictiveness, porousness, and elasticity – applies just as well to the borders of literary history, which are so often taken as natural features of the scholarly landscape? The applicability of recent work on American literature's spatiotemporal dimensions to the study of periodicity is underscored not only by the spatialized language that is frequently used to plot literary history (for instance, scaling and rescaling, margins and peripheries) – which, as Doreen Massey writes, transforms "geography into history" through a conceptual "sleight of hand" – but also by the central role that timelines play in shaping the nation's mythologies.[2] Nationalism is conceptually rooted in historical narratives that endow the state with a kind of mnemonic life and false sense of natural development, and those narratives are almost necessarily reproduced whenever literary history is presented as a product of fixed eras or progressive sequences. To continue reimagining American literature beyond the nation therefore requires us to approach periodicity itself with the same revisionary sensibility that has enabled scholars to rethink and rescale American literature in motley ways.

Such reperiodizations, of course, fill out the preceding pages. The transbellum texts, visions, and careers we have examined offer numerous alternative ways in which the Civil War, as well as the broader era of which it is a part, can be reread. If we take Melville to his limits, we discover an account not just of the war but of human experience that is structured around an almost endlessly repeating transnational and transhistorical cycle. The historical sensibility that is cultivated in *Battle-Pieces*, *Clarel*, and *Timoleon* even extends far beyond the nineteenth century – the loose periodic container that frames this book – by folding the American and European conflicts of 1860s and 1870s into ancient upheavals and medieval conquests. Whitman and Douglass, meanwhile, invite us to think about the war as an uncompleted, and perhaps uncompletable, project – not so much part of a long nineteenth century as part of a long modernity that is still very much ongoing. And Dickinson's poetic erasures encourage us to view American literary history in ways that are decoupled from time and space almost altogether, yoking the Civil War – at least as Dickinson renders it – to Edgar Allan Poe's "Material Nihility," Henry David Thoreau's "interior chart[s]," and countless other leaps into the desublimated or the unknown.[3]

However, these nonstandard accounts of the Civil War and the shape of American literary history are hardly exhaustive. Romanticism, for example, provides a rather attractive throughline for reading across the nineteenth century while acknowledging the war's multilinear impact. Rather than being decimated by the war or supplanted by realism (as it is often reputed to be), romanticism takes shape in a multiplicity of eras, places, and print media, connecting the United States to Russia, Europe, and South America; literature to painting and the other arts; and the age of revolution to the age of emancipation. In the United States, Romanticism is most popularly taken up by the Transcendentalists, but its halflife is remarkably long and complex. Many of the poets who wrote during the ascent of realism and naturalism, from Joaquin Miller to Emma Lazarus, borrow from and innovate upon their Romantic forebears, crafting poems that revel in nature's ability to "shape a poet's heart"; the world's musicality; and the artist's Whitmanian need, as Miller puts it in "A Song of Creation" (1909), for boundless "room [...] not only the latitude but even the longitude of all known oceans and of all glorious nature."[4] Much of the science fiction of the late nineteenth and early twentieth centuries similarly hinges on – indeed, is conceptually predicated upon – Romantic fantasies of literary transport and imaginative change. (Hence the stories by H.G. Wells, Jules Verne, and Edgar Rice Burroughs about time-machines, psychic experiences, and Confederate veterans who are suddenly teleported to Mars.) And a great deal of Civil War literature, in all of its generic and regional variety, traffics heavily in Romantic ideas and investments, from the higher law philosophy that fuels numerous abolitionist writings to the emphasis placed on nature, sentiment, and ideality in so many wartime texts, both Northern and Southern.

Still other borderlands are located along the margins of economic history. Many scholars have examined American literature's evolving relation to the productive economies that subtend it – from the market revolution to the industrial revolution and the ensuing ages of incorporation, Fordism, and post-Fordism – but the history of downturns and recessions might provide a better rubric for organizing literary history. The latter could be reconceived as part of a recurring recession culture that extends nonsequentially across time and interlinks disparate eras and authors. Many of the writings from the 1836–43 recession, such as Poe's short stories and Emerson's early essays, are fueled by an interest in character and credibility that also marks William Dean Howells's realist novels, Horatio Alger's "Luck and Pluck" series, and other products of the 1873–9 recession. Similarly, despite their decades-long removal from one another, the depressions of the 1890s and the 1920s were both accompanied by literatures keenly interested in determination and agency, from Stephen Crane and Theodor Dreiser's novels about doomed soldiers and prostitutes to John Steinbeck and Ellen Glasgow's stories about migrant workers and poor farmers. The centrifugal force of such reperiodizations would certainly pull against the Civil War's gravitational hold, but the war would also need to be foregrounded in any such recession narrative, not only because it occasioned a decades-long era of deflation but also because so many wartime writings – especially those of slaves, soldiers, and Southerners – are marked by deprivation. Reading Civil War literature in this manner, as a kind of cognate or offshoot of depression literature, would also deemphasize the war's militarized violence, which grounds almost every ideological reading of the war, and instead highlight the rhythms of everyday life and the ways they inflect wartime writing.

Transbellum literary histories also take shape through the long careers of far less canonical writers, such as Frances Ellen Watkins Harper. After publishing her first collection of poems, *Forest Leaves*, in 1845, she continued to write for nearly 60 years, producing seven more books of poetry, four novels, and dozens of speeches, essays, and short stories. Those various works, from *Poems on Miscellaneous Subjects* (1854) to *Idylls of the Bible* (1901), are often associated with the reform movements to which Harper devoted so much of her time: abolitionism, temperance, women's suffrage, black civil rights. But the imaginative worlds she creates tend to revolve, either structurally or philosophically, around the Civil War. Whether she is writing about the Confederacy's afterlives in "Words for the Hour" (1871), or racial passing and inheritance in *Minnie's Sacrifice* (1869), or the relation between "the Negro," the "Brahmin," the "Bhuddist," and the "sons of far Cathay" in "The Present Age" (1895), the Civil War resurfaces again and again as an open-ended upheaval that is tied to the modern world's political and religious struggles.[5]

The Civil War's transbellum trajectories are particularly crucial to Harper's most well-known book, *Iola Leroy, Or Shadows Uplifted* (1892). That novel focuses on the life of its eponymous heroine, a "mulatta" who – along with her brother, Harry – is born to an enslaved mother but raised as if she were free, at least until her father dies. After that, she is separated from her family, reenslaved, and "subjected to cruel indignities," from which she is eventually rescued.[6] Upon returning to the North, she nurses Union soldiers back to health, becomes a teacher during Reconstruction and, at the end of the book, reunites with her family and weds a mixed-race doctor. One is thus tempted to read *Iola Leroy*, by way of our common periodizing practices, as a postbellum novel of the 1890s, when stories about passing and racial uplift were quite common. But that reading is contravened by the Civil War's centrality to the story, which is registered in its wartime setting; its references to Fort Sumter, Bull's Run, Sherman's march, and the battles at Vicksburg, Five Forks, and Port Hudson; and its chapter titles (for example, "Contraband of War," "Arrival of the Union Army," "After the Battle"). In fact, the narrative structure of Harper's tale – like the fates of her characters – is utterly warped by the war and its influence: the first several chapters take place amidst the conflict, and as the ensuing parts either rewind back to the

1840s or fast forward to Reconstruction, it becomes clear that *Iola Leroy* is less of a historical novel than a counterhistorical novel that pivots on emancipation's *longue durée*. Indeed, the collective impression imparted by the narrative's storylines is that emancipation, instead of abruptly and miraculously arriving in 1865, is an ongoing and still-unaccomplished act of reunion.

Such altered chronologies are extraordinarily difficult to narrate, or even plot out. The centuries-long story told in "William the Silent," the temporal somersaults of *Battle-Pieces* and *Iola Leroy*, the anxious anticipations of *Leaves of Grass*, and the deathly absences in Dickinson's poems are nearly impossible to fit into a linear story about the war and its place in American literary history. But that is precisely why these timelines are so important. They contain other, hitherto elided accounts of the Civil War – accounts that, instead of marching through the nation's sequenced history, radically reimagine it. And by doing so, they provide us, the latter-day heirs of this struggle, with temporalities that cut across our most entrenched periodic ideas, categories, and a priori assumptions, which all too often blind us to the war's myriad times and durations.

Notes

INTRODUCTION: TRANSBELLUM AMERICAN LITERATURE

1 The Norton, Heath, Wadsworth, and Bedford anthologies establish different chronological subdivisions – the Norton volumes, for instance, proceed from colonization to 1820, from 1820 to 1865, and from 1865 to 1914, while Bedford splits its volumes at 1865 – but they all frame the war as a single, chronologically discrete periodic boundary. One finds similar temporal fencing in such critical overviews as *The Cambridge History of American Literature*, which divides American prose at 1860; companions such as G.R. Thompson's *Reading the American Novel, 1865–1914* (Malden, MA: Wiley-Blackwell, 2012); and monographs such as Kevin Pelletier's *Apocalyptic Sentimentalism: Love and Fear in U.S. Antebellum Literature* (Athens: University of Georgia Press, 2015) and Lara Langer Cohen's *The Fabrication of American Literature: Fraudulence and Antebellum Print Culture* (Philadelphia: University of Pennsylvania Press, 2011).

2 Robert Penn Warren, *The Legacy of the Civil War: Meditations on the Centennial* (New York: Random House, 1961), 4.

3 Considering the strange history of these terms, it is more than a little surprising that they eventually became such fixtures in our critical nomenclature. "Antebellum," for instance, first appeared – in its longer, legal version – in a variety of Civil War-era articles, essays, and letters. As Samuel S. Cox put it in one of his Congressional speeches: "Conquest by force is only physical: subjugation does not imply mental acquiescence on the part of the vanquished in the ideas of the victor. Such a war, therefore, will produce only the *status quo ante bellum*, leaving an absolute reciprocal negation; each party denying the claims of the other, and leaving no common ground for a truce." *Eight Years in Congress, from 1857 to 1865* (New York: D. Appleton and Co., 1865), 387. Shortly after the war, the phrase began to be condensed into a single word, *ante-bellum*, which was typically used to describe something that was both Southern and outmoded. Writers in the late nineteenth century used the truncated term to discuss prewar Southern politics, cooking, culture, and law, and to title novels, memoirs, and histories about the prewar South. That association of antebellumness with pastness and Southernness was preserved when literary critics repurposed the term in the twentieth century. Early surveys of American literature, such as Thomas Wentworth Higginson and Henry Walcott Boynton's

Reader's History of American Literature (Boston: Houghton, Mifflin, and Co., 1903), construed antebellum literature as an exclusively Southern phenomenon ("there were [...] three or four ante-bellum writers who attempted to give literary expression to the Southern life or the Southern spirit" [203–4]), and that emphasis on Southern archaism was reiterated in scholarly histories, such as the *Cambridge History of American Literature* (1917). The idea of the antebellum era thereby entered literary studies as a marker of otherness, as an expression of distance and unbelonging. And that changed only relatively recently. In fact, the concept of a *national* antebellum literature did not crystallize until the mid-to-late twentieth century, when the United States became a global superpower during the Cold War. The first articles and monographs on "antebellum American literature" appeared in the 1970s, and the term acquired its greatest currency only after that, when the category of the American Renaissance began to be critiqued by the New Americanists. To challenge Matthiessen's narrow canon, and the senses of literary nationalism that it ostensibly promoted, the New Americanists initiated a large-scale move away from the idea of the Renaissance in favor of the idea of the antebellum. The essays in Walter Benn Michaels and Donald Pease's *The American Renaissance Reconsidered* (Baltimore: Johns Hopkins University Press, 1985) and Sacvan Bercovitch and Myra Jehlen's *Ideology and Classic American Literature* (New York: Cambridge University Press, 1986), for instance, focus almost exclusively on texts written and published between the 1830s and the Civil War, and for good reason: the New Americanists effectively replaced an authorial canon with a periodic canon, encapsulated by the terms "antebellum" and "postbellum."

4 As Christopher Hager and I have argued, the Civil War is best grasped as "both a rupture *and* an occasion for extension," the impact of which "can be properly accounted for only if we grasp duration and rupture as codependent, unfixed coordinates along a series of diachronic lines" (260, 266). See Christopher Hager and Cody Marrs, "Against 1865: Reperiodizing the Nineteenth Century," *J19: The Journal of Nineteenth-Century Americanists* 1.2 (October 2013): 259–84.

5 Walt Whitman, *Notebooks and Unpublished Prose Manuscripts*, 6 vols., ed. Edward F. Grier (New York: New York University Press, 1984), vol. 6, 2011.

6 William H. Seward, "The Irrepressible Conflict" (1858), in *The Works of William H. Seward*, ed. George E. Baker, vol. 4 (Boston: Houghton, Mifflin, & Co., 1884), 292.

7 *The Poems of Emily Dickinson: Reading Edition*, ed. R.W. Franklin (Cambridge: Harvard University Press, 1999), poems 1551 and 1212. Hereafter cited parenthetically as F.

8 I am thinking of the following studies, to which I am very much indebted: Faith Barrett, *To Fight Aloud is Very Brave: American Poetry and the Civil War* (Amherst: University of Massachusetts Press, 2012); Kathleen Diffley, *Where My Heart is Turning Ever: Civil War Stories and Constitutional Reform, 1861–1876* (Athens: University of Georgia Press, 1992); Alice Fahs, *The Imagined Civil War: Popular Literature of the North and South, 1861–1865* (Chapel Hill: University of North Carolina Press, 2001); Randall Fuller,

From Battlefields Rising: How the Civil War Transformed American Literature (New York: Oxford University Press, 2011); Coleman Hutchison, *Apples and Ashes: Literature, Nationalism, and the Confederate States of America* (Athens: University of Georgia Press, 2012); Deak Nabers, *Victory of Law: The Fourteenth Amendment, the Civil War, and American Literature, 1852–1867* (Baltimore: Johns Hopkins University Press, 2006); Shirley Samuels, *Facing America: Iconography and the Civil War* (New York: Oxford University Press, 2004); Julia Stern, *Mary Chesnut's Civil War Epic* (Chicago: University of Chicago Press, 2010); Timothy Sweet, *Traces of War: Poetry, Photography, and the Crisis of the Union* (Baltimore: Johns Hopkins University Press, 1990); and Elizabeth Young, *Disarming the Nation: Women's Writing and the American Civil War* (Chicago: University of Chicago Press, 1999).

9 Wai Chee Dimock, *Through Other Continents: American Literature Across Deep Time* (Princeton: Princeton University Press, 2007), 4; Elizabeth Freeman, *Time Binds: Queer Temporalities, Queer Histories* (Durham: Duke University Press, 2010), 23; Philip Fisher, *The Vehement Passions* (Princeton: Princeton University Press, 2002); Thomas M. Allen, *A Republic in Time: Social Imagination in Nineteenth-Century America* (Chapel Hill: University of North Carolina Press, 2008), 4; Dana Luciano, *Arranging Grief: Sacred Time and the Body in Nineteenth-Century America* (New York: New York University Press, 2007), 6. See also Lloyd Pratt, *Archives of American Time: Literature and Modernity in the Nineteenth Century* (Philadelphia: University of Pennsylvania Press, 2010).

10 On the slave narrative's bellum and postbellum forms, see Christopher Hager, *Word by Word: Emancipation and the Act of Writing* (Cambridge: Harvard University Press, 2013) and William L. Andrews, Introduction to *Slave Narratives After Slavery* (New York: Oxford University Press, 2011), vii–xxxii.

11 Diffley, "Home from the Theatre of War: The *Southern Magazine* and Recollections of the Civil War," in *Periodical Literature in Nineteenth-Century America*, ed. Kenneth M. Price and Susan Belasco Smith (Charlottesville: University of Virginia Press, 1995), 184. Some of these veterans' autobiographies were published in *Century Magazine* as part of their "Battles and Leaders of the Civil War" series (1884–1887), which was so popular that it made the monthly circulation almost double within a year. (See Fahs, *The Imagined Civil War*, 314.) The autobiographies to which I refer parenthetically are Ulysses S. Grant's *Personal Memoirs* (1885), James Longstreet's *From Manassas to Appomattox: Memoirs of the Civil War in America* (1896), John Singleton Mosby's *Memoirs* (1917), William Watson's *The Adventures of a Blockade Runner* (1892), Samuel S. Hildebrand's *Autobiography* (1870), James Morris Morgan's *Recollections of a Rebel Reefer* (1917), Allan Pinkerton's *The Spy of the Rebellion* (1883), and Mark Twain's "The Private History of a Campaign that Failed," *Century Magazine* 31 (December 1885): 193–204.

12 Visual records of the war, such as Alexander Gardner's *Photographic Sketch Book* (1866) and Benson J. Lossing's three-volume *Pictorial History of the Civil War* (1866–69), appeared shortly after the Confederacy's defeat. Popular

histories also abounded, ranging from Horace Greeley's *The American Conflict* (1864 and 1866) to John William Draper's three-volume *History of the American Civil War* (1867–70). The war was also exhaustively recorded from Confederate perspectives in histories like Edward A. Pollard's *The Lost Cause* (1866) and Jefferson Davis's *The Rise and Fall of the Confederate Government* (1881), and in anthologies like William Gilmore Simms's *War Poetry of the South* (1867). In the late nineteenth century, there were also efforts to retrieve and record the contributions of women and African Americans; see, for example, Linus Pierpont Brockett and Mary C. Vaughan, ed., *Woman's Work in the Civil War* (1867), and George Washington Williams, *A History of the Negro Troops in the War of the Rebellion* (1887).

13 Marshall Brown, "Periods and Resistances," *MLQ* 62.4 (December 2001): 313.

14 Jonathan Arac, *The Emergence of American Literary Narrative, 1820–1860* (Cambridge: Harvard University Press, 2005), 2–3, 4.

15 Ibid., 234, 230–1.

16 Norman Foerster, *The Reinterpretation of American Literature* (New York: Harcourt, Brace, and Co., 1928), 15; Edmund Wilson, *Patriotic Gore: Studies in the Literature of the American Civil War* (New York: Norton, 1962), 636, 638; Martha Banta, "Literature and Culture," in *The Columbia Literary History of the United States*, ed. Emory Elliott (New York: Columbia University Press, 1988), 467; Louis Menand, *The Metaphysical Club: A Story of Ideas in America* (New York: Farrar, Straus, and Giroux, 2001), x–xi; Randall Fuller, *From Battlefields Rising*, 221.

17 These reconsiderations of the American Renaissance are too eclectic to be neatly summarized, but some of the most formative statements include Charlene Avallone, "What American Renaissance? The Gendered Genealogy of a Critical Discourse," *PMLA* 112.5 (October 1997): 1102–20; Russ Castronovo, "Death to the American Renaissance: History, Heidegger, Poe," *ESQ: A Journal of the American Renaissance* 49.1–3 (2003): 179–92; Jay Grossman, *Reconstituting the American Renaissance: Emerson, Whitman, and the Politics of Representation* (Durham: Duke University Press, 2003); Michaels and Pease, eds., *The American Renaissance Reconsidered*; and David S. Reynolds, *Beneath the American Renaissance: The Subversive Imagination in the Age of Emerson and Melville* (New York: Oxford University Press, 1988).

18 On American literature's early institutionalization, see in particular Elizabeth Renker, *The Origins of American Literary Studies: An Institutional History* (New York: Cambridge University Press, 2007) and Claudia Stokes, *Writers in Retrospect: The Rise of American Literary History, 1875–1900* (Chapel Hill: University of North Carolina, 2006).

19 Matthiessen, *The American Renaissance: Art and Expression in the Age of Emerson and Whitman* (New York: Oxford University Press, 1941), xv.

20 Barrett Wendell, *A Literary History of America* (New York: Scribner's, 1901), 440; Fred Lewis Pattee, *A History of American Literature Since 1870* (New York: The Century Co., 1917), 3, 7; Norman Foerster, *The Reinterpretation of American Literature*; Granville Hicks, *The Great Tradition: An Interpretation of American Literature since the Civil War* (New York: Macmillan, 1933), 5.

21 Van Wyck Brooks, *The Flowering of New England, 1815–1865* (New York: E.P. Dutton and Co., 1936), 526, and *New England: Indian Summer, 1865–1915* (New York: E.P. Dutton and Co., 1940), 1. Matthiessen, of course, faulted Brooks for providing too much "synthesis" and not enough literary and aesthetic "analysis" (xiv). Their respective chronologies are nonetheless identical.

22 Kathleen Davis, *Periodization and Sovereignty: How Ideas of Feudalism and Secularization Govern the Politics of Time* (Philadelphia: University of Pennsylvania Press, 2008), 6.

23 On the blind-spots produced by such a periodization, see also Russ Castronovo, "Death to the American Renaissance." The "temporal effects of [the idea of the] 'Renaissance,'" he points out, "do damage to the past, present, and future of American literature, amputating what, from a rigidly historicist perspective that rests on periodization, seem like far-flung and non-empirical connections that span decades and even centuries" (181).

24 Brooks, *The Flowering*, 526–7.

25 Oswald Spengler, *The Decline of the West: Form and Actuality*, vol. 1, trans. Charles Francis Atkinson (New York: Knopf, 1926), 3, 21, 106 (original emphasis).

26 Timothy J. Reiss, "Perioddity: Considerations on the Geography of Histories," *MLQ* 62.4 (December 2001): 433.

27 Caroline Levine, "Infrastructuralism, or the Tempo of Institutions," in *On Periodization: Selected Essays from the English Institute*, ed. Virginia Jackson (ACLS Humanities E-Book, 2010), 53, 60; Eric Hayot, "Against Periodization; or, On Institutional Time," *New Literary History* 42.4 (Autumn 2011): 740; Russell Berman, "Politics: Divide and Rule," *MLQ* 62.4 (December 2001): 328; David Perkins, *Is Literary History Possible?* (Baltimore: Johns Hopkins University Press, 1993), 6; Katie Trumpener, "On Living in Time," in *On Periodization*, ed. Jackson, 194.

28 Reinhart Koselleck, *Futures Past: On the Semantics of Historical Time*, trans. Keith Tribe (New York: Columbia University Press, 2004), 195.

29 James Chandler, *England in 1819: The Politics of Literary Culture and the Case of Romantic Historicism* (Chicago: University of Chicago Press, 1998), xv.

30 Melville, *Battle-Pieces and Aspects of the War* (1866), in *Published Poems*, vol. II of *The Writings of Herman Melville*, ed. Robert C. Ryan, Harrison Hayford, Alma MacDougall Reising, and G. Thomas Tanselle (Evanston and Chicago: Northwestern University Press and the Newberry Library, 2009), 54–5. This edition of *Battle-Pieces* will hereafter be cited parenthetically as *BP*.

31 On the broader uses and history of periodization, see also Ted Underwood, *Why Literary Periods Mattered: Historical Contrast and the Prestige of English Studies* (Stanford: Stanford University Press, 2013). Periodization's lasting appeal, he notes, has to do not with the act of "boundary-drawing" but, instead, with the idea that literature has the power to "mediate historical change and transmute it into community" – a power that "depends on vividly particularizing and differentiating vanished eras, contrasting them implicitly against the present as well as against each other" (3).

32 Michael T. Gilmore, *The War on Words: Slavery, Race, and Free Speech in American Literature* (Chicago: University of Chicago Press, 2010), 2, 4.

33 Maurice Lee, *Uncertain Chances: Science, Skepticism, and Belief in Nineteenth Century American Literature* (New York: Oxford University Press, 2011), 4, 186, 11.

34 On the non-linear evolution of literary genres, see Margaret Cohen, *The Novel and the Sea* (Princeton: Princeton University Press, 2012); Lloyd Pratt, *Archives of American Time*; Max Cavitch, *American Elegy: The Poetry of Mourning from the Puritans to Whitman* (Minneapolis: University of Minnesota Press, 2007); and Christopher N. Phillips, *Epic in American Culture: Settlement to Reconstruction* (Baltimore: Johns Hopkins University Press, 2012). On the nonsequential temporalities of the affects, see Dana Luciano, *Arranging Grief*; Philip Fisher, *The Vehement Passions*; Justine Murison, *The Politics of Anxiety in Nineteenth-Century American Literature* (New York: Cambridge University Press, 2011); and Sianne Ngai, *Ugly Feelings* (Cambridge: Harvard University Press, 2005). On the politics and print cultures of nineteenth-century poetry, see Paula Bennett, *Poets in the Public Sphere: The Emancipatory Project of American Women's Poetry, 1800–1900* (Princeton: Princeton University Press, 2003); Michael C. Cohen, *The Social Lives of Poems in Nineteenth-Century America* (Philadelphia: University of Pennsylvania Press, 2015); Virginia Jackson, *Dickinson's Misery: A Theory of Lyric Reading* (Princeton: Princeton University Press, 2005); Mary Loeffelholz, *From School to Salon: Reading Nineteenth-Century American Women's Poetry* (Princeton: Princeton University Press, 2004); Meredith McGill, ed., *The Traffic in Poems: Nineteenth-Century Poetry and Transatlantic Exchange* (New Brunswick: Rutgers University Press, 2008); Eliza Richards, *Gender and the Poetics of Reception in Poe's Circle* (New York: Cambridge University Press, 2004); and Ivy G. Wilson, *Specters of Democracy: Blackness and the Aesthetics of Politics in the Antebellum U.S.* (New York: Oxford University Press, 2011), 59–102.

35 On the relation between reading practices and the evolution of a career, see in particular Douglas Anderson, *The Radical Enlightenments of Benjamin Franklin* (Baltimore: Johns Hopkins University Press, 1997).

1 WALT WHITMAN'S DIALECTICS

1 Walt Whitman, "A Backward Glance O'er Travel'd Roads" (1891), in *Prose Works 1892*, 2 vols., ed. Floyd Stovall (New York: New York University Press, 2009), vol. 2, 712–14, 727. Hereafter cited parenthetically as *PW*.

2 The Civil War's formative influence on Whitman has been rigorously expounded by each of these critics. In *Tomorrow's Parties: Sex and the Untimely in Nineteenth-Century America* (New York: New York University Press, 2013), Peter Coviello examines how the war, in spite of destroying "Whitman's expressivist utopianism," nonetheless strengthens his poetic and philosophical "vision of sex" (49). In *Whitman and the Romance of Medicine* (Berkeley and Los Angeles: University of California Press, 1997), Robert Leigh Davis construes Whitman's wartime experiences – especially in

the hospitals – as generative of a renewed sense of democracy. In *Whitman the Political Poet* (New York: Oxford University Press, 1989), Betsy Erkkila argues that Whitman's wartime sense that he "was living at a crossroad of history" and had suddenly "touched the pulse of the nation" (198) shaped his writing for decades afterwards, from *Drum-Taps* to *Democratic Vistas* and beyond. In *Disseminating Whitman: Revision and Corporeality in* Leaves of Grass (Cambridge: Harvard University Press, 1991), Michael Moon posits that the "two rhetorics" of *Drum-Taps* (i.e., the poems about the war itself and the poems about "the political attitudes that led up to it") are evidence not of "an aesthetic failing," but, instead, of the wartime "intensification" of Whitman's practice of "revising contemporary conceptions of the range and meaning of bodily experience" (173). And in *The Lunar Light of Whitman's Poetry* (Cambridge: Harvard University Press, 1987), M. Wynn Thomas situates *Drum-Taps* within Whitman's career-long struggle to bridge, via his democratic poetry, the class divisions that defined nineteenth-century society. The Civil War's influence has also been the subject of recent scholarship on Whitman's Reconstruction-era politics and poetics. See Martin Buinicki, *Walt Whitman's Reconstruction: Poetry and Publishing between Memory and History* (Iowa City: University of Iowa Press, 2011); Luke Mancuso, *The Strange Sad War Revolving: Walt Whitman, Reconstruction, and the Emergence of Black Citizenship* (Columbia, SC: Camden House Press, 1997); Cristanne Miller, "*Drum-Taps*: Revisions and Reconciliation," *Walt Whitman Quarterly Review* 26 (Spring 2009): 171–96; and Ed Folsom, "Lucifer and Ethiopia: Whitman, Race, and Poetics before the Civil War and After," in *A Historical Guide to Walt Whitman*, ed. David S. Reynolds (New York: Oxford University Press, 2000), 45–96. Whitman refers to the war as the "umbilicus" of his "whole career" in one of his many conversations with Horace Traubel. See Traubel, *With Walt Whitman in Camden*, 9 vols. (New York: Mitchell Kennerley, 1906–1996), vol. 3, 95.

3 *Oxford English Dictionary*, 7th ed.
4 Whitman, *Leaves of Grass: A Textual Variorum of the Printed Poems*, 3 volumes, ed. Sculley Bradley, Harold W. Blodgett, Arthur Golden, and William White (New York: New York University Press, 1980), vol. 2, 292 (hereafter cited parenthetically as *LG*); *Memoranda during the War*, ed. Peter Coviello (New York: Oxford University Press, 2004), 125.
5 Whitman's postwar poetic self, Ed Folsom observes, resembles that of an "old soldier, seeking out ways to make the country pay its obligation of memory." According to M. Wynn Thomas, postwar Whitman becomes a "prophet of the past" in order to process the war that had "threatened his mental equilibrium." Martin Buinicki similarly discerns in Whitman's Reconstruction-era writing and politics a strong pull toward continuous recollection, as the poet attempts to "reconstruct his experiences as they slip inexorably into the past." Luke Mancuso – drawing from Svetlana Boym's philosophy of memory – considers Whitman's nostalgia to be "restorative," and thus conservative, whereas for Cristanne Miller it is "reflective," and at moments even quite subversive. See Folsom, "Lucifer and Ethiopia," 75; Thomas, *The Lunar*

Light of Whitman's Poetry, 278, 217; Buinicki, *Walt Whitman's Reconstruction*, 8; Mancuso, "Civil War," in *A Companion to Walt Whitman*, ed. Donald D. Kummings (Malden, MA and Oxford: Blackwell, 2009), 295; and Miller, "*Drum-Taps*: Revisions and Reconciliation," 171.

6 Whitman, letter to Louisa Van Velsor Whitman (December 29, 1862), in *The Correspondence*, ed. Edwin Haviland Miller, 7 vols. (New York: New York University Press, 1961–77), vol. 1, 58.

7 Whitman, letter to Thomas Jefferson Whitman (March 6, 1863), in *The Correspondence*, vol. 1, 77; Traubel, *With Walt Whitman in Camden*, vol. 2, 137.

8 William Dean Howells, "Drum-Taps," *Round Table* 2 (November 11, 1865): 147–48, rpt. in *Walt Whitman: The Contemporary Reviews*, ed. Kenneth M. Price (Cambridge: Cambridge University Press, 1996), 114; Henry James, "Mr. Walt Whitman," *Nation* 1 (November 16, 1865): 625–6, rpt. in *The Contemporary Reviews*, 116 and 117.

9 See Ted Genoways, "The Disorder of *Drum-Taps*," *Walt Whitman Quarterly Review* 24 (Fall 2006/Winter 2007): 98–116, and Miller, "*Drum-Taps*: Revision and Reconciliation." On the circumstances surrounding *Drum-Taps'* composition, see also Roy Morris, Jr., *The Better Angel: Walt Whitman in the Civil War* (New York and Oxford: Oxford University Press, 2000), 184–5, 215–21, and David Reynolds, *Walt Whitman's America: A Cultural Biography* (New York: Random House, 1995), 413–47.

10 Whitman, letter to William D. O'Connor (January 6, 1865), in *The Correspondence*, vol. 1, 246–7 (emphasis added).

11 Michael Warner, "Civil War Religion and Whitman's *Drum-Taps*," in *Walt Whitman: Where the Future Becomes Present*, ed. David Haven Blake and Michael Robertson (Iowa City: University of Iowa Press, 2008), 84, 86.

12 *Memoranda*, 148.

13 Warner, "Civil War Religion," 84.

14 Wells, *Civil War Time: Temporality and Identity in America, 1861–1865* (Athens: University of Georgia Press, 2005), 9, 5; Whitman, *Memoranda*, 8.

15 Matthew Brown, "BOSTON/SOB NOT': Elegiac Performance in Early New England and Materialist Studies of the Book," *American Quarterly* 50.2 (June 1998): 322. The poem's regularity is also stressed by Helen Vendler, who describes the meter and rhyme as "a form of populist expression"; Betsy Erkkila, who notes Whitman's "artistic control" and desire to keep "Lincoln's death distant, contained, and safe"; and Ed Folsom, who underscores its "repetitive stability and predictability." See, respectively, "Poetry and the Mediation of Value: Whitman on Lincoln," *Michigan Quarterly Review* 39 (Winter 2000): 16; *Whitman the Political Poet*, 238; and "Lucifer and Ethiopia," in *A Historical Guide*, 54.

16 *With Walt Whitman in Camden*, vol. 3, 23. The aesthetics of such photographic poems are also bound up with the aesthetics of war itself, since, as Shirley Samuels points out, "the difficulty with war and photography alike is that the repetition of singular acts of appearance and identity blurs the

singularity of choice" and conjures up the problem of a given experience's repeatability (or lack thereof). See Samuels, *Facing America*, 6.

17 Martin Buinicki also notes that information itself acquires a war-like quality in the poem, since it "is not imparted so much as it is deployed as if for battle": other than the word "columns," the "the entire structure [of the opening lines] suggests someone observing the field of combat, [and] considering the divided forces" (*Walt Whitman's Reconstruction*, 93).

18 Cavitch, *American Elegy*, 239. On these efforts at quantifying the war, see also James Dawes, *The Language of War: Literature and Culture in the U.S. from the Civil War to World War II* (Cambridge: Harvard University Press, 2004), 24–68.

19 *Memoranda*, 102–3.

20 Menand, *The Metaphysical Club*, 3.

21 Morris, Jr., *The Better Angel*, 130; Davis, *Whitman and the Romance of Medicine*, 71; Kerry Larson, *Whitman's Drama of Consensus* (Chicago: University of Chicago Press, 1988), 234.

22 *Notebooks and Unpublished Prose Manuscripts*, vol. 1, 62, 75, 104.

23 Whitman's syntax, Wai Chee Dimock observes, provides a verbal and poetic structure for his democratic politics, since, in Whitman's sentences, all are "admitted as strict equals" by "a poetic syntax which greets each of them in exactly the same way, as a grammatical unit, equivalently functioning and structurally interchangeable." *Residues of Justice: Literature, Law, Philosophy* (Berkeley and Los Angeles: University of California Press, 1996), 115. On Whitman's shifting modes of address, see also Tenney Nathanson, *Whitman's Presence: Body, Voice, and Writing in Leaves of Grass* (New York: New York University Press, 1994), and Peter Coviello, *Intimacy in America: Dreams of Affiliation in Antebellum Literature* (Minneapolis: University of Minnesota Press, 2005), 127–56.

24 David M. Potter, *The Impending Crisis, 1848–1861* (New York: HarperCollins, 1976), 113. On the political aftermath of the Compromise, see also Elizabeth R. Varon, *Disunion!: The Coming of the American Civil War, 1789–1859* (Chapel Hill: University of North Carolina Press, 2008), 199–336. On the literary and rhetorical dimensions of these prewar political divides, see Christopher Hanlon, *America's England: Antebellum Literature and Atlantic Sectionalism* (New York and Oxford: Oxford University Press, 2013).

25 Letter to O'Connor, in *The Correspondence*, vol. 1, 247.

26 Burroughs, *Notes on Walt Whitman as Poet and Person* (New York: American News, 1867), 12.

27 Folsom, *Whitman Making Books / Books Making Whitman* (Iowa City: Obermann Center for Advanced Studies and the University of Iowa, 2005), 28.

28 Thomas, *The Lunar Light*, 254.

29 Frederic H. Hedge, *Prose Writers of Germany* (Philadelphia: Carey & Hart, 1848), 450–1. As Whitman recounted in 1890, "I am personally greatly indebted to Hedge – have been for 40 years. He was the man [who] opened

German literature to me." *Prose Writers of Germany*, he explained, "was a great book for me – I shall not forget its influence. It was a necessity, nobly answered [... and it] became indispensible"; it "has been one of my longest treasures. I can never be shaken from my love for it. I can hardly tell how many years it has been inspiration, aid, sunlight." See Traubel, *With Walt Whitman in Camden*, vol. 7, 76, III. The meaning that Whitman attached to Hegel is also connected to the meaning that he attached to the material book itself. He received his copy of Hedge's *Prose Writers of Germany* from Fred Gray, a close friend and associate from Pfaff's pub who, right before leaving to fight for the Union Army, gave Whitman this book as a token of remembrance. After fighting at the Battle of Antietam, Gray returned to New York where he met up with Whitman and recalled the slaughter. "He gave me," Whitman inscribed in the margins of his book, "a fearful account of the battlefield at ½ past 9 the night following the engagement – He crossed it on duty." As Ted Genoways notes, the scene witnessed by Gray and recounted to Whitman "must have been difficult to comprehend. Upwards of twenty thousand men had been left sprawled, dead or wounded, on the field that night, more than the ambulance trains could carry away." See Genoways, *Walt Whitman and the Civil War: America's Poet During the Lost Years of 1860–1862* (Berkeley and Los Angeles: University of California Press, 2009), 167. Stephanie M. Blalock also discusses the Whitman-Hedge-Gray connection in "'Tell what I meant by *Calamus*': Walt Whitman's Vision of Comradeship from Fred Vaughan to the Fred Gray Association," in *Whitman Among the Bohemians*, ed. Joanna Levin and Edward Whitley (Iowa City: University of Iowa Press, 2014), 172–91.

30 "America," Hegel writes, "is the country of the future, and its world-historical importance has yet to be revealed in the ages which lie ahead [...] It is a land of desire for all those who are weary of the historical arsenal of old Europe. Napoleon is said to have remarked: *Cette vieille Europe m'ennuie*. It is up to America to abandon the ground on which world history has hitherto been enacted. What has taken place there up to now is but an echo of the Old World and the expression of an alien life; and as a country of the future, it is of no interest to us here, for prophecy is not the business of the philosopher." G.W.F. Hegel, *Lectures on the Philosophy of World History*, trans. H.B. Nisbet (Cambridge and New York: Cambridge University Press, 1975), 170–1.

31 Michael Moon's distinction between Whitman's clusters and annexes informs my claim here. The "transformation of *Drum-Taps* from unassimilable 'annex' to assimilated 'cluster,'" he argues, has to be understood in terms of the difference between these two organizational forms, since the first (i.e., the annex) is a separative mode and the second (i.e., the cluster) is an "'organic procedure" that Whitman linked to the "'dilation' of his own 'limbs' and veins' with '[t]he blood of the world'" (*Disseminating Whitman*, 200–1).

32 Miller, "*Drum-Taps*," 172, 179.

33 Reynolds, *Walt Whitman's America*, 449–50. That "philosophical consolation" is also connected to the dismantling of Radical Reconstruction and black civil rights in the 1870s and 1880s. Whitman's recasting of the war as a dialectical

struggle between "the paradoxes of one and the same identity" is largely contiguous with the forms of collective memory that construed the war – as we will see in Chapter 2 – not as a battle over racial slavery but as a domestic conflict within a single white family. By pushing his poetic vision off to the future and reclaiming democracy as history's "central and never-broken unity," Whitman seems to erase the story of black freedom – which was pivotal to *Leaves'* genesis and early development – from his poetry and prose almost entirely. For a fuller account of the relation between race and poetics in Whitman's thought, see Martin Klammer, *Whitman, Slavery, and the Emergence of Leaves of Grass* (University Park: Pennsylvania State University Press, 1995), and "Slavery and Race," in *A Companion to Walt Whitman*, ed. Kummings, 101–121; Ed Folsom, "Lucifer and Ethiopia"; Karen Sánchez-Eppler, *Touching Liberty: Abolition, Feminism, and the Politics of the Body* (Berkeley and Los Angeles: University of California Press, 1993), 50–82; Ivy Wilson, *Specters of Democracy*, 80–102; and the essays in Ivy Wilson, ed., *Whitman Noir: Black America and the Good Gray Poet* (Iowa City: University of Iowa Press, 2014).

34 Scarry, *The Body in Pain: The Making and Unmaking of the World* (New York: Oxford University Press, 1985), 124.

35 On Whitman's lifelong interested in workers, see also M. Wynn Thomas, "Labor and Laborers," in *A Companion to Walt Whitman*, ed. Kummings, 60–75.

36 Whitman, *The Journalism: 1846–1848*, ed. Herbert Bergman, Douglas A. Noverr, and Edward J. Recchia (New York: Peter Lang, 1998), 197.

37 On these politico-economic changes, see Eric Foner, *Reconstruction: America's Unfinished Revolution, 1863–1977* (New York: HarperCollins, 1988), 392–411, 461–8, 512–23, and Rendigs Fels, *American Business Cycles, 1865–1897* (Chapel Hill: University of North Carolina Press, 1959), 107–8.

38 U.S. Bureau of the Census, *Compendium of the Tenth Census*, vol. 2 (Washington: Government Printing Office, 1880), 926–8; "Our Working Classes," *New York Times* (February 22, 1869).

39 Whitman, *Notebooks and Unpublished Prose Manuscripts*, vol. 1, ed. Edward F. Grier (New York: New York University Press, 1984), 67.

40 "A Day of Fighting in Chicago," *New York Times* (July 27, 1877); James Dabney McCabe, *The History of the Great Riots* (Philadelphia, Chicago, St. Louis, and Dayton: National Publishing Co., 1877), 91; Frances Parkman, "The Failure of Universal Suffrage," *North American Review* 127 (July–August 1878): 4. On the history of these revolts, see Philip Foner, *The Great Labor Uprising of 1877* (New York: Monad Press, 1977) and David O. Stowell, *Streets, Railroads, and the Great Strike of 1877* (Chicago: University of Chicago Press, 1999).

41 These lines are part of Whitman's 1871 revisions to "To a Foil'd European Revolutionaire," a poem that he initially inserted into *Leaves of Grass* in 1856 ("Liberty Poem for Asia, Africa, Europe, America, Australia, Cuba, and The Archipelagoes of the Sea"), and then rewrote in 1860 ("To a Foiled Revolter or Revoltress"), 1867 ("To a Foil'd Revolter or Revoltress"), and 1871. After

the Civil War, the poem still retains its original references to the mid-century revolts in France, Hungary, and Italy, but its new and altered lines also take up the politico-economic struggles of the late-nineteenth-century United States. On this cluster and its relation to Whitman's postwar politics, also see Betsy Erkkila, *Whitman the Political Poet*, 263–5, and Martin Buinicki, *Walt Whitman's Reconstruction*, 78–80.

42 *Walt Whitman's Workshop: A Collection of Unpublished Manuscripts*, ed. Clifton Joseph Furness (Cambridge: Harvard University Press, 1928), 229. As he told Traubel in one of their many interviews, "I suppose ever since time was known, or man, this labor question has been agitated, stirring [… but] now it is more on top – is more palpable than ever before […] I am in favor of agitation – agitation – agitation and agitation: without the questioner, the agitator, the disturber, to hit away at our complacency, we'd get into a pretty pass indeed." *With Walt Whitman in Camden*, vol. 5, 14.

43 "Sunday Evening Lectures," *Notebooks and Unpublished Prose Manuscripts*, vol. 6, 2011–12.

44 *Memoranda During the War*, 130–1, 133.

2 FREDERICK DOUGLASS'S REVISIONS

1 Douglass invokes the "logic of events" in letters, like his 1861 missive to Samuel J. May ("I wait and work relying more upon the stern logic of events than upon any disposition of the Federal army towards slavery"); in essays about emancipation ("the 'inexorable logic of events' will force it upon them [that is, the American people] in the end […] that the war now being waged in this land is a war for and against slavery") and the Confederacy's political aims ("[One] cannot fail to read in the stern logic of passing events, the resolute determination on the part of the South to subjugate every other section of the country"); and in speeches supporting black enlistment ("[The Confederates want] to make the slavery of the African race universal and perpetual on this continent. It is not only evident from the history and logic of events, but the declared purpose of the atrocious war now being waged against the country"). See, respectively, "To the Rev. Samuel J. May, August 30, 1861," "Nemesis" (1861), "The Past and Present" (1861), and "Address for the Promotion of Colored Enlistments" (1863), in *Frederick Douglass: Selected Speeches and Writings*, ed. Philip S. Foner and Yuval Taylor (New York: Lawrence Hill Books, 1999), 470, 451, 535. Hereafter cited parenthetically as *SS*.

2 For most Northerners, the war was a struggle not over slavery but over national unity and Constitutional authority. See Gary W. Gallagher, *The Union War* (Cambridge: Harvard University Press, 2011). In contrast, Douglass and other antislavery advocates viewed the conflict as an abolitionist struggle because, as he put it, "the lesser is included in the greater": "You cannot have the Union […] until you have stricken down that damning curse, and put it beyond the pale of the Republic." "Our Work is Not Done" (1863), *SS*, 548.

3 Frederick Douglass, "Our Composite Nationality" (1869), in *The Frederick Douglass Papers*, ed. John W. Blassingame, Series 1: Speeches, Debates, and Interviews, 5 vols. (New Haven: Yale University Press, 1979–1992), vol. 4, 245. Hereafter cited parenthetically as *FDP*.

4 See David W. Blight, *Frederick Douglass' Civil War: Keeping Faith in Jubilee* (Baton Rouge: LSU Press, 1989); Carolyn Karcher, "White Fratricide, Black Liberation: Melville, Douglass, and Civil War Memory," in *Melville and Douglass: Essays in Relation*, ed. Robert S. Levine and Samuel Otter (Chapel Hill: University of North Carolina Press, 2008), 349–68; Maurice Wallace, "Riveted to the Wall: Covetous Fathers, Devoted Sons, and the Patriarchal Pieties of Melville and Douglass," in *Melville and Douglass*, ed. Levine and Otter, 300–28; Michael T. Gilmore, *The War on Words*, 123–39; Gene Jarrett, "Douglass, Ideological Slavery, and Postbellum Racial Politics," in *The Cambridge Companion to Frederick Douglass*, ed. Maurice Lee (New York: Cambridge University Press, 2009), 158–72; Robert S. Levine, "Frederick Douglass, War, Haiti," *PMLA* 124.5 (October 2009): 1864–8, and *Dislocating Race and Nation: Episodes in Nineteenth-Century American Literary Nationalism* (Chapel Hill: University of North Carolina Press, 2008), 179–236; Ifeoma Nwankwo, *Black Cosmopolitanism* (Philadelphia: University of Pennsylvania Press, 2005), 114–52; Paul Giles, "Douglass's Black Atlantic: Britain, Europe, Egypt," in *The Cambridge Companion*, ed. Lee, 132–45; and Maurice Lee, *Uncertain Chances*, 89–119. Despite this scholarship, most anthologies, syllabi, and monographs still tend to focus on the "antebellum" texts that fit into the field's extant chronological fencing: *Narrative of the Life of Frederick Douglass, an American Slave* (1845), *My Bondage and My Freedom* (1855), "The Heroic Slave" (1853), and "What to the Slave is the Fourth of July?" (1852). A search on the MLA International Bibliography, for instance, currently yields the following hits: 209 for the 1845 *Narrative*; 84 for *My Bondage and My Freedom*; 39 for *The Life and Times*; and only 12 for "Frederick Douglass and the Civil War."

5 Lincoln, "First Inaugural Address" (1861), in *Speeches and Writings, 1859–1865*, ed. Roy P. Basler (New York: Library of America, 1989), 414. For a fuller account of Redpath's colonization plan and Douglass's role in it, see John McKivigan, *Forgotten Firebrand: James Redpath and the Making of Nineteenth-Century America* (Ithaca: Cornell University Press, 2008), 61–83.

6 On the history and consequences of these revolutions, see Jonathan Sperber, *The European Revolutions, 1848–1851* (Cambridge: Cambridge University Press, 1994) and Priscilla Robertson, *Revolutions of 1848: A Social History* (Princeton: Princeton University Press, 1952). On Douglass's responses to these revolts, see also Cody Marrs, "Frederick Douglass in 1848," *American Literature* 85.3 (Fall 2013): 447–73.

7 Karcher, "White Fratricide, Black Liberation," in *Frederick Douglass and Herman Melville*, ed. Levine and Otter, 354, 357. In *Frederick Douglass' Civil War*, David Blight also merges Douglass into an apocalyptic tradition, arguing that he "garnered long-range hope for the cause of black freedom from

faith" not simply from the "divine direction of human affairs," but from the existence of "an apocalyptic God who could enter history and force nations, like individuals, to chart a new course" (8, 6).

8 The phrase upon which Douglass draws here (and in many other writings) is Childe Harold's insurrectionary plea, "Slaves who would be free / must themselves strike the blow!" See *Childe Harold's Pilgrimage* (1818), in *The Complete Poetical Works*, ed. Frederick Page and John Jump (Oxford: Oxford University Press, 1970), lines 720–1.

9 See Koselleck, *Futures Past*, 43–57, and *The Practice of Conceptual History: Timing History, Spacing Concepts* (Stanford: Stanford University Press, 2002), 148–69. On the nationalist discourse of revolution, see Russ Castronovo, *Fathering the Nation: American Genealogies of Slavery and Freedom* (Berkeley and Los Angeles: University of California Press, 1995).

10 Karl Marx and Friedrich Engels, *The German Ideology* (1845), in *Karl Marx: A Reader*, ed. Joel Elster (Cambridge: Cambridge University Press, 1999), 186; Emerson, "Divinity School Address" (1838), in *The Collected Works*, vol. 1, ed. Alfred Riggs Ferguson, Joseph Slater, Jean Ferguson Carr (Cambridge: Harvard University Press, 1971), 89; Dickinson, "Revolution is the Pod" (F 1044).

11 Wilson, *Specters of Democracy*, 19; Douglass, "The Reasons for Our Troubles" (1862), in *The Life and Writings of Frederick Douglass*, ed. Philip S. Foner, 5 vols. (New York: International, 1950–1975), vol. 3, 196–7.

12 Douglass, "Letter to James Redpath" (1860), "The Work of the Future" (1862), and "Reconstruction" (1866) in *SS*, 396, 522, 594. This rhetorical framing was also a response to the countless Southern claims about the Confederacy's Revolutionary lineage. Cognates of James Wilkes Booth's famous cry, after assassinating Lincoln, "Sic semper tyrannis" ("Thus always to tyrants"), can be found in numerous Confederate essays, poems, stories, orations, and songs that described the North in general, and Lincoln in particular, as tyrannical.

13 Douglass reads the Abolition War through the Norman Conquest, for instance, in "The Future of the Negro People of the Slave States" (1862). Drawing on Augustin Thierry's *History of the Conquest of England* (1825), Douglass observes that the Saxon, too, was once "of no account": "In the case of the Saxon, we have a people held in abject slavery, upon their own native soil, by strangers and foreigners [...] They were bought and sold like the beast of the field, and their offspring born and to be born doomed to the same wretched condition [...] The misfortunes of my one race in this respect are not singular [...] The Jews, the Indians, the Saxons and the ancient Britons, have all had a taste of this bitter experience" (*SS*, 481–2).

14 "The Proclamation and a Negro Army" (1863), in *The Life and Writings*, ed. Foner, vol. 3, 332–3. Douglass's proclamation also shores up Christopher Hanlon's claim that the Civil War, like the politico-regional divides that preceded it, was "not *simply* codified as an internecine struggle" but as a "conflict over sectional preeminence [... that] was articulated through terms that bound the United States to a larger and more complex North Atlantic entity" (*America's England*, 12).

15 "The Irrepressible Conflict," 292.

16 See the book inventory, or "Title List of Douglass Library," in The Frederick Douglass Papers at the Library of Congress: http://hdl.loc.gov/loc.mss/mfd.16007.

17 Douglass, "Shall Slavery Survive the War?" (1861), in *The Life and Writings*, ed. Foner, vol. 3, 144. Douglass advances a similar claim in "The Proclamation and a Negro Army," an essay that appeared in *Douglass' Monthly* shortly after emancipation took effect in 1863. "Our trouble," he writes, "is a logical part of the conflict of ages, past, present, and future. It will go on […] The moral chemistry of the universe makes peace between Liberty and Slavery impossible […] The conflict has changed its form from words to blows, and it may change again from blows to words; but the conflict itself, in one form or the other, will go on till truth is slain or error is driven from the field" (*FDP*, 3:550).

18 *Frederick Douglass' Civil War*, 6.

19 Douglass rearticulated this view of the war in a lecture that he delivered two years later, explaining: "There was never any physical reason for the dissolution of the Union. The geographical and topographical conditions of the country all served to unite rather than to divide the two sections. It was moral not physical dynamite that blew the two sections asunder" (*FDP*, 5:175).

20 Lee, *Uncertain Chances*, 98, 108.

21 Nabers, *Victory of Law*, 8; Norris, *The Octopus: A Story of California* (New York: Viking, 1996), 634. Noting that Douglass's accounts of "just force […] almost always include some reference to what 'lessons' are 'taught' by the enforcement of law," Nicholas Buccola argues that Douglass's interest in force has to do primarily with its "educative value." See *The Political Thought of Frederick Douglass* (New York: New York University Press, 2012), 130. That sense of law, I am arguing, expands through the Civil War so as to recast force as something that is at once legal and extra-legal – indeed, as something that inheres in the very physical and moral fabric of the universe.

22 See Humboldt, *Kosmos: A General Survey of the Physical Phenomena of the Universe*, vol. 1 (London: Hippolyte Ballière, 1845), 155; Agassiz, *Geological Sketches* (Boston: Ticknor and Fields, 1866), *Contributions to the Natural History of the United States of America* (Boston: Little, Brown, 1857–62), and *Principles of Zoology* (Boston: Gould, Kendall and Lincoln, 1848); Faraday, *A Course of Six Lectures on the Various Forces of Matter, and Their Relations to Each Other* (New York: Harper & Brothers, 1860), vii; and Faraday as quoted in *Popular Science Monthly*, ed. E.L. Youmans, vol. 1 (New York: D. Appleton and Co., 1872), 751.

23 See, for instance, "The Progress of the Electric Telegraph," *Atlantic Monthly* (March 1860): 290–8; "Meteorology," *Atlantic Monthly* (July 1860): 1–15; Robert J. Walker, "American Slavery and Finances," *The Continental Monthly* (July 1864): 22–34; and Charles Collins, "The Values of Accident," *Atlantic Monthly* (February 1870): 172–9.

24 See Emerson, "Moral Forces" (April 1862) and "Perpetual Forces" (November 1862), in *The Later Lectures of Ralph Waldo Emerson*, vol. 2, ed. Ronald A.

Bosco and Joel Myerson (Athens: University of Georgia Press, 2001), 274–86, 287–301. The quotes come from 289 and 292.

25 "Perpetual Forces," 299–300. It is impossible to know whether or not Douglass knew about these wartime speeches, but we do know that Douglass frequently referenced and refashioned Emerson's ideas throughout his career. Upon returning from his travels abroad in the late 1880s, Douglass remarked that he considered *English Traits* (1856) to be "one of the best books written by an American tourist" (*FDP*, 5:281). And that interest in Emerson commenced decades earlier. As Lawrence Buell notes in *Emerson* (Cambridge: Harvard University Press, 2004), Douglass praised Emerson's "American Slavery" (1855) speech in the pages of *Frederick Douglass' Paper*; wrote a letter to Emerson to request a copy of *Representative Men* (1850) almost as soon as it was published; and drew upon Emerson's theory of the poet in "Pictures," his 1864 speech about pictorial consciousness and social transformation (256–7). On Douglass's relationship to romanticism more generally, see Jared Hickman, "Douglass Unbound," *Nineteenth-Century Literature* 68.3 (December 2013): 323–62; Bill E. Lawson, "Douglass among the Romantics," in *The Cambridge Companion to Frederick Douglass*, ed. Lee, 118–31; and John Stauffer, "Frederick Douglass and the Aesthetics of Freedom," *Raritan* 25.1 (Summer 2005): 114–36.

26 Emerson – and perhaps Douglass, too – turned to Faraday because his ideas represented what, according to Laura Dassow Walls, Humboldt's ideas represented to many other Romantic writers: a scientific account of the universe's perfect harmony and interconnectedness – in short, an empirical verification of transcendentalism. See Walls, *The Passage to Cosmos: Alexander Von Humboldt and the Shaping of America* (Chicago: University of Chicago, 2009), 251–82.

27 Spencer, *Synthetic Philosophy*, vol. 1 (London: Williams and Norgate, 1867), 185, 188, 183. According to the Library of Congress's inventory of his Cedar Hill library, Douglass owned a copy of *Synthetic Philosophy*. He also kept photographs of some of the images in Spencer's book.

28 Fichte, *The Destination of Man*, trans. Percy Sinnett (London: Chapman, 1846), 6–8. This book – a gift from John Chapman – also appears on the library inventory. Douglass may have been introduced to Fichte's philosophy by Ottilie Assing, the German émigrée and intellectual with whom Douglass established "a salon for two," as Henry Louis Gates puts it. See Gates, "A Dangerous Literacy: The Legacy of Frederick Douglass," *New York Times Book Review* (May 28, 1995): 3. As Maria Diedrich notes in *Love Across Color Lines: Ottilie Assing and Frederick Douglass* (New York: Hill and Wang, 1999), Assing belonged to a circle of feminists whose theory of womanhood was grounded in the Romantic philosophies of Fichte, Schlegel, Schiller, and Goethe (69).

29 Post-emancipation ideas of freedom, Amy Dru Stanley observes, were almost always articulated through a "language of contract" that rhetorically and conceptually "reconciled human autonomy and obligation, imposing social order

through personal volition rather than external force. To contract" – or, to follow Douglass's analogy, to get baptized – "was to incur a duty purely by choice and establish its terms without the constraints of status or legal pre-scription." *From Bondage to Contract: Wage Labor, Marriage, and the Market in the Age of Slave Emancipation* (New York: Cambridge University Press, 1998), 2.

30 Wallace, "Violence, Manhood, and War in Douglass," in *The Cambridge Companion*, 86. Douglass recalls Godwyn again, for instance, in "The United States Cannot Remain Half-Slave and Half-Free" (1883), "Good Men are God in the Flesh" (1890), "The Negro Problem" (1890), and in both editions of *The Life and Times*. In each of these references, Godwyn's relation to the present indexes the shape of history itself. As Douglass put it in 1883, "What baptism and church membership were for the Negro in the days of Godwin, the ballot and civil rights were for the Negro in the days of Sumner. Though standing two centuries apart these two men are, nevertheless, conspicuous links in the great chain of causes and events which raised the Negro to his present level of freedom in this and other lands" (*SS*, 664).

31 James Monroe Gregory, *Frederick Douglass the Orator* (Springfield: Willey & Co., 1893), 177.

32 Reginald F. Davis, *Frederick Douglass: A Precursor of Liberation Theology* (Macon, GA: Mercer University Press, 2005). Douglass also seems to have been influenced, in this regard, by Ludwig Feuerbach. He kept a bust of the atheistic philosopher in his study and, as Ottilie Assing told Feuerbach him-self, Douglass's views were transformed by reading *The Essence of Christianity* (1841): "we read the [English translation] together [... and it] resulted in a total reversal of his [religious] attitudes [...] For the satisfaction of seeing a superior man won over for atheism, and through that to have gained a faithful, valuable friend for myself, I feel obliged to you, and I cannot deny myself the pleasure of expressing my gratitude." Diedrich, *Love across Color Lines*, 365.

33 This rough outline of the Dutch revolts draws upon Maarten Prak, *The Dutch Republic in the Seventeenth Century* (Cambridge: Cambridge University Press, 2005); Geoffrey Parker, *The Dutch Revolt* (Ithaca: Cornell University Press, 1977); and the editorial headnote to "William the Silent" (*FDP*, 4:186–7).

34 Robert Purvis, "Address," in *In Memoriam: Frederick Douglass*, ed. Helen Douglass (Philadelphia: John C. Yorston & Co., 1897), 214.

35 Emerson, *Representative Men: Seven Lectures* (London: Routledge, 1850), 4; McCune Smith, Introduction to *My Bondage and My Freedom*, in *The Autobiographies*, ed. Henry Louis Gates, Jr. (New York: Library of America, 1996),132. William L. Andrews similarly points out that in *My Bondage and My Freedom* Douglass's "symbolic" self not only ranks "among the great 'I-narrators' of the American Renaissance" but also makes Douglass's personal experiences "nationally significant, [and] revelatory of the complex mean-ing of slavery and freedom in the North as well as the South." See Andrews, "*My Bondage and My Freedom* and the American Literary Renaissance of

the 1850s," in *Critical Essays on Frederick Douglass*, ed. William L. Andrews (Boston: G.K. Hall, 1991), 133–34.

36 Susan Gilman, "Afterword: The Times of Hemispheric Studies," in *Hemispheric American Studies*, ed. Caroline Levander and Robert S. Levine (New Brunswick: Rutgers University Press, 2008), 330.

37 The Richmond *Daily Dispatch* (January 4, 1865): 2.

38 On this transformation of Civil War memory, see David Blight, *Race and Reunion: The Civil War in American Memory* (Cambridge: Harvard University Press, 2001).

39 Oliver Wendell Holmes, Jr., *The Occasional Speeches of Justice Oliver Wendell Holmes, Jr.*, ed. Mark De Wolfe Howe (Cambridge: Harvard University Press, 1962), 15, 76; Whitman, *Memoranda during the War*, 5. For an alternative reading of Holmes's relation to Douglass, and their mutual interest in empiricism, see Lee, *Uncertain Chances*, 114–119.

40 Richard Henry Stoddard, "Decoration Day," *Magazine of American History* 20 (July-December 1888): 151.

41 Luciano, *Arranging Grief*, 172, 173.

42 Douglass, *The Life and Times of Frederick Douglass*, in *The Autobiographies*, ed. Gates, 896; henceforth referred to as *LT*.

43 Abrams, *Landscape and Ideology in American Renaissance Literature: Topographies of Skepticism* (New York: Cambridge University Press, 2004), 112.

44 Bromell, "A 'Voice from the Enslaved': The Origins of Frederick Douglass's Political Philosophy of Democracy," *American Literary History* 23.4 (Winter 2011): 702.

45 Douglass, *My Bondage and My Freedom*, in *Autobiographies*, ed. Gates, 352.

46 Paul Giles discusses the philosophical conservatism of *The Life and Times* in "Douglass's Black Atlantic: Britain, Europe, Egypt," 140; John Stauffer examines Douglass's later, "whiter" self in "Frederick Douglass and the Aesthetics of Freedom," 134–5; William L. Andrews assesses Douglass's relative detachment from the post-Reconstruction struggles of "the black rank and file" in his Introduction to *Slave Narratives After Slavery*, xxiv; and Michael Bennett considers the later Douglass's political apostasy in *Democratic Discourses: The Radical Abolition Movement and Antebellum American Literature* (Cambridge: Harvard University Press, 2005), 116. Several other critics have advanced similar readings of *The Life and Times*, including James Oakes, who frames postwar Douglass as a lapsed radical who is "still committed to equal justice, but always by means of party politics," and Rafia Zafar, who emphasizes the many connections, both explicit and implicit, between *The Life and Times* and Benjamin Franklin's *Autobiography* (1793). See, respectively, *The Radical and the Republican: Frederick Douglass, Abraham Lincoln, and the Triumph of Antislavery Politics* (New York: Norton, 2007), 281, and "Franklinian Douglass: The Afro-American as Representative Man," in *Frederick Douglass: New Literary and Historical Essays*, ed. Eric Sundquist (Cambridge: Cambridge University Press, 1990), 99–117.

47 Levine, *Dislocating Race and Nation*, 229.

48 In doing so, *The Life and Times* repeats with a difference the shift that, according to Eric Sundquist, marks Douglass's move from the first to the second autobiography. "Although it sacrifices some of the immediacy and visceral simplicity of the *Narrative*," he posits, the "*My Bondage and My Freedom* develops a philosophical frame and psychological depth for Douglass's moving autobiography and is a classic text of the American Renaissance – not least because of the literal rebirth into freedom it records and the rebirth, the reawakening, of revolutionary principles it advocates." See Sundquist, "Slavery, Revolution and the American Renaissance," in *The American Renaissance Reconsidered*, 23. In *The Life and Times*, I would suggest, Douglass revises that "philosophical frame and psychological depth" by way of the Abolition War and the ideas about history, progress, and force to which it led him.

49 Fahs, *The Imagined Civil War*, 314. On the Southern versions of these memoirs, and the ways in which they both memorialize and reimagine the Confederacy, see Coleman Hutchison, *Apples and Ashes*, 173–204.

50 Longstreet, *From Manassas to Appomattox: Memoirs of the Civil War in America* (Philadelphia: J.P. Lippincott Co., 1896), v.

3 HERMAN MELVILLE'S CIVIL WARS

1 Melville's post-*Battle-Pieces* writings also include several projects that he left either unpublished or uncompleted, including the Burgundy Club sketches; the *Parthenope* manuscript; *Weeds and Wildings*; and several other poems, stories, and experiments. On these works, and Melville's later career more broadly, see William B. Dillingham, *Melville and His Circle: The Last Years* (Athens: University of Georgia Press, 1995); Edgar Dryden, *Monumental Melville: The Formation of A Literary Career* (Stanford: Stanford University Press, 2004), 101–94; Sanford E. Marovitz, ed., *Melville as Poet: The Art of "Pulsed Life"* (Kent: Kent State University Press, 2013); Elizabeth Renker, "Melville the Poet in the Postbellum World," in *The New Cambridge Companion to Herman Melville*, ed. Robert S. Levine (Cambridge: Cambridge University Press, 2013), 127–41; and the essays in *Leviathan: A Journal of Melville Studies*, special issue on "Late Melvilles," ed. Cody Marrs (forthcoming), and *Essays in Arts and Sciences* 15 (June 1986), special issue on "Melville's Later Life and Work," ed. Douglas Robillard.

2 Raymond M. Weaver, *Herman Melville: Mariner and Mystic* (New York: George H. Doran, 1921), 348, 350. The other quotes come, respectively, from Stanton Garner, *The Civil War World of Herman Melville* (Lawrence: University of Kansas Press, 1993), 43; Andrew Delbanco, *Melville: His World and Work* (New York: Knopf, 2005), 7, 269; Nina Baym, "Melville's Quarrel with Fiction," *PMLA* 94.5 (October 1979): 921; and Robert Penn Warren, Introduction to *Selected Poems of Herman Melville* (New York: Random House, 1970), 26. Melville's postwar decline is also

emphasized by Michael Paul Rogin, who reads *Battle-Pieces* as evidence of Melville's gradual reconciliation with the power of the state; by Carolyn Karcher, who construes Melville's poetry as an outgrowth of his increasingly anti-democratic politics; and by Daniel Aaron, who finds Southern sympathies, as well as a distrust of radicalism *tout court*, in *Battle-Pieces* and *Clarel*. See Rogin, *Subversive Genealogy: The Politics and Art of Herman Melville* (Berkeley: University of California Press, 1985), 257–87; Karcher, *Shadow Over the Promised Land: Slavery, Race, and Violence in Melville's America* (Baton Rouge: Louisiana State University Press, 1980), 258–308, and "The Moderate and the Radical: Melville and Child on the Civil War and Reconstruction," *ESQ: A Journal of the American Renaissance* 45 (1999): 187–257; and Daniel Aaron, *The Unwritten War: American Writers and the Civil War* (Madison: University of Wisconsin Press, 1987), 75–90.

3 See Deak Nabers, *Victory of Law*, 19–47; Eliza Richards, "Correspondent Lines: Poetry and Journalism in the US Civil War," *ESQ: A Journal of the American Renaissance* 54.1–4 (2008): 144–69; Michael Warner, "What Like a Bullet Can Undeceive," *Public Culture* 15.1 (Winter 2003): 41–54; Dennis Berthold, *American Risorgimento: Herman Melville and the Cultural Politics of Italy* (Columbus: Ohio State University Press, 2009); Lawrence Buell, "Melville and the Question of Decolonization," *American Literature* 64.2 (June 1992): 215–37, and "Melville the Poet," in *The Cambridge Companion to Herman Melville*, ed. Robert S. Levine (Cambridge: Cambridge University Press, 1998), 135–56; Timothy Marr, *The Cultural Roots of American Islamicism* (New York: Cambridge University Press, 2006), 239–61; Peter Coviello, "Battle Music: Melville and the Forms of War," in *Melville and Aesthetics*, ed. Samuel Otter and Geoffrey Sanborn (New York: Palgrave, 2011), 193–212; Samuel Otter, "How *Clarel* Works," in *A Companion to Herman Melville*, ed. Wyn Kelley (London: Blackwell, 2006), 467–81; and Elizabeth Renker, "Melville the Realist Poet," in *A Companion to Herman Melville*, ed. Kelley, 482–96, and "Melville the Poet in the Postbellum World." Scholars have also examined *Battle-Pieces'* Miltonic debts and resonances; the volume's politico-ethical dimensions; and Melville's relation to the epic tradition. See, respectively, Robin Grey, "Annotations on Civil War: Melville's *Battle-Pieces* and Milton's War in Heaven," *Leviathan: A Journal of Melville Studies* 4.1–2 (March 2002): 51–70; Ian Finseth, "On *Battle-Pieces*: The Ethics of Aesthetics in Melville's War Poetry," *Leviathan: A Journal of Melville Studies* 12.3 (October 2010): 71–89; and Christopher N. Phillips, *Epic in American Culture*, 253–84.

4 *White-Jacket; Or, the World in a Man-of-War*, vol. 5 of *The Writings of Herman Melville*, ed. Harrison Hayford, Hershel Parker, and G. Thomas Tanselle (Evanston and Chicago: Northwestern University Press and The Newberry Library, 1970), 190–1; letter to Nathaniel Hawthorne (June 1851), in *Correspondence*, vol. 14 of *The Writings of Herman Melville*, ed. Lynn Horth (Evanston and Chicago: Northwestern University Press and The Newberry Library, 1993), 191; *Weeds and Wildings Chiefly: With a Rose or Two*, in *Poems*, vol. 16 of *The Works of Herman Melville* (New York: Russell & Russell, 1963), 303.

5 Cohen, Introduction to *The Battle-Pieces of Herman Melville* (New York: Thomas Yoseloff, 1963), 15. Retrospection and anticipation, of course, only converge in that most entangled and obscured figure, John Brown. As Virginia Jackson notes, the poem seems to be about "the obscurity of consciousness [itself], about our lack of access to the historical experience of John Brown." That access only becomes available – albeit partially, and in fragments – in the poems that follow, which present the Civil War as an episode of cyclical declension. See Jackson, "Who Reads Poetry?," *PMLA* 123.1 (January 2008): 184.

6 Vendler, "Melville and the Lyric of History," *Southern Review* 35.3 (Summer 1999): 580.

7 Stanton Garner, *The Civil War World of Herman Melville*, 253–4.

8 Foner, *Reconstruction*, 32. On the 1863 draft riots, which were especially massive in New York City but also sprang up in other parts of the U.S., see Iver Bernstein, *The New York City Draft Riots: Their Significance for American Society and Politics in the Age of the Civil War* (New York: Oxford University Press, 1990), and Leslie M. Harris, *In the Shadow of Slavery: African Americans in New York City, 1626–1863* (Chicago: University of Chicago Press, 2004), 279–88.

9 John Froissart, *Chronicles*, trans. Geoffrey Brereton (New York: Penguin, 1978), 151–2.

10 Ibid., 152–3.

11 Dryden, *Monumental Melville*, 77.

12 Gilles Deleuze, *Difference and Repetition*, trans. Paul Patton (New York: Columbia University Press, 1994), 1. Deleuze's notion of "complex repetition" revises Nietzsche's theory of the "eternal return," according to which the world "lacks the power of [...] renewal" and, consequently, is marked not by "development" but by recurrence. *The Will to Power: An Attempted Transvaluation of All Values*, vol. 15 of *The Complete Works of Friedrich Nietzsche*, ed. Oscar Levy, trans. Anthony M. (London: T. N. Foulis, 1910), 430–2. Amending this idea that disorder and reiteration are linked, Deleuze argues that complex repetition is always internally differentiated, and that this is precisely what renders it transgressive: "It puts law into question, it denounces its nominal or general character in favor of a more profound and more artistic reality" (*Difference and Repetition*, 3). In Melville's poetry, this inner severing also distinguishes his representations of historical change not only from premodern and classical notions of temporal cyclicality, such as Aristotle's schema of political transformation, but also from eighteenth- and nineteenth-century Euro-American Enlightenment models of history, which tend to imagine time along a common historical plane.

13 This fascination with circles and cycles, of course, has precedents in Melville's earlier work, and as Jennifer Greiman has argued, it is deeply bound up with – and even structurally expressive of – Melville's theory of democracy. See Greiman, "Circles Upon Circles: Tautology, Form, and the Shape of Democracy in Tocqueville and Melville," *J19: The Journal of Nineteenth-Century Americanists* 1.1 (Spring 2013): 131–46.

14 William Shurr, *The Mystery of Iniquity: Melville as Poet, 1857–1891* (Lexington: University Press of Kentucky, 1972), 42. On the relation between Melville's poem and the Battle of the Crater, see David Cody, " 'So, then, Solidity's a Crust': Melville's 'The Apparition' and the Explosion of the Petersburg Mine," *Melville Society Extracts* 78 (September 1989): 1, 4–8.

15 Of course, rhyme and meter are also part of the cyclical history that *Battle-Pieces* so richly and repeatedly evokes. In "The Apparition," Melville enlists a modified ballad form (*abccb*) that he likely gleaned from either *Lyrical Ballads* (1798) or Scott's *Minstrelsy of the Scottish Border* (1802–3), and then uses that extra c-line to meditate on the shape of historical time, the limits of perception, and the periodicity of the Civil War.

16 See Sweet, *Traces of War*, 170–2.

17 For a fuller account of Melville's aesthetic and philosophical responses to Turner, see Robert K. Wallace, *Melville and Turner: Spheres of Love and Fright* (Athens: University of Georgia Press, 1992).

18 *Poems*, 424, 356, 358.

19 *Clarel: A Poem and Pilgrimage in the Holy Land*, ed. Hershel Parker (Chicago: Northwestern University Press, 2008), 1.10.1–17.

20 Melville likely got his history about this history from several sources, including William Bartlett's *Walks about the City and Environs of Jerusalem* (1844) and *Forty Days in the Desert* (1860); Arthur Stanley's *Sinai and Palestine in Connection with their History* (1863); William Thomson's *The Land and the Book* (1859); and Edward Palmer's *The Desert of the Exodus* (1872). On the poem's relation to other late-nineteenth-century literature about the Holy Land, see Hilton Obenzinger, *American Palestine: Melville, Twain, and the Holy Land Mania* (Princeton: Princeton University Press, 1999), and Basem L. Ra'ad, "Ancient Lands," in *A Companion to Herman Melville*, ed. Kelley, 129–45.

21 See Christopher Freeburg, *Melville and the Idea of Blackness* (New York: Cambridge University Press, 2012).

22 Ahab's monomania, Ishmael is careful to note, did not take "instant rise at the precise time" of Ahab's "bodily dismemberment": it was only in the "long months and days" afterwards, when "Ahab and anguish lay stretched together in one hammock," that his "torn body and gashed soul bled into one another," ushering in the monomania that eventually took over his head and heart. *Moby-Dick*, vol. 6 of *The Writings of Herman Melville*, ed. Harrison Hayford, Hershel Parker, and G. Thomas Tanselle (Chicago: Northwestern University Press and The Newberry Library, 1988), 184–5.

23 On the politico-religious dimensions of the poem, see especially William Potter, *Melville's Clarel and the Intersympathy of Creeds* (Kent, OH: Kent State University Press, 2004), and Zach Hutchins, "Miscegenetic Melville: Race and Reconstruction in *Clarel*," *ELH* 80.4 (Winter 2013): 1173–1203.

24 See Walter Cowen, *Melville's Marginalia*, vol. 2 (New York and London: Garland, 1987), 308–34, as well as *Melville's Marginalia Online*, ed.

Steven Olsen-Smith, Peter Norberg, and Dennis C. Marnon: http://melvilles-marginalia.org/front.php.

25 Arthur   Schopenhauer, *The World as Will and Idea*, trans. R.B. Haldane and J. Kemp, 3 vols. (Boston: Ticknor and Co., 1888), vol. 1, 236; *Counsels and Maxims*, in *Complete Essays of Schopenhauer*, trans. T. Bailey Saunders (New York: Willey Book Co., 1942), 1. The third quote, about art, is from a passage in the translator's commentary (which Melville scored twice) in *The Wisdom of Life*, trans. T. Bailey Saunders (London: Sonnenschein, 1891), x–xi.

26 Schopenhauer, *Studies in Pessimism*, in *Complete Essays*, 1, 12, 43; *Parerga and Paralipomena*, trans. E.F.J. Payne (Oxford: Clarendon Press, 1974), 301.

27 *The World as Will and Idea*, vol. 3, 52.

28 *The World as Will and Idea*, vol. 3, 225–7. Melville scored the following sentences, which appear right before Schopenhauer's commentary on a "true philosophy of history": "Fools [...] imagine that something must first become and happen. Therefore they [... view history as a] preconceived plan of the world, according to which everything is ordered for the best, which is then supposed *finaliter* to appear, and will be a glorious thing. Accordingly they take the world as perfectly real, and place the end of it in the poor earthly happiness, which, however much it may be fostered by men and favored by fate, is a hollow, deceptive, decaying, and sad thing, out of which neither constitutions and legal systems nor steam-engines and telegraphs can ever make anything that is essentially better. The said philosophers and glorifiers of history are accordingly [...] dull fellows and incarnate philistines; and besides are really bad Christians, for the true spirit and kernel of Christianity, as also of Brahmanism and Buddhism, is the knowledge of the vanity of earthly happiness, the complete contempt for it, and the turning away from it to an existence of another, nay, an opposite, kind." *The World as Will and Idea*, vol. 3, 226; Cowen, *Melville's Marginalia*, 330.

29 *The World as Will and Idea*, vol. 1, 469. To be sure, the Schopenhauerian resonances in Melville's late works neither begin nor end with *Timoleon*. As William B. Dillingham has demonstrated, Melville likely draws from Schopenhauer in "After the Pleasure Party," *John Marr*, and *Billy Budd*. The character of Claggart, he notes, "is so similar" to the "person Schopenhauer describes in [his essay] 'Human Nature'" – the the man who envies beauty until "nothing remains but [...] a bitter and irreconcilable hatred of the person who possesses [it]," and "hides his feelings as carefully as if they were secret sins" – that there must be either "direct influence" or "a remarkable affinity between the two authors." See Dillingham, *Melville and His Circle*, 61, and Schopenhauer, *Essays*, trans. T. Bailey Saunders (London: George Allen and Unwin, 1951), 20.

30 *Studies in Pessimism*, in *Complete Essays*, 20.

31 *The World as Will and Idea*, vol. 1, 469.

32 *Moby-Dick*, 188. This dimension of Melville's writing has been well documented. Critics have examined Melville's "immanent manipulat[ions]" of language and discourse; his tendency to simultaneously invite "an allegorical

reading and subvert the very terms of its consistency"; the "oscillating unde-cidability" of his tone; and his commitment to uncertainty, which contin-uously "unsettles distinctions" and shapes his "multifarious encounters with chance." See Samuel Otter, *Melville's Anatomies* (Berkeley and Los Angeles: University of California Press, 1999), 6; Barbara Johnson, "Melville's Fist: The Execution of Billy Budd," in *Deconstruction: Critical Concepts in Literary and Cultural Studies*, ed. Jonathan D. Culler (London: Routledge, 2003), 216; Nancy Fredericks, *Melville's Art of Democracy* (Athens: University of Georgia Press, 1995), 78; John Evelev, *Tolerable Entertainment: Herman Melville and Professionalism in Antebellum New York* (Amherst: University of Massachusetts Press, 2006), 149; and Maurice Lee, *Uncertain Chances*, 49. On Melville's hermeneutic entanglements, see also Elizabeth Duquette, "*Pierre's* Nominal Conversions," in *Melville and Aesthetics*, ed. Otter and Sanborn, 117–35.

33 John Keats, "Ode on a Grecian Urn," in *Ode on a Grecian Urn, The Eve of St. Agnes, and Other Poems* (Boston: Houghton Mifflin, 1901), 14.

34 This investment in art also shapes the volume's structural organization and movement. As Elizabeth Renker notes, Melville's interests in art, distance, and perspective are addressed "metapoetically" in *Timoleon*, which presents its poems "as a set of objects carefully constructed on the page for (presumed) readers to encounter visually." "Melville the Poet in the Postbellum World," in *The New Cambridge Companion*, ed. Levine, 137. On the volume's broader aesthetic engagements, see also Douglas Robillard, "Wrestling with the Angel: Melville's Use of the Visual Arts in *Timoleon*," in *Savage Eye: Melville and the Visual Arts*, ed. Christopher Sten (Kent: Kent State University Press, 1991), 246–56, and Sanford E. Marovitz, "Connecting by Contrast: The Art of *Timoleon, Etc.*," in *Melville as Poet*, 125–148.

35 Coleridge, *Biographia Literaria*, ed. J. Shawcross (Oxford: Clarendon Press, 1907), vol. 2, 253; Arnold, "Preface" to *Poems* (London: Longman, Brown, Green, and Longmans, 1853), x; Emerson, "Initial, Daemonic and Celestial Love," in *Poems* (Boston: James Munroe and Co., 1847), 172–3.

36 *The World as Will and Idea*, vol. 1, 240.

4 EMILY DICKINSON'S ERASURES

1 Letter to Higginson (April 25, 1862), in *The Letters of Emily Dickinson*, ed. Thomas Johnson (Cambridge: Harvard University Press, 1986), 261.

2 Thomas Johnson, Introduction to *The Letters of Emily Dickinson* (Cambridge: Harvard University Press, 1958), xx; Daniel Aaron, *The Unwritten War*, 355–358; Edmund Wilson, *Patriotic Gore*, 488; Christopher Benfey, *American Audacity: Literary Essays North and South* (Ann Arbor: University of Michigan Press, 2008), 52.

3 See Shira Wolosky, *Emily Dickinson: A Voice of War* (New Haven: Yale University Press, 1984) and "Public and Private in Emily Dickinson's

War Poetry," in *A Historical Guide to Emily Dickinson*, ed. Vivian Pollack (New York: Oxford University Press, 2004), 103–132; Karen Dandurand, "New Dickinson Civil War Publications," *American Literature* 56.1 (March 1984): 17–27; and Barton Levi St. Armand, *Emily Dickinson and Her Culture: The Soul's Society* (Cambridge and New York: Cambridge University Press, 1984). The quote from Wolosky appears on xviii of *A Voice of War*.

4 See Faith Barrett, *To Fight Aloud*, 130–86, "'Drums off the Phantom Battlements': Dickinson's War Poems in Discursive Context," in *A Companion to Emily Dickinson*, ed. Martha Nell Smith and Mary Loeffelholz (New York and London: Blackwell, 2008), 107–32, and "Slavery and the Civil War," in *Emily Dickinson in Context*, ed. Eliza Richards (New York: Cambridge University Press, 2013), 206–15; Benjamin Friedlander, "Emily Dickinson and the Battle of Ball's Bluff," *PMLA* 124.5 (October 2009): 1582–99; Tyler Hoffman, "Emily Dickinson and the Limit of War," *The Emily Dickinson Journal* 3.2 (Fall 1994): 1–18; Michelle Kohler, *Miles of Stare: Transcendentalism and the Problem of Literary Vision in Nineteenth-Century America* (Tuscaloosa: University of Alabama Press, 2014), 115–19; Dominic Mastroianni, *Politics and Skepticism in Antebellum American Literature* (Cambridge and New York: Cambridge University Press, 2014), 119–68; Cristanne Miller, *Reading in Time: Emily Dickinson in the Nineteenth Century* (Amherst: University of Massachusetts Press, 2012), 147–75; Eliza Richards, "'How News Must Feel When Traveling': Dickinson and Civil War Media," in *A Companion to Emily Dickinson*, ed. Smith and Loeffelholz, 157–80, and "Weathering the News in US Civil War Poetry," in *The Cambridge Companion to Nineteenth-Century American Poetry*, ed. Kerry Larson (Cambridge and New York: Cambridge University Press, 2012), 113–34; and Coleman Hutchison, "'Eastern Exiles': Dickinson, Whiggery, and War," *The Emily Dickinson Journal* 13.2 (Fall 2004): 1–26.

5 See, for instance, Victoria N. Morgan, *Emily Dickinson and Hymn Culture: Tradition and Experience* (Burlington: Ashgate, 2010); Domhnall Mitchell, *Emily Dickinson: Monarch of Perception* (Amherst: University of Massachusetts Press, 2000), 112–53; Robert McClure Smith, *The Seductions of Emily Dickinson* (Tuscaloosa: University of Alabama Press, 1996); William Merrill Decker, *Epistolary Practices: Letter Writing in America Before Telecommunications* (Chapel Hill: University of North Carolina Press, 1998), 141–75; and Daneen Wardrop, *Emily Dickinson and the Labor of Clothing* (Lebanon: University of New Hampshire Press, 2009). My argument, of course, is not with any of these particular scholarly accounts, but with the periodic framework that collectively bounds them.

6 Matthiessen, *The American Renaissance*, 115. On Dickinson's early reception, see Willis J. Buckingham's extensive documentary history, *Emily Dickinson's Reception in the 1890s* (Pittsburgh: University of Pittsburgh Press, 1989). Barton Levi St. Armand notes that part of the reason why Dickinson was so enthusiastically received in the 1890s was the "renewed vogue" in New England for "'antiquities' of all kinds." Amidst this craze, "Dickinson was

hailed as the last fading flower of American Puritanism" (*Emily Dickinson and Her Culture*, 3).

7 Letter to Higginson (February 1863), in *Letters of Emily Dickinson*, ed. Johnson, 423.

8 Hoffman, "Emily Dickinson and the Limit of War," 2; Richards, "'How the News Must Feel,'" 164.

9 Lincoln, "Gettysburg Address," in *Speeches and Writings*, 536; Douglass, "There was a Right Side in the Late War" (1878), *SS*, 631.

10 As Coleman Hutchison writes, "Dickinson studies would do well to ask, what does 'Civil War poetry' look like? Could 'Civil War poetry' include poems that, in one way or another, address the political intercourses and discourses that led to or perpetuated war?" ("'Eastern Exiles,'" 18). This chapter is, among other things, an extended answer in the affirmative, as well as a rearticulation of this same question vis-à-vis Dickinson's later poems.

11 On the political and historical resonances of "The Black Berry – wears a Thorn in his Side –" (F 548), see Eliza Richards's account of how the poem "offers both a spectacle of racist dehumanization and its critique" (172) in "Emily Dickinson and Civil War Media," 170–3. See also John Shoptaw's reading the poem as more explicitly abolitionist "tribute" (3) to a black soldier in "Dickinson's Civil War Poetics: From the Enrollment Act to the Lincoln Assassination," *The Emily Dickinson Journal* 19.2 (2010): 1–19, and Cristanne Miller's meditation on the role of sympathy in the poem in *Reading in Time*, 13–17. On the abolitionist dimensions of "As the Starved Maelstrom laps the Navies" (F 1064), see Richards, "Emily Dickinson and Civil War Media," and Erica Fretwell, "Emily Dickinson in Domingo," *J19: The Journal of Nineteenth-Century Americanists* 1.1 (Spring 2013): 71–96. On the wartime contexts of "The name – of it – is 'Autumn' –" (F 465) and "It feels a shame to be Alive –" (F 524), see, respectively, Tyler Hoffman, "Emily Dickinson and the Limit of War," and Benjamin Friedlander, "Emily Dickinson and the Battle of Ball's Bluff." On Dickinson's response to Frazer's death, see Faith Barrett, "'Drums off the Phantom Battlements,'" 109–11; Randall Fuller, *From Battlefields Rising*, 84–6; and Barton Levi St. Armand, *Emily Dickinson and Her Culture*, 104–13.

12 Letter to Louise and Frances Norcross (March 1862), in *The Letters of Emily Dickinson*, ed. Johnson, 397–8.

13 There is also the significant problem of determining when exactly Dickinson wrote her poems. Although the fascicles create a rough sense of chronological order – which I, like many other scholars, use to ascribe certain poems to certain years – that is only an approximation, and many of the poems remain undated. To associate her poetic response to the Civil War exclusively to the years between 1861 and 1865 thus contravenes Dickinson's own compositional practices.

14 As Dana Luciano has demonstrated, grief took shape in the nineteenth century as an affective alternative to the standardized forms of time-keeping that were increasingly enacted by the modern development of the clock, the

railroad, and the state. Mourning in particular generated psychic temporalities that were "collective rather than productive, repetitive rather than linear, [and] reflective rather than forward-moving" (*Arranging Grief*, 6).

15 Higginson, "Leaves from an Officer's Journal," *Atlantic Monthly* (November 1864): 521.

16 See, for instance, Benson Lossing's articles on Shays' Rebellion and the War of 1812 in the 1862 and 1863 issues of *Harper's Magazine*. *The North American Review* published pieces on "Giuseppe Garibaldi" (January 1861) and "The Foundation of the Roman Empire" (January 1865). Frank Moore, prior to compiling *The Rebellion Record*, also published a two-volume compendium of founding documents: the *Diary of the American Revolution, from Newspapers and original Documents* (New York: Scribner, 1860). Such historical comparisons were often used by Northern writers to present the Confederacy as devoid of any political lineage. As Higginson writes: "The most bigoted royal house in Europe never dreamed of throwing down the gauntlet for the actual ownership of man by man. Even Russian never fought for serfdom, and Austria has only enslaved nations, not individuals [...] The more strongly the Secessionists state their cause, the more glaringly it is seen to differ from any cause for which any sane person has taken up arms since the Roman servile wars." "The Ordeal by Battle," *Atlantic Monthly* (July 1861): 89.

17 Hawthorne, "Chiefly about War-Matters," *Atlantic Monthly* (July 1862): 43–61 (the quote comes from 58–9). Justine Murison provides a trenchant reading of this essay – in all of its ambiguity – in "Feeling out of Place: Affective History, Nathaniel Hawthorne, and the Civil War," *ESQ: A Journal of the American Renaissance* 59.4 (2013): 519–51.

18 Alice Fahs provides an overview of these histories, and their place in the book markets of the late 1860s, in *The Imagined Civil War*, 287–310. On the rise of Southern histories and anthologies, and their relation to postwar ideas about American literary nationalism, see Coleman Hutchison, *Apples and Ashes*, 139–142, 176–179.

19 "[This is] without question," the President declared, "the most valuable contemporary History ever prepared." As for the War Department's documents: they were released from 1880 until 1901 under the title *The War of the Rebellion: A Compilation of the Official Records of the Union and Confederate Armies*. The first series – which includes formal reports of property seizures, campaigns, and military operations – clocks in at 53 volumes.

20 See Lloyd Pratt, *Archives of American Time* (the quote appears on 6); Dana Luciano, *Arranging Grief*; and Thomas M. Allen, *A Republic in Time*.

21 "Dickinson's Poems in Discursive Context," 108.

22 "The Aurora Borealis," *Atlantic Monthly* (December 1859): 748.

23 Michelle Kohler similarly observes that the poem enlists "competing visions of time," but in her reading the tension is between linearity and cyclicality (or as she puts it, between "teleological" and "regenerative" time). See Kohler, "Dickinson and the Poetics of Revolution," *The Emily Dickinson Journal* 19.2 (2010): 25–6.

24 Pabor, "Emancipation," and Timrod, "Ethnogenesis," in *"Words for the Hour": A New Anthology of American Civil War Poetry*, ed. Faith Barrett and Cristanne Miller (Amherst: University of Massachusetts Press, 2005), 93, 313; Richards, "'How the News Must Feel,'" 116.

25 *Oxford English Dictionary*, 7th ed.

26 Shelley, "Mutability" and "Ode to the West Wind," in *The Poetical Works* (London: Edward Moxon, 1861), 360, 486; Keats, "Hyperion" and "I Stood Tip-Toe upon a Little Hill," in *Complete Poems*, ed. Jack Stillinger (Cambridge: Harvard University Press, 2003), 262, 51; Thoreau, *Walden*, ed. Jeffrey S. Cramer (New Haven: Yale University Press, 2004), 82, 298; Emerson, "Musketaquid," in *Complete Poems and Translations*, ed. Harold Bloom and Paul Kane (New York: Library of America, 1994), 114.

27 Hoffman, "Emily Dickinson and the Limit of War," 4; Cameron, *Lyric Time: Dickinson and the Limits of Genre* (Baltimore: Johns Hopkins University Press, 1979), 38.

28 Of course, this sequence is not limited to just these three poems. "Whole Gulfs – of Red," for instance, is preceded by a poem (F 467) that spiritualizes the idea of "dwelling in possibility," comparing the growth of the soul to the ripening of a plant in the sun; and it is followed by a poem (F 469) in which Dickinson connects her "Garden" (which is often a figure for poetry itself) to the "Sea" (which she just described as a vast ocean of blood).

29 Cameron, *Choosing Not Choosing*, 3–4; Socarides, *Dickinson Unbound: Paper, Process, Poetics* (New York: Oxford University Press, 2012), 14.

30 Martha Nell Smith, *Rowing in Eden: Rereading Emily Dickinson* (Austin: University of Texas Press, 1992), 39.

31 R.W. Franklin, Introduction to *The Poems*, 3; Lee Rust Brown, Introduction to *Battle-Pieces* (New York: Da Capo, 1995), iii. See also, in this same vein, Cynthia Wolff's reading of the later Dickinson as a "disenfranchised singer" (481) in *Emily Dickinson* (New York: Knopf, 1988), 449–520.

32 See Bennett, *Poets in the Public Sphere*, 70–76, 181–204, and Miller, *Reading in Time*, 176–196. On Dickinson's later poems, see also Marta Werner, *Open Folios: Scenes of Reading, Surfaces of Writing* (Ann Arbor: University of Michigan Press, 1995), 11–54.

33 Franklin, Introduction to *The Poems*, 4.

34 "Public and Private in Dickinson's War Poems," 10.

35 *Dickinson's Misery*, 6.

36 Theodor Adorno, "On Lyric Poetry and Society," in *Notes to Literature*, vol. 1, ed. Rolf Tiedemann, trans. Shierry Weber Nicholsen (New York: Columbia University press, 1991), 37–54.

37 Anne-Lise François, *Open Secrets: The Literature of Uncounted Experience* (Stanford: Stanford University Press, 2008), xvi, 10.

38 Miller, *Reading in Time*, 180.

CODA: OTHER NINETEENTH CENTURIES

1 Giles, *The Global Remapping of American Literature* (Princeton: Princeton University Press, 2012), 1.

2 Massey, *For Space* (London: SAGE, 2005), 5. Although Massey's subject is globalization and the manner in which it conceptually secures its own inevitability, nationalism also converts "geography into history," and in remarkably similar ways.

3 Poe, *Eureka: A Prose Poem* (1848), in *Poetry and Tales*, ed. Patrick F. Quinn (New York: Library of America, 1984), 1355; Thoreau, *Walden*, ed. William Rossi (New York: Norton, 2008), 215.

4 Lazarus, "Chopin" (1879), in *Selected Poems and Other Writings*, ed. Gregory Eiselein (Toronto: Broadview, 2002), 82; Miller, "A Song for Creation," in *Poems: Songs of the American Seas* (San Francisco: The Whitaker and Ray Co., 1909), 133.

5 "The Present Age" (1895), in *Complete Poems*, ed. Maryemma Graham (New York: Oxford University Press, 1988), 172. On Harper's politics and literary career, see Faith Barrett, *To Fight Aloud*, 87–129; Hazel Carby, *Reconstructing Womanhood: The Emergence of the Afro-American Woman Novelist* (New York: Oxford University Press, 1987), 62–94, and Andreá N. Williams, *Dividing Lines: Class Anxiety and Postbellum Black Fiction* (Ann Arbor: University of Michigan Press, 2013), 25–52.

6 Harper, *Iola Leroy, or Shadows Uplifted* (Philadelphia: Garrigues Brothers, 1892), 114.

Index